———

FRIEDRICH NIETZSCHE
Thus Spoke Zarathustra

CAMBRIDGE TEXTS IN THE
HISTORY OF PHILOSOPHY

Series editors

KARL AMERIKS
Professor of Philosophy at the University of Notre Dame

DESMOND M. CLARKE
Professor of Philosophy at University College Cork

The main objective of Cambridge Texts in the History of Philosophy is to expand the range, variety, and quality of texts in the history of philosophy which are available in English. The series includes texts by familiar names (such as Descartes and Kant) and also by less well-known authors. Wherever possible, texts are published in complete and unabridged form, and translations are specially commissioned for the series. Each volume contains a critical introduction together with a guide to further reading and any necessary glossaries and textual apparatus. The volumes are designed for student use at undergraduate and postgraduate level and will be of interest not only to students of philosophy, but also to a wider audience of readers in the history of science, the history of theology, and the history of ideas.

For a list of titles published in the series, please see end of book.

FRIEDRICH NIETZSCHE

Thus Spoke Zarathustra
A Book for All and None

EDITED BY

ADRIAN DEL CARO

University of Colorado at Boulder

ROBERT B. PIPPIN

University of Chicago

TRANSLATED BY

ADRIAN DEL CARO

CAMBRIDGE
UNIVERSITY PRESS

CAMBRIDGE
UNIVERSITY PRESS

University Printing House, Cambridge CB2 8BS, United Kingdom

One Liberty Plaza, 20th Floor, New York, NY 10006, USA

477 Williamstown Road, Port Melbourne, VIC 3207, Australia

314–321, 3rd Floor, Plot 3, Splendor Forum, Jasola District Centre,
New Delhi – 110025, India

103 Penang Road, #05-06/07, Visioncrest Commercial, Singapore 238467

Cambridge University Press is part of the University of Cambridge.

It furthers the University's mission by disseminating knowledge in the pursuit of
education, learning and research at the highest international levels of excellence.

www.cambridge.org
Information on this title: www.cambridge.org/9780521602617

© Cambridge University Press 2006

First published 2006
Reprinted with corrections 2012
14th printing 2022

Printed in Great Britain by Ashford Colour Press Ltd.

A catalogue record for this publication is available from the British Library

ISBN-13 978-0-521-84171-9 Hardback
ISBN-13 978-0-521-60261-7 Paperback

Contents

Contents

Introduction

The text

Nietzsche published each of the first three parts of *Thus Spoke Zarathus-tra* (TSZ hereafter) separately between 1883 and 1885, during one of his most productive and interesting periods, in between the appearance of *The Gay Science* (which he noted had itself marked a new beginning of his thought) and *Beyond Good and Evil*. As with the rest of his books, very few copies were sold. He later wrote a fourth part (called "Fourth and Final Part") which was not published until 1892, and then privately, only for a few friends, by which time Nietzsche had slipped into the insanity that marked the last decade of his life.[1] Not long afterwards an edition with all four parts published together appeared, and most editions and translations have followed suit, treating the four parts as somehow belonging in one book, although many scholars see a natural ending of sorts after Part III and regard Part IV as more of an appendix than a central element in the drama narrated by the work. Nietzsche, who was trained as a classicist, may have been thinking of the traditional tragedy competitions in ancient Greece, where entrants submitted three tragedies and a fourth play, a comic and somewhat bawdy satyr play. At any event, he thought of this final section as in some sense the "Fourth Part" and any interpretation must come to terms with it.

---

[1] Nietzsche went mad in January 1889. For more on the problem of Part IV, see Laurence Lampert's discussion in *Nietzsche's Teaching: An Interpretation of "Thus Spoke Zarathustra"* (New Haven: Yale University Press, 1986), pp. 287–91. For a contrasting view (that Part IV is integral to the work and a genuine conclusion), see Robert Gooding-Williams, *Zarathustra's Dionysian Modernism* (Stanford: Stanford University Press, 2001).

TSZ is unlike any of Nietzsche's other works, which themselves are unlike virtually anything else in the history of philosophy. Nietzsche himself provides no preface or introduction, although the section on TSZ in his late book, *Ecce Homo*, and especially its last section, "Why I am a Destiny," are invaluable guides to what he might have been up to. Zarathustra seems to be some sort of prophet, calling people, modern European Christian people especially, to account for their failings and encouraging them to pursue a new way of life. (As we shall discuss in a moment, even this simple characterization is immediately complicated by the fact that Nietzsche insists that this has nothing to do with a "replacement" religion, and that the book is as much a parody of a prophetic view as it is an instance of it.)[2] In *Ecce Homo* Nietzsche expresses some irritation that no one has wondered about the odd name of this prophet. Zarathustra was a Persian prophet (known to the Greeks as Zoroaster)[3] and he is important for Nietzsche because he originally established that the central struggle in human life (even cosmic life) was between two absolutely distinct principles, between good and evil, which Nietzsche interpreted in Christian and humanist terms as the opposition between selflessness and benevolence on the one hand and egoism and self-interest on the other. Nietzsche tells us two things about this prophet:

> Zarathustra created this fateful error of morality: this means he has to be the first to recognize it.[4]

(Nietzsche means that Zarathustra was the first to recognize its calamitous consequences.) And:

> [t]he self-overcoming of morality from out of truthfulness; the self-overcoming of the moralists into their opposite – into me – that is what the name Zarathustra means coming from my mouth.[5]

That is, we can now live, Zarathustra attempts to teach, freed from the picture of this absolute dualism, but without moral anarchy and without sliding into a bovine contentment or a violent primitivism. Sometimes, especially in the first two parts, this new way of living is presented

---

[2] Cf. Friedrich Nietzsche, *Ecce Homo* (hereafter EH), in *The Anti-Christ, Ecce Homo, Twilight of the Idols*, trans. Judith Norman (Cambridge: Cambridge University Press, 2005), §6, pp. 129–31.
[3] Estimates about when Zarathustra actually lived vary from 6000 BCE to 600 BCE. Somewhere between 1500 BCE and 1000 BCE would appear the safest guess. Nietzsche, however, evinces virtually no interest in the historical Zarathustra or the actual religion of Zoroastrianism.
[4] EH, §3, p. 145.   [5] Ibid.

in sweeping and collective, historical terms, as an epochal transition from mere human being to an "overman," virtually a new species. This way of characterizing the problem tends to drop out after Part II, and Zarathustra focuses his attention on what he often calls the problem of self-overcoming: how each of us, as individuals, might come to be dissatisfied with our way of living and so be able to strive for something better, even if the traditional supports for and guidance toward such a goal seem no longer credible (e.g. the idea of *the* purpose of human nature, or what is revealed by religion, or any objective view of human happiness and so forth). And in Part III Zarathustra asks much more broadly about a whole new way of thinking about or imagining ourselves that he believes is necessary for this sort of re-orientation. He suggests that such a possibility depends on how we come to understand and experience temporality at a very basic level, and he introduces a famous image, "the eternal return of the same" (which he elsewhere calls Zarathustra's central teaching), to begin to grapple with the problem. He himself becomes deathly ill in contemplating this cyclical picture; not surprisingly since it seems to deny a possibility he himself had hoped for at the outset – a *decisive* historical revolution, a time after which all would be different from the time before. Many of the basic issues in the book are raised by considering what it means for Zarathustra to suffer from and then "recover" from such an "illness."

The interpretive problem

TSZ is often reported to be Nietzsche's most popular and most read book, but the fact that the book is so unusual and often hermetic has made for wildly different sorts of reception. Here is one that is typical of the kind of popular reputation Nietzsche has in modern culture:

> Together with Goethe's *Faust* and the New Testament, *Zarathustra* was the most popular work that literate soldiers took into battle for inspiration and consolation [in WW I – RP]. The "beautiful words" of Zarathustra, one author wrote, were especially apt for the Germans who "more than any other Volk possessed fighting natures in Zarathustra's sense." About 150,000 copies of a specially durable wartime *Zarathustra* were distributed to the troops.[6]

[6] Steven Aschheim, *The Nietzsche Legacy in Germany, 1890–1990* (Berkeley: University of California Press, 1992), p. 135. The quotation cited is from Rektor P. Hoche, "Nietzsche und der deutsche Kampf," *Zeitung für Literatur, Kunst und Wissenschaft* 39:6 (12 March 1916).

Now it is hard to imagine a book less suitable for such a purpose than Nietzsche's *Thus Spoke Zarathustra*. It is true that Zarathustra had famously said, "You say it is the good cause that hallows even war? I tell you: it is the good war that hallows any cause" (p. 33), but even that passage is surrounded by claims that the highest aspiration is actually to be a "saint of knowledge," and that only failing that should one become a warrior (what sort of continuum could this be?), and that the "highest thought" of such warriors should be one commanded by Zarathustra, and it should have nothing to do with states and territory but with the injunction that human being shall be overcome. (What armies would be fighting whom in such a cause?)[7] Moreover one wonders what "inspiration and consolation" our "literate soldiers" could have found in the Fellini-esque title character,[8] himself hardly possessed of a "warlike nature," chronically indecisive, sometimes self-pitying, wandering, speechifying, dancing about and encouraging others to dance, consorting mostly with animals, confused disciples, a dwarf, and his two mistresses. And what could they have made of the speeches, with those references to bees overloaded with honey, soothsayers, gravediggers, bursting coffins, pale criminals, red judges, self-propelling wheels, shepherds choking on snakes, tarantulas, "little golden fishing rods of wisdom," Zarathustra's ape, Zarathustra speaking too "crudely and sincerely" for "Angora rabbits," and the worship of a jackass in Part IV, with that circle of an old king, a magician, the last pope, a beggar, a shadow, the conscientious of spirit, and a sad soothsayer?

What in fact could *anyone* make of this bewildering work, parts of which seem more hermetic than Celan, parts more self-indulgent and bizarre than bad Bob Dylan lyrics? Do we know what we are *meant* to make of it? Nietzsche himself, in *Ecce Homo*, was willing to say a number of things about the work, that in it he is the "inventor of the dithyramb,"[9] that with

---

[7] In EH, §1, p. 144 when Nietzsche says that after Zarathustra "the concept of politics will have then merged entirely into a war of spirits" he does not pause to tell us what a war, not of bodies, but of *spirits* might be. And he goes on to say "there will be wars such as the earth has never seen," and we might note that he seems to mean that different sorts, *types* of "wars" will make up "great politics."

[8] Cf. EH, §1, p. 144: "I do not want to be a saint, I would rather be a buffoon . . . Perhaps I am a buffoon . . . And yet in spite of this or rather not in spite of this – because nothing to date has been more hypocritical than saints – the truth speaks from out of me. – But the truth is *terrible*: because *lies* have been called truth so far."

[9] A dithyramb was a choral hymn sung in the classical period in Greece by fifty men or boys to honor the god Dionysus.

TSZ he became the "first tragic philosopher," and that TSZ should be understood as "music." When it is announced, as the work to follow *The Gay Science*, we are clearly warned of the difficulty that will challenge any reader. Section §342 had concluded the original version of *The Gay Science* with "Incipit tragoedia," and then the first paragraph of TSZ's Prologue. Nietzsche's warning comes in the second edition Preface:

> "*Incipit tragoedia*" [tragedy begins] we read at the end of this suspiciously innocent book. Beware! Something utterly wicked and mischievous is being announced here: *incipit parodia* [parody begins], no doubt."[10]

Are there other works that could be said to be both tragedies and parodies? *Don Quixote*, perhaps, a work in many other ways also quite similar to TSZ?[11] If Nietzsche announced that his TSZ can and should be read as a parody, what exactly would that mean? I do not mean what it would mean to find parts of it funny; I mean trying to understand *how* it could be both a prophetic book and a kind of send-up of a prophetic book. How it could both present Zarathustra as a teacher and parody his attempt to play that role? Why has the work remained for the most part a place simply to mine for quotations in support of Nietzschean "theories" of the overman, the Eternal Return of the Same, and the "last human beings"; all as if the theories were contained inside an ornate literary form, delivered by Nietzsche's surrogate, an ancient Persian prophet? At the very least, especially when we look also to virtually everything written after the later 1870s, when Nietzsche in effect abandoned the traditional essay form in favor of less continuous, more aphoristic, and here parabolic forms, it is clear that Nietzsche wanted to resist incorporation into traditional philosophy, to escape traditional assumptions about the writing of philosophy. In a way that point is obvious, nowhere more obvious than in the form of TSZ, even if the steady stream of books about Nietzsche's metaphysics, or value theory, or even epistemology shows no sign of abating. The two

---

[10] Friedrich Nietzsche, *The Gay Science* (hereafter GS), edited by Bernard Williams (Cambridge: Cambridge University Press), §1, p. 4.

[11] The intertwining of the two dramatic modes of tragedy and comic parody appear throughout the text. A typical example is at the end of "The Wanderer" in Part III, when Zarathustra laughs in a kind of self-mocking and then weeps as he remembers the friends he has had to leave behind. (p. 123). It is also very likely that Nietzsche, the "old philologist," is referring to the end of Plato's *Symposium*, where Socrates claims that what we need is someone who can write both tragedies and comedies, that the tragic poet might also be comic (*Symposium*, 223c–d).

more interesting questions are rather, first, what one takes such resistance to mean, what the practical point is, we might say, of the act of so resisting, what Nietzsche is trying to *do* with his books, as much as what his books mean, if we are not to understand them in the traditional philosophical sense. (It would have been helpful if, in *Ecce Homo*, Nietzsche had not just written the chapter "Why I Write Such Good Books," but "Why I Write Books At All.") Secondly, why has this resistance been so resisted, to the point that there are not even many disputes about TSZ, no contesting views about what *parodia* might have meant?

One obvious answer should be addressed immediately. It may be so hard to know what TSZ is for, and so easy simply to plunder it unsystematically, because the work is in large part a failure. TSZ echoes Romantic attempts at created mythologies, such as William Blake's, as well as Wagner's attempt to re-work Teutonic myth, but it remains so sui generis and unclassifiable that it resists even the broadest sort of category and does not itself instruct us, at least not very clearly or very well, about how to read it. That it is both a tragedy and a parody helps little with the details. Large stretches of it seem ponderous and turgid, mysteriously abandoning Nietzsche's characteristic light touch and pithy wit. The many dreams and dream images appealed to by Zarathustra jumble together so much (in one case, grimacing children, angels, owls, fools, and butterflies as big as children tumble out of a broken coffin) that an attempt at interpretation seems beside the point. (When a disciple tries to offer a reading of this dream – and seems to do a pretty fair job of it – Zarathustra ultimately just stares into this disciple's face and shakes his head with apparent deep disappointment.) These difficulties have all insured that TSZ is not read or studied in university philosophy departments anywhere near as often as the Nietzschean standards, *The Birth of Tragedy*, *The Uses and Disadvantages of History*, *Beyond Good and Evil*, and *The Genealogy of Morals*.

This is understandable, but such judgments may be quite premature. Throughout the short and extremely volatile reception of his work, Nietzsche may not yet have been given enough leeway with his various experiments in a new kind of philosophical writing, may have been subject much too quickly to philosophical "translations." This is an issue – how to write philosophy under contemporary historical conditions, or even how to write "philosophically" now that much of traditional philosophy itself is no longer historically credible – that Nietzsche obviously devoted a great deal of thought to, and it is extremely unlikely that his conclusions would not show up in worked out, highly crafted forms. They ask of the reader something different than traditional reading and understanding, but they are asking for some effort, even demanding it, from readers. This is especially at issue in TSZ since in so far as it could be said to have a dominant theme, it is *this* problem, Zarathustra's problem: who is his audience? What is he trying to accomplish? How does he think he should go about this? While it is pretty clear what it means for his teaching to be rejected, he seems himself very unsure of what would count as having that teaching understood and accepted. (The theme – the question we have to understand first before anything in the work can be addressed – is clearly announced in the subtitle: *A Book for All and None*. How *could* a book be for all and none?)

Thus Spoke Zarathustra as a work of literature?

On the face of it at least some answers seem accessible from the plot of the work. Zarathustra leaves his cave to revisit the human world because he wants both to prophesy and help hasten the advent of something like a new "attempt" on the part of mankind, a post "beyond" or "over the human" (*Übermensch*) aspiration. Such a goal would be free of the psychological dimensions that have led the human type into a state of some crisis (made worse by the fact that most do not think a crisis has occurred or that any new attempt is necessary). Much of the first two parts is thus occupied with setting out these failings, and the various human types who most embody them, railing against them by showing what they have cost us, and intimating how things might be different. Some such failings, like having the wrong sort of relation to oneself, or being burdened with a spirit of revenge against time itself, are particularly important. So we are treated to brief characterizations of the despisers of the body, the pale criminal, the preachers of death, warriors, chastity, the pitying, the hinterworldly, the bestowers of virtue, women, priests, the virtuous, the rabble, the sublime ones, poets, and scholars. Along the way these typologies, one might call them, are interrupted by even more figurative parables (On the Adder's Bite, the Blessed Isles, Tarantulas, the Stillest Hour), by highly figurative homilies on such topics as friends, marriage, a free death, self-overcoming, redemption, and prudence, as well as by three songs, Night Song, Dance Song, and Grave Song.

However, we encounter a very difficult issue right away when we try to take account of the fact that in all these discussions, Zarathustra's account is throughout so highly parabolic, metaphorical, and aphoristic. Rather than state various claims about virtues and the present age and religion and aspirations, Zarathustra speaks about stars, animals, trees, tarantulas, dreams, and so forth. Explanations and claims are almost always analogical and figurative. (In his discussion of TSZ in *Ecce Homo*, Nietzsche wrote, "The most powerful force of metaphor that has ever existed is poor and trivial compared with the return of language to the nature of imagery.")[12] Why is his message given in such a highly figurative, literary way? It is an important question because it goes to the heart of Nietzsche's own view of his relation to traditional philosophy, and how the literary and rhetorical form of his books marks whatever sort of new beginning he thinks he has made. Philosophy after all has traditionally thought of itself as clarifying what is unclear, and as attempting to justify what in the everyday world too often passes without challenge. Philosophy tries to reveal, we might say in general, what is hidden (in presuppositions, commitments, folk wisdom, etc.). If we think of literature in such traditional ways, though, then there is a clear contrast. A literary work does not assert anything. "Meaning" in a poem or play or novel is not only hidden, and requires effort to find; our sense of the greatness of great literature is bound up with our sense that the credibility and authority of such works rests on how much and how complexly meaning is both profoundly and unavoidably hidden and enticingly intimated, promised; how difficult to discern, but "there," extractable in prosaic summaries only with great distortion. Contrary to the philosophical attempt (or fantasy) of freeing ordinary life from illusions, confusions and unjustified presuppositions, one way in which a literary treatment departs from ordinary life lies in its great compression of possible meanings, defamiliarization, "showing" paradoxically how much *more* is hidden, mysterious, sublime in ordinary life than is ordinarily understood. (One thinks of Emily Dickinson's pithy summary: "Nature is a haunted house, but art is a house that wants to be haunted.")[13]

---

[12] EH, §6, p. 130.

[13] Emily Dickinson, *Emily Dickinson: Selected Letters*, ed. T. H. Johnson (Cambridge: Harvard University Press, 1958), p. 236. There is another text by a "Nietzschean" author that might also serve as, might even have been, a commentary on this aspect of TSZ – Kafka's famous parable, "On Parables:"

What would it mean to present a "teaching" with so many philosophical resonances, so close to the philosophy we might call "value theory," in a way that not only leaves so much hidden, but that in effect heightens our sense of the interpretive work that must be done before philosophical reflection can hope to begin (if even then), and even further impedes any hermeneutic response by inventing a context so unfamiliar and often bizarre? There is a famous claim concerning truth and appearance and a set of complex images that are both relevant to this question.[14]

Truth, appearance, and the failure of desire

In more traditional philosophical terms, Nietzsche often stresses that we start going wrong when we become captured by the picture of revealing "reality," the "truth," beneath appearances, in mere opinions. This can be particularly misleading, Nietzsche often states, when we think of ourselves in post-Kantian modernity as having exposed the supposed groundlessness "underneath" the deceptive appearances of value and purpose, when we think that we have rendered impossible any continuation of Zarathustra's pronounced love of human beings, life, and the earth. Some impasse in the possible affirmation of value (what Zarathustra calls

Many complain that the words of the wise are always merely parables and of no use in daily life, which is the only life we have. When the sage says, "Go over," he does not mean that we should cross to some actual place, which we could do anyhow if the labor were worth it; he means some fabulous yonder [Drüben], something unknown to us, something that he cannot designate more precisely either, and therefore cannot help us here in the very least. All these parables set out to say merely that the incomprehensible is incomprehensible, and we know that already. But the cares we have to struggle with every day; that is a different matter.

Concerning this a man once said: Why such reluctance? If you only followed the parables you yourselves would become parables and with that rid of all your daily cares.

Another said: I bet that is also a parable.

The first said: You have won.

The second said: But unfortunately only in parable.

The first said: No, in reality; in parable you have lost.

Franz Kafka, *The Basic Kafka* (New York: Pocket Books, 1979), p. 58. It is well known that Kafka read and admired Nietzsche. The story about his vigorous defense of Nietzsche against Max Brod's charge that Nietzsche was a "fraud" is often cited. See Klaus Wagenbach, *Kafka*, trans. Ewald Osers (Cambridge: Harvard University Press, 2003), p. 41.

[14] I pass over here another complex dimension of Nietzsche's literary style. Zarathustra is not Nietzsche, any more than Prospero is Shakespeare, and appreciating the literary irony of the work is indispensable to a full reading. I have tried to sketch an interpretation along these lines in "Irony and Affirmation in Nietzsche's *Thus Spoke Zarathustra*," in *Nietzsche's New Seas: Explorations in Philosophy, Aesthetics, and Politics*, ed. Michael Allen Gillespie and Tracy Strong (Chicago: University of Chicago Press, 1988), pp. 45–74.

"esteeming") *has* been reached ("nihilism") but this "radical enlighten-ment" picture is not the right description. (See Zarathustra's attack on the "preachers of death" and his rejection there of the melancholy that might result when "they encounter a sick or a very old person or a corpse, and right away they say, 'life is refuted'" (p. 32).) And Nietzsche clearly wants to discard as misleading that simple distinction between appearance and reality itself. He is well known for claiming, in his own mini-version of the self-education of the human spirit in *The Twilight of the Idols*, that

> We have abolished the real world: what world is left? The apparent world perhaps? . . . But no! *with the real world we have also abolished the apparent world.*[15]

However, even if this sort of suspicion of the everyday appearances (that they are merely a pale copy of the true world, the true ideal, etc.) is rejected, it is very much not the case that Nietzsche wants to infer that we are therefore left merely to achieve as much subjectively mea-sured happiness as possible, nor does he intend to open the door to a measureless, wildly tolerant pluralism. As he has set it out, Nietzsche's new philosophers (or post-philosophers) are still driven by what he calls a modern "intellectual conscience":[16] they want to know if what matters to them now ought to matter, whether there might be more important things to care about. Even though not driven by an otherworldly or tran-scendent or even "objective" ideal beneath or above the appearances, they should still be able to "overcome themselves" and in this way, to escape "wretched contentment." That is, they cannot orient themselves from the question, "What matters *in itself?*" as if a reality beneath the appearances, but even without reliance on such a reality, a possible self-dissatisfaction and striving must still be possible if an affirmable, especially what

---

[15] Friedrich Nietzsche, *Twilight of the Idols*, in *Twilight of the Idols and The Anti-Christ*, transl. R. J. Hollingdale (Harmondsworth: Penguin Books, 1968), p. 50.

[16] GS, §2, p. 29. See also the remark in *Daybreak*, about how the drive to knowledge

> has become too strong for us to be able to want happiness without knowledge or [to be able to want the happiness] of a strong, firmly rooted delusion; even to imagine such a state of things is painful to us! Restless discovering and divining has such an attraction for us, and has grown as indispensable to us as is to the lover his unrequited love, which he would at no price relinquish for a state of indifference – perhaps, indeed, we too are unrequited lovers. (Friedrich Nietzsche, *Daybreak: Thoughts on the Prejudices of Morality*, trans. R. J. Hollingdale and ed. Maudemarie Clark and Brian Leiter (Cambridge: Cambridge University Press, 1997), §429, p. 184)

Nietzsche sometimes calls a "noble" life, is still to be possible. And he clearly believes that the major element of this possibility is *his* own effect on his listeners. A great deal depends *on him* (just as in the "tragic age of the Greeks," Socrates was able to create, to legislate a new form of life). In what way, goes the implied question or experiment, can a human being now tied to the "earth" still aspire to be ultimately "over-man," *Übermensch*? How could one come to *want* such an earthly self-overcoming in these post-death-of-God conditions? Whence the right sort of contempt for one's present state, and aspiration for some future goal? Whatever the answer to such questions, Nietzsche clearly thinks that the character of Zarathustra's literary rhetoric must be understood in terms of this goal.

Parallel to the paradox of a book for all and none, this problem suggests the paradox of how Zarathustra by "going *under*" and by destroying hopes for a "hinterworld" in the names of "earth" and "life" can prepare the way for a new form of "going *over*," can prepare the transition between human beings as they now are and an "overman." One final version of essentially the same paradox: how can Zarathustra inspire and shame without being imitated, without creating disciples?[17]

For example, in the Preface to *Beyond Good and Evil*, Nietzsche notes that our long struggle with and often opposition to and dissatisfaction with our own moral tradition, European Christianity, has created a "magnificent tension (*Spannung*) of the spirit in Europe, the likes of which the earth has never known: with such a tension in our bow we can now shoot at the furthest goals." But, he goes on, the "democratic Enlightenment" also sought to "unbend" such a bow, to "make sure that spirit does not experience itself so readily as 'need.'"[18] This latter formulation coincides with a wonderfully lapidary expression in *The Gay Science*. In discussing "the millions of Europeans who cannot endure their boredom and themselves," he notes that they would even welcome "a craving to suffer" and so "to find in their suffering a probable reason for action, for

---

[17] In EH, what distinguishes Zarathustra is said to be his capacity for contradictions like this (EH, §6, pp. 129–130). See also section I, "On Great Longing," references to "loving contempt" (p. 179) and to the intertwining of love and hate for life in "The Other Dance Song" (p. 181). This is also the problem of "exemplarity" in Nietzsche's *Schopenhauer as Educator* essay. There is an illuminating essay on this issue, "Nietzsche's Perfectionism: A Reading of *Schopenhauer as Educator*," of great relevance to TSZ, by James Conant in *Nietzsche's Postmoralism: Essays on Nietzsche's Prelude to Philosophy*, ed. R. Schacht (Cambridge: Cambridge University Press, 2001), pp. 180–257.

[18] Friedrich Nietzsche, *Beyond Good and Evil*, transl. Judith Norman, ed. Rolf-Peter Horstmann and Judith Norman (Cambridge: Cambridge University Press, 2002), preface, p. 4.

deeds." In sum: "neediness is needed!" ("Not ist nötig")[19] In TSZ, the point is formulated in a similar way:

> Beware! The time approaches when human beings no longer launch the arrow of their longing beyond the human, and the string of their bow will have forgotten how to whir!
>
> Beware! The time approaches when human beings will no longer give birth to a dancing star. Beware! The time of the most contemptible human is coming, the one who can no longer have contempt for himself. [p. 9][20]

In these terms Nietzsche is trying to create something like a living model for a new, heroic form of affirmation of life (something like the way Montaigne simply offered himself to his readers),[21] and by means of this model to re-introduce this "tension" of spirit so necessary for self-overcoming. This picture of a living, complex Zarathustra and his unsettledness, his inability to rest content either in isolation or in society, his uncertainty about a form of address, his apostrophes to various dimensions of himself, his illness and recovery, are all supposed to provide us with both an archetypal picture of the great dilemma of modernity itself (the problem of affirmation, a new striving to be "higher"), but also to inspire the kind of thoughtfulness and risk taking Zarathustra embodies. In his more grandiose moments Nietzsche no doubt thought of Zarathustra's struggles and explorations as reaching for us the same fundamental level as Homer's Odysseus, as Moses, as Virgil's Aeneas, as Christ. TSZ is somehow to be addressed to the source of whatever longing, striving, desire gives life a direction, inspires sacrifice and dedication. And it will be a very difficult task. There is a clear account of the basic issue in *Ecce Homo*:

> The psychological problem apparent in the Zarathustra type is how someone who to an unprecedented degree says no and *does* no to everything everyone has said yes to so far, – how somebody like this can nevertheless be the opposite of a no-saying spirit.[22]

[19] GS, §56.
[20] See also "On Unwilling Bliss" in the third part, where Zarathustra speaks of the "desire for love" (p. xxx).
[21] For more on Nietzsche's relation to Montaigne and the French psychological tradition, see my *Nietzsche moraliste français. La conception nietzschéenne d'une psychologie philosophique*, forthcoming, 2005, Odile Jacob. Emerson is also clearly a model as well. See Conant, *Nietzsche's Postmoralism*.
[22] EH, §6, pp. 130–131.

And this way of putting the point makes it clear that Nietzsche also imagines that the experiment in so addressing each other might easily and contingently fail and fail catastrophically; it may just be the case that a sustainable attachment to life and to each other requires the kind of more standard, prosaic "illusion" (a lie) that we have also rendered impossible. The possibility of such a failure is also an issue that worries Zarathustra a great deal, as we shall see.

The problem, then, that Zarathustra must address, the problem of "nihilism," is a kind of collective failure of desire, bows that have lost their tension, the absence of "need" or of any fruitful self-contempt, the presence of wretched contentment, "settling" for too little. And these discussions of desire and meaning throw into a different light how he means to address such a failure. As we have seen, even texts other than TSZ are overwhelmingly literary, rhetorically complex, elliptical, and always a matter of adopting personae and "masks," often the mask of a historian or scientist.[23] He appears to believe that this is the only effective way to reach the level of such concern – to address an audience suffering from failed desire (without knowing it). Nietzsche clearly thinks we cannot understand such a possibility, much less be both shamed and inspired by it, except by a literary and so "living" treatment of such an existential possibility. And Nietzsche clearly thinks he has such a chance, in the current historical context of crisis, collapse, boredom, and confusion, a chance of shaming and cajoling us away from commitments that will condemn us to a "last man" or "pale atheist" sort of existence, and of inspiring a new desire, a new "tension" of the spirit. Hence the importance of these endless pictures and images: truth as a woman, science as gay, troubadours, tomb robbers, seduction, romance, prophets, animals, tightrope walkers, dwarves, beehives, crazy men, sleep, dreams, breeding, blonde beasts, twilight of the gods, and on and on. (It makes *all* the difference in the world if, having appreciated this point, we then appreciate that such notions as "the will to power" and "the eternal return of the same" *belong on this list*, are not independent "philosophical" explanations of the meaning of the list. It is not an accident that Nietzsche often introduces these notions with the same hypothetical indirectness that he uses for the other images.)

---

[23] For an extensive discussion of the issue of masks in TSZ see Stanley Rosen, *The Mask of Enlightenment: Nietzsche's Zarathustra* (Cambridge: Cambridge University Press, 1995).

The dramatic action (Prologue and Part I)

However, as in many dramatic and literary presentations of philosophy (such as Platonic dialogues, Proust's novel, Beckett's plays, and so forth) there are not only things said, but things done, and said and done by characters located somewhere and at a time, usually within a narrative time that is constantly changing contexts, conditions of appropriateness, aspects of relevance, and the like. On the face of it this means that one ought to be aware of who says what to whom when, and what is shown rather than said by what they do and what happens to them. In this case, Zarathustra had left the human world when he was thirty and stayed ten years in the mountains. We are not told why, although it is implied that he had psychologically "burned up"; he carried his own "ashes" up to the mountain. In the section "The Hinterworldly" he also tells us that he managed to free himself (he does not tell us how) from the view that the finite human world was an imperfect copy of something better, "the work of a suffering and tortured god," that such views were a kind of disease he had recovered from, and that he now speaks of "the meaning of the earth" (p. 6). But we are not told exactly when this event occurred, before or after his voluntary exile, and the speech can be misleading unless, as just discussed above, it is read together with a number of others about self-overcoming. That is, it turns out not at all to be *easy*, having abandoned a transcendent source of ideals, to live in a way true to this meaning of the earth or to understand in what sense this is a "self-overcoming" way. The latter is not a mere "liberationist" project, but one that in some ways is even more difficult than traditional self-denying virtue.

We also have no clear sense of what Zarathustra did all day, every day for ten years; he seemed mostly to think, contemplate, and talk to animals, especially his favorites, his snake and eagle (already an indication of a link between the low and the high in all things human). But we do know that something happened to him one day, his "heart transformed," and he resolved to re-enter the human world. We might assume, given Nietzsche's own diagnosis of the age, that this change was brought about by a sense of some coming crisis among humans. That is, Nietzsche is well known for calling this crisis "nihilism," and eventually many of Zarathustra's speeches express this urgency about our becoming the "last human beings," humans who can no longer "overcome themselves." But initially Zarathustra's return is promoted by motives that are explicit and somewhat harder to understand. He had become "weary" of the wisdom gained while in isolation and needs to distribute it, much as the sun gratuitously "overflows" with warmth and light for humans; he would be in some way fatigued or frustrated by not being able to share this overflow. In a brief exchange with a hermit on the way down, we learn two further things about Zarathustra's motives. His generosity is prompted by *a love of human beings*, and those who remain in hermit-like isolation can do so only because they have not heard that "God is dead."

These references to love, gift-giving, and Zarathustra's potential weariness are quite important since they amount to his further figurative answers to questions about the intended function and purpose of TSZ; it is a gift of love and meant to inspire some erotic longing as well. (This assumes that Zarathustra's fate in some way allegorizes what Nietzsche expects the fate of TSZ to be and, while this seems credible, Nietzsche also ironicizes Zarathustra enough to give one pause about such an allegory.) The images suggest that the lassitude, smug self-satisfaction, and complacency that Zarathustra finds around him in the market place and later in the city define the problem he faces in the unusual way suggested above. It again suggests that what in other contexts he could call the problem of nihilism is not so much the result of some discovery, a new piece of knowledge (that God is dead, or that values are ungrounded, contingent psychological projections), nor merely a fearful failure of will, a failing that requires the rhetoric of courage, a call to a new kind of strength. As noted, the problem Zarathustra confronts seems to be a failure of desire; nobody wants what he is offering, and they seem to want very little other than a rather bovine version of happiness. It is that sort of failure that proves particularly difficult to address, and that cannot be corrected by thinking up a "better argument" against such a failure.

The events that are narrated are also clearly tied to the question of what it means for Zarathustra to have a teaching, to try to impart it to an audience suffering in this unusual way, suffering from complacency or dead desire. Only at the very beginning, in the Prologue, does he try to "lecture publicly," one might say, and this is a pretty unambiguous failure. He is jeered at and mocked and he leaves, saying "I am not the mouth for these ears" (p. 9). The meaning of his attempt, however, seems to be acted out in an unusual drama about a tightrope walker who mistakenly thinks he is being called to start his act, does so, and then is frightened into a fall by a "jester" who had attempted to leap over the tightrope walker. It is not uncommon in TSZ that Zarathustra later returns to some of these early images and offers an interpretation. In Part III, in the section called "On Old and New Tablets," Zarathustra remarks,

> This is what my great love of the farthest demands: *do not spare your neighbor!* Human being is something that must be overcome.
> There are manifold ways and means of overcoming: *you* see to it! But only a jester thinks: "human being can also be *leaped over*." (p. 159)

This is only one of many manifestations of the importance of understanding Zarathustra's "love" and his intimations of the great difficulty involved in his new doctrine of self-overcoming. Here it is something that must be accomplished by each ("*you* see to it!") and even more strikingly, the reminder here of the Prologue appears to indicate that Zarathustra himself had portrayed his own teaching in a comically inadequate way, preaching to the multitudes as if people could simply begin to overcome themselves by some revolutionary act of will, as if the overman were a new species to be arrived at by "overleaping" the current one. We come closer here to the parodic elements of the text; in this case a kind of self-parody.

The wandering Zarathustra (Part II)

The other plot events in the book also continue to suggest a great unsettledness in Zarathustra's conception and execution of his project, rather than a confident manifesto by Nietzsche through the persona of Zarathustra. He had shifted from market place preaching to conversations with disciples in Part I, and at the end of that Part I he decides to forgo even that and to go back to his cave alone, and warns his disciples to "guard" themselves against him, and even "to be ashamed of him" (p. 59). At the beginning of Part II he begins to descend again, and again we hear that he is overfull and weary with his gifts and with love (the image of love has changed into something more dramatic: "And may my torrent of love plunge into impasses!"), but now we hear something new, something absent from his first descent: he is also concerned and impatient. "My enemies have become powerful and have distorted the image of my teaching." He will seek out his friends and disciples again (as well as his enemies this time, he notes) but he seems to have realized that part of the problem with the dissemination of his teachings and warnings lies in him, and not just the audience. He admits that his wisdom is a "wild" wisdom that frightens, and that he might scare everyone off, even his friends. "If only my lioness-wisdom could learn to roar tenderly!" he laments, a lesson he clearly thinks he has not yet learned.

The crucial dramatic event in Part II is what occurs near the end. Until then many of Zarathustra's themes had been similar to, or extensions of, what he had already said. Again he seeks to understand the possibility of a form of self-dissatisfaction and even self-contempt that is not based on some sense of *absence* or incompleteness, a natural gap or imperfection that needs to be filled or completed, and so a new goal that can be linked with a new *kind* of desire to "overcome." He discusses that issue here in terms of "revenge," especially against time, and he begins to worry that, with no redemptive revolutionary hope in human life, no ultimate justice in the after-life, and no realm of objective "goods in themselves" or any natural right, human beings will come to see a finite, temporally mutable, contingent life as a kind of burden, or curse, or purposeless play, and they will exact revenge for having been arbitrarily thrown into this condition. What he means to say in the important section "On the Tarantulas" is something he had not made clear before, least of all to himself. Indeed, he had helped create the illusion he wants to dispel. He now denies that he, Zarathustra, is a historical or revolutionary figure who will somehow save all of us from this fate, and he denies that the overman is a historical goal (in the way a prophet would foretell the coming of *the* redeemer) but a personal and quite elusive, very difficult new kind of ideal for each individual. In this sense TSZ can be a book for all, for anyone who is responsive to the call to self-overcoming, but for none, in the sense that it cannot offer a comprehensive reason (for anyone) to overcome themselves and cannot offer specific prescriptions. (It is striking that, although Zarathustra opens his speeches with the call for an overman, that aspect of his message virtually drops out after Part II.)[24] Indeed Zarathustra's role as such an early prophet is again part of what makes his early manifestation comic, a *parodia*. He is clearly pulling back from such a role:

> But so that I do *not* whirl, my friends, bind me fast to the pillar here!
> I would rather be a stylite than a whirlwind of revenge!

---

[24] For more detail on the relation between the first two parts and the last two, see Pippin, "Irony and Affirmation."

> Indeed, Zarathustra is no tornado or whirlwind; and if he is a
> dancer, nevermore a tarantella dancer! (p. 79)

Even so, this dance of some escape from revenge is hardly an automatic affirmation of existence as such. Throughout Part II, there are constant reminders of how *hard* this new sort of self-overcoming will be. The "Famous Wise Men" did not know the first thing about what "spirit" truly was:

> Spirit is life that itself cuts into life; by its own agony it increases its
> own knowledge – did you know that?
> And the happiness of spirit is this: to be anointed and consecrated
> by tears to serve as a sacrificial animal – did you know that? (p. 80)

Other dimensions of this "agony," and the failed hopes of the beginning of his project start appearing. He says that "My happiness in bestowing died in bestowing, my virtue wearied of itself in its superabundance" (p. 82). Paradoxical (to say the least) formulations arise. "At bottom I love only life – and verily, most when I hate it!"

The problem of self-overcoming

But he seems also to be gaining some clarity about his earlier aspirations and about the nature of the theme that plays the most important role in TSZ, "self-overcoming." In a passage with that name, he comments on the doctrine most associated with Nietzsche, "the will to power." But again everything is expressed figuratively. He says that all prior values had been placed in a "skiff" as a result of the "dominating will" of the inventors of such values and he suggests that this "river of becoming" has carried those values to a disturbingly unexpected fate. He counsels these "wisest ones" not to think of this historical and largely uncontrollable fate as dangerous and the end of good and evil; rather the river itself (not a psychological will for power on the part of the creators) is the will to power, the "unexhausted begetting will of life," the current of radical historical change "upon" which or in terms of which obeying and esteeming and committing must always go on. And he notes that he has learned three things about this process. (1) Life itself (that is the possibility of *leading* a life) always requires "obedience," that is, the possibility of commitment to a norm or goal and the capacity to sustain such commitment.

(2) "The one who cannot obey himself is commanded." (If we do not find a way of leading our life, it will be led for us one way or another.) And (3) "Commanding is harder than obeying." He then adds what is in effect a fourth point to these, that the attempt to exercise such command is "an experiment and a risk"; indeed a risk of life. He tells us that with these questions he is at the very "heart of life and into the roots of its heart" (p. 89). There, in this heartland, he again confronts the problem he had discussed earlier in many different ways, the wrong sort of self-contempt, the absence of any arrows shot beyond man, no giving birth to stars, the bovine complacency of the last human beings. He asks again, that is, *the* question: without possible reliance on a faith in divine purposes or natural perfections (that river has "carried" us beyond such options), how should we now understand the possibility of the "intellectual conscience" without which we would be beneath contempt? That is, whence the experience that we are *not* as we could be, that what matters to me now might not be what should matter most, that our present state, for each individual, must be "overcome?" Why? Since the summary "secret" that Zarathustra has learned from life is expressed this way – "And this secret life itself spoke to me: 'Behold,' it said, 'I am that *which must always overcome itself*,'" – it appears that what is at stake for him is the possibility of coming to exercise power *over oneself*; that is, to lead one's life both by sustaining commitments (right "to the death," he often implies, suggesting that being able to lead a life in such a whole-hearted way is much more to be esteemed than merely staying alive) and by finding some way to endure the altering historical conditions of valuing, esteeming, such that one can "overcome" the self so committed to prior values and find a way to "will" again. One could say that what makes the "overman" (*Übermensch*) genuinely self-transcending is that he can over-come himself, accomplish when necessary this self-transcending (*Selbst-Überwindung.*) He thereby has gained power "over" himself and so realized his will to power:

> That I must be struggle and becoming and purpose and the contradiction of purposes – alas, whoever guesses my will guesses also on what *crooked* paths it must walk!
>
> Whatever I may create and however I may love it – soon I must oppose it and my love, thus my will wants it. (pp. 89–90)

Likewise, Zarathustra stresses that good and evil, any life-orienting normative distinctions, are hardly everlasting; rather they "must overcome themselves out of themselves again and again." That is, self-overcoming is not transcending a present state for the sake of an ideal, stable higher state (as in a naturally perfected state or any other kind of fixed telos). All aspirations to be more, better than one is, if they are possible at all in present conditions, are provisional, will always give rise to further transformed aspirations. Zarathustra's questions about this do not so much concern traditional philosophical questions about such a form of life but a much more difficult one to address: could we *bear, endure* such a fate? Clearly Zarathustra's own starts and stops, and the effect these have on him, are meant to raise such an issue dramatically. (And it is not at all clear that this issue is in any way resolved, or that a resolution is even relevant.)

Two other things are quite striking about these formulations. The first, as the autobiographical inflection of such passages makes clear, is that we have to see Zarathustra as embodying this struggle, and thus must note that this possibility – the heart of everything, the possibility of self-overcoming – seems thereby also tied somehow to *his* problems of rhetoric, language, of audience, friends, his own loneliness, and occasional bitterness and pity. Some condition of success in self-overcoming is linked to achieving the right relation to others (and so, by implication, is inconsistent with a hermit-like, isolated life). The second emerges quickly from the first. We have to note that Zarathustra, as the embodiment of this struggle, whatever this relation to others turns out to be, is completely uninterested in gaining power *over others*, subjecting as much or as many as possible to his control or command. ("I lack the lion's voice for all commanding" (p. 116).) *Self*-commanding (and, dialectically, self-obeying) are the great problems. (In fact he keeps insisting that the *last* thing he wants is the ability to command them. His chief problem is that whenever he hears them re-formulate what he thinks he has said or dreamt, he is either disappointed, or perhaps anxious that he does not understand his own "doctrine"; they may be right, he may be wrong, and no intellectual conscience could sustain a commitment that was suspected of being delusory.) Even when he appears to discuss serving or mastering others, he treats it as in the service of self-mastery and so again possible self-overcoming. ("[A]nd even in the will of the serving I found the will to be master" (p. 89).)[25]

---

[25] There are of course other passages in Nietzsche which seem to encourage a violent upheaval, all so that the strong can rule over the weak and so forth. I have only space to say that if we use TSZ

These are less formulations of a position than fragmentary and largely programmatic aspects of Zarathustra's self-diagnosis and the cure he at least aspires to. Many philosophical questions arise inevitably. *What* would be amiss, lost, wrong in a life not fully or not at all "led" by a subject? How could this aspiration towards something believed to be higher or more worthy than what one is or has now *be directed*, if all the old language of external or objective forms of normative authority is now impossible? On what grounds can one say that a desire to cultivate a different sort of self, to overcome oneself, is really in the service of a "higher" self? Higher in what sense? What could be said to be responsible for (relied on for) securing this obedience, for helping to ward off skepticism when it arises? Under what conditions can such commitments and projects be said to lose their grip on a subject, fail, or die?

In general Zarathustra does not fully accept the burden of these questions as ones he must assume. For one thing he clearly does not believe that the inspiration for such an attempt at self-direction and something like "becoming better at becoming who one is"[26] can be provided by an argument or a revelation or a command. One would already have had to measure oneself and one's worth against "arguments" or "revelation" or "authoritative commands" for such different calls to be effective and it is to *that* prior, deepest level of commitment that Zarathustra, however indirectly and figuratively, is directing his rhetoric. And given the great indeterminateness of his approach, he is clearly much more interested in the qualitative characteristics of such commitments than with their content. The quality he is most interested in turns out to be extremely complex: on the one hand, "whole-heartedness" and an absorbed or passionate "identification" with one's higher ideal; on the other hand, a paradoxical capacity to "let go" of such commitments and pursue other ideals when the originals (somehow) cease to serve self-overcoming and self-transcendence, when they lead to complacency and contentment.

However, to come to by far the most complicated issue introduced by Zarathustra's speeches, he clearly also thinks that such qualitative considerations – the chief topic of the book, the qualitative dimensions

as a model for reading Nietzsche, and attend to issues like voice, persona, irony, and context, we will see a Nietzsche very different from the traditional one. For more on the political issues in Nietzsche, see my "Deceit, Desire, and Democracy: Nietzsche on Modern Eros," *International Studies in Philosophy*, 32:3 (March, 2000), pp. 63–70.

[26] That is, better at becoming who one truly is, beyond or over one's present state.

of a self-relation that will in the present circumstances make possible a yearning for a self-overcoming and escape from mere contentment – will also *rule out various contents*. It is clear that he, and in this case Nietzsche as well, thinks that one cannot whole-heartedly and "self-overcomingly" *be* a "last human being" or any of its many manifestations (a petty tyrant, a pale atheist, a "reactive" type, a modern ascetic). Such types embody forms of a "negative" self-relation that are "reactive" and self-denying in a way that makes true self-overcoming and self-affirmation impossible and so will not allow that form of identification with one's deeds that Zarathustra suggests should be like the way a "mother" sees herself in her "child." ("I wish *your* self were in the deed like the mother is in the child; let that be *your* word on virtue" (p. 74).) Yet it is also clear that one cannot simply *will* "to have contempt for oneself as Zarathustra recommends." The right relation between shame and yearning is as delicate and elusive as are Zarathustra's strange speeches and dreams and visions. And, as we have been seeing, he also clearly thinks (or he experiences in his own adventures) that only *some kinds of relations to others* are consistent with the possibility of such genuine self-direction. Merely commanding others, discipleship, indifference, or isolation are all ruled out. Since we also do not ever get from Nietzsche a discursive account of what distinguishes a genuine form of self-direction and self-overcoming from an illusory or self-deceived one (whatever such a distinction amounts to, it is not of the kind that could be helped, would be better realized, by such a theory), elements of how he understands that distinction emerge only indirectly and, together with a clearer understanding of self-overcoming and the social relations it requires, would all have to be reconstructed from a wide variety of contexts and passages. Moreover, to make everything even more complicated, Nietzsche also clearly believes that such a whole-hearted aspiration to self-overcoming is also consistent with a certain level of *irony*, some distance from one's ideals, the adoption of personae and masks, and even a kind of esotericism when addressing different audiences.

Illness and convalescence (Part III)

But while Zarathustra does not treat these issues as discursive problems, as if they were problems about skepticism or justification, he does *suffer* from them, suffer from the burden that the thought of such contingency imposes on any possibly worthy life. He becomes ill, apparently ill with the human condition as such, even disgusted by it, and a great deal of the latter four speeches of Part II and the majority of Part III involve his possible recovery from such an illness, his "convalescing." There is in effect a kind of mini-narrative from the speech called "The Soothsayer" in Part II until the speech "On Unwilling Bliss" in Part III that is at the center of the work's drama, and the re-orientation effected there is played out throughout the rest of Part III, especially in "The Convalescent." Dramatically, at the end of Part II Zarathustra again resolves to return home, and in Part III he is underway back there, and finally reaches his cave and his animals.

"The Soothsayer" begins with remarks about the famous doctrine mostly attributed to Nietzsche, but here expressed by a soothsayer and quoted by Zarathustra. (In *Ecce Homo*, the idea is called the "basic idea" and "fundamental thought" of the work.)[27] This notion, that "Everything is empty, everything is the same, everything was!" is promptly interpreted in a melancholic way, such that "We have become too weary to die; now we continue to wake and we live on – in burial chambers" (p. 106). It is this prophecy that "went straight to his [Zarathustra's] heart and transformed him." He does not eat or drink for three days, does not speak, and does not sleep. In typically figurative language he explains the source of his despair in a way that suggests a kind of self-critique. He had clearly earlier placed his hopes for mankind in a dramatic historical, epochal moment, the bridge from man to the overman, and he now realizes that it was a mistake to consider this a historical goal or broad civilizational ideal, that such a teleology is a fantasy, that rather "all recurs eternally," that the last human being cannot be overcome in some revolutionary moment. In the language of his strange dream he finds that he does not, after all, have the "keys" to open the relevant historical gate (he thought he did, thought he need not only keep watch over, but could open up, what had gone dead), that it is a matter of chance or a sudden wind whether or not a historical change will occur within individuals, and if it does, it might be nothing but the release of what had been dead. His disciples promptly interpret the dream in exactly the opposite way, as if Zarathustra himself were "the [liberating] wind." Zarathustra merely shakes his head in disappointment and continues his wandering home.

---

[27] EH, §1, pp. 123 and 124.

The details of Zarathustra's re-evaluation of what is required now of him and his addressees in order, in effect, to "take up the reins" of a life and live it better, to embody a commitment to constant self-transcendence, instead of merely suffering existence, involve scores of images and parables. Zarathustra will not now see himself as removing the deformity from "cripples." That is useless, he implies; they must do that for themselves. Or Zarathustra must learn to be silent often, to teach by not teaching, and this occasions the clearest expressions, even at this late date, of the ambiguities in Zarathustra's role and self-understanding:

> Is he a promiser? Or a fulfiller? A conqueror? Or an inheritor? An autumn? Or a plow? A physician? Or a convalescent?
>
> Is he a poet? Or a truthful man? A liberator? Or a tamer? A good man? Or an evil man?
>
> I walk among human beings as among fragments of the future; the future that I see. (p. 110)

Yet again, the question of who Zarathustra is, what he stands for, what his purpose is, remains a puzzling question *for Zarathustra himself*. Zarathustra, in other words, cannot understand what it means to be a "spokesman" for Zarathustra. We are obviously very far from being able to see him as a spokesman for Nietzsche.

This is all also said to effect a kind of "reconciliation" with circular, repetitive time. He will encourage a liberation in which what we took to be what merely happened to us in the past can be assumed as the burden of one's own doing, that one will heroically take on what merely "was" as one's own and so transform it into "thus I willed it." (This might be likened to a Greek tragic hero who takes on more of a burden of what was done than can be strictly attributed to his deed, someone like Oedipus or Ajax.[28]) He does not need the "lion's voice" of commanding: "The stillest words are those that bring the storm. Thoughts that come on the feet of doves steer the world" (p. 117).

Throughout Part III, Zarathustra speaks mostly to himself; he learns that his greatest danger is "love," "the danger of the loneliest one, love of everything *if only it lives!*" (p. 123). He must struggle with a "spirit of gravity," his own reflective doubt that he will be "dragged down"

---

[28] See Bernard Williams, *Shame and Necessity* (Berkeley: University of California Press, 1994).

by the "abysmal thought" of the Eternal Return. It is in this struggle that he realizes that the way in which the meaning of the absence of historical revolution or redemption is lived out or embodied in a life is not something that can be easily read off from the mere doctrine itself. There is no clear, unavoidable inference either to despair, indifference, or affirmation. The dwarf, the spirit of gravity, does that (reads despair as the implication) and "makes it too easy on himself" (p. 126). And Zarathustra again tries to "dream" his way out of his sadness by dreaming himself as a young shepherd "choking" on his own "circular" doctrine, the Eternal Return, but one who succeeds in "biting off the head of the snake" that had crawled into his throat, and so emerged "a transformed, illuminated, laughing" being (p. 127). Just how exactly the despair-inducing features of there being no temporal redemption and a ceaseless return of even the last men are transformed into an affirmative vision, and just how *this* is captured by "biting the head off the snake" is not clear. When that very question comes up much more explicitly in "The Convalescent" (Zarathustra fasts again for seven days and when he resumes speaking he mentions again the "nausea" that the thought of the Eternal Return occasioned), the attempt by his animals to attribute the Eternal Return to Zarathustra as a "teaching" is met first by his complaint that they are turning him and his struggle into a "hurdy-gurdy song" and when they go on and interpret the doctrine as a kind of immortality teaching (that Zarathustra will return), Zarathustra ignores them, communes only with his soul. Also, given that aspects of Zarathustra's own despair *return* after this, the image of recovery might be as much wishful thinking, or at least the expression of a mere faint hope as it is a settled event.

Zarathustra's tragic end? Parables and parody (Part IV)

This dialogue with his disciples also shows that one of the things that recurs repeatedly for Zarathustra are his own words; that he cannot prevent the "literalization" of his parabolic speech. His disciples are not dense or merely mistaken; they are simply trying to understand what Zarathustra means. When repeated as a teaching or a doctrine, Zarathustra's parabolic speech becomes parodic, comic. But he has no option other than saying nothing (and he has found that he cannot live in such isolation) or preaching more directly, in which case his disciples would be (even more than they already are) following him, not themselves. The parodic return of his own words is thus the heart of his tragedy.[29]

After this expression of his putative, perhaps short-lived new self-understanding, he believes he can say such things as "I gave it [chance] back to all things, I redeemed them from their servitude under purpose" (p. 132). Having done so, a "homecoming" back with his animals is now possible, he thinks, and he expresses the relation to others, here his animals, that he would have wanted "down there," but failed to achieve: "We do not implore one another, we do not deplore one another, we walk openly with one another through open doors" (p. 147). Thus, as we drift towards the end of the Part III, which Nietzsche at one time clearly conceived as the end of the book, Zarathustra's despair at any change in the collective or individual lives of human beings seems at its darkest. However, as is so typical of the wandering eros of Zarathustra, within a few speeches he announces yet again "I want to return to mankind once more" (p. 156).

He does not, however, and at the beginning of the Part IV, Zarathustra is still alone, and he is old now. He re-encounters the soothsayer but one cannot see in their confrontation that anything decisive is settled. And, although Zarathustra begins to talk with and assemble a wide variety of what are called "higher human beings" (kings, an old magician, the pope, the voluntary beggar, the shadow, the conscientious of spirit, the sad soothsayer, and the ass), his own "teaching" about overcoming and the higher seems here yet again parodied rather than celebrated. As noted, Part IV reads more like a comic, concluding satyr play to a tragic trilogy than a real conclusion. It is especially self-parodic when all these so-called higher types end up worshipping a jackass, presumably because the ass can at least make a sound that articulates what all have been seeking, a mode of affirmation and commitment. The ass can say Hee-yaw, that is, ja, or Yes!

So we end with the same problem. Zarathustra must report, "But I still lack the proper human beings." However, when a "cloud of love" descends around him,[30] and he hears a lion's roar (a "sign" that takes us back to

---

[29] On this point I am grateful to conversations with David Wellbery.

[30] Compare, "*it is only in love,* only when shaded by the illusions produced by love, that is to say in the unconditional faith in right and perfection, that man is creative." Friedrich Nietzsche, "On the Uses and Disadvantages of History for Life," in *Untimely Meditations,* trans. R. J. Hollingdale, ed. Daniel Breazeale (Cambridge: Cambridge University Press, 1997), §7, p. 95.

the three metamorphoses of the first speech), he also believes that "My children are near, my children," and yet again he leaves his cave, "glowing and strong, like a morning sun that emerges from dark mountains" (p. 266). But by this point we are experiencing as readers our own eternal return, the cycle of hope and despair, descent and return, sociality and isolation, love and contempt, parable and parody, lower and higher, earth and heaven, snake and eagle, that we have been reading about throughout. The "ending" in other words is meant to suggest a cyclical temporality, as if to pose for us the question Zarathustra continually has to ask himself. The question is oriented from the now familiar assumptions: no redemptive or revolutionary moment in human time, no re-assurance about or reliance on the naturally right or good; no revelations from God; and the eventual return of everything we have tried to overcome. Given such assumptions, the question is whether the self-overcoming Zarathustra encourages, the desire for some greater or better form of self-direction, assuming the full burden of leading a life, is practically possible, from the lived viewpoint of the agent.

In keeping with the unsystematic form of the clear models for TSZ – biblical wisdom literature, the French moral psychologists of the sixteenth and seventeenth centuries (Montaigne, Pascal, La Rochefoucauld), Emerson, Goethe – it is of course appropriate that we be "taught" nothing about this by Zarathustra, "taught" if at all only by his ultimate silence about this new possibility and so its challenge to us, to make it "our own." No lessons can be drawn from it, no summary credo articulated, no justification for a position formulated, any more than any "gift of love" like this, any image of a life worth living under these conditions, can be interrogated in this way. The work seems to function as the same kind of "test" for the reader as the soothsayer's doctrine for Zarathustra. Either the temper and credibility of Zarathustra's constant return to the ultimately unredeemable human world will strike the chord Nietzsche hoped still existed, or it will not; either there are such "children" as Zarathustra sees in his final vision, or they will seem like the illusions that so many of Zarathustra's hopes have proven to be from the beginning. Or to adopt the language of Zarathustra, and in this case at least, Nietzsche himself, perhaps such children do have the status of mere dreams, but they thereby also might satisfy what Nietzsche once described as the conditions of contemporary self-overcoming: the ability to "dream" without first having to "sleep."[31]

Robert B. Pippin

[31] GS, §59. A re-orientation of some sort that would permit the entertaining of some aspiration or ideal, some inspiring picture that would not (given our intellectual conscience) have to be treated as a distortion or fantasy or merely utopian (that we would not have to "sleep," shut off our conscience) in order to dream in this way, is at the heart of the Kafka fable cited in n. 13 above. From what has become the ordinary viewpoint, parables are a waste of time (What is Nietzsche's proposal? His plan? How does he want us to live?), and the right understanding would be to *live out* the parable; but, paradoxically, not "*as* a parable," as if a self-conscious idealization. That would be "correct," from the viewpoint of reality, but a destruction of the parable's function; one would have "lost."

Chronology

task and truly metaphysical activity of his life"; devastating reviews follow.

1873 Publishes "David Strauss, the Confessor and the Writer," the first of his *Untimely Meditations*; begins taking books on natural science out of the Basle library, whereas he had previously confined himself largely to books on philological matters. Writes "On Truth and Lying in a Non-Moral Sense."

1874 Publishes two more *Meditations*, "The Uses and Disadvantages of History for Life" and "Schopenhauer as Educator."

1876 Publishes the fourth *Meditation*, "Richard Wagner in Bayreuth," which already bears subtle signs of his movement away from Wagner.

1878 Publishes *Human, All Too Human* (dedicated to the memory of Voltaire); it praises science over art as the high culture and thus marks a decisive turn away from Wagner.

1879 Terrible health problems force him to resign his chair at Basle (with a small pension); publishes "Assorted Opinions and Maxims," the first part of vol. II of *Human, All Too Human*; begins living alone in Swiss and Italian boarding-houses.

1880 Publishes "The Wanderer and His Shadow," which becomes the second part of vol. II of *Human, All Too Human*.

1881 Publishes *Daybreak*.

1882 Publishes *Idylls of Messina* (eight poems) in a monthly magazine; publishes *The Gay Science* (first edition); friendship with Paul Rée and Lou Andreas-Salomé ends badly, leaving Nietzsche devastated.

1883 Publishes the first two parts of *Thus Spoke Zarathustra;* learns of Wagner's death just after mailing Part I to the publisher.

1884 Publishes Part III of *Thus Spoke Zarathustra*.

1885 Publishes Part IV of *Zarathustra* for private circulation only.

1886 Publishes *Beyond Good and Evil*; writes prefaces for new releases of: *The Birth of Tragedy, Human, All Too Human*, vols. I and II, and *Daybreak*.

1887 Publishes expanded edition of *The Gay Science* with a new preface, a fifth book, and an appendix of poems; publishes *Hymn to Life*, a musical work for chorus and orchestra; publishes *On the Genealogy of Morality*.

1888   Publishes *The Case of Wagner*, composes a collection of poems, *Dionysian Dithyrambs*, and four short books: *Twilight of Idols*, *The Antichrist*, *Ecce Homo*, and *Nietzsche contra Wagner*.

1889   Collapses physically and mentally in Turin on 3 January; writes a few lucid notes but never recovers sanity; is briefly institutionalized; spends remainder of his life as an invalid, living with his mother and then his sister, who also gains control of his literary estate.

1900   Dies in Weimar on 25 August.

Further reading

Thus Spoke Zarathustra has attracted the most attention of all of Nietzsche's works, it is therefore his most popular in terms of printings and sales, and his most critically acclaimed. Attempts to do justice to the richness and strangeness of this work by providing detailed commentary on each chapter began early, in the nineteenth century, with Gustav Naumann's *Zarathustra-Commentar* (4 vols., Leipzig: H. Haessel, 1899–1901). Naumann's commentary addresses each chapter of *Zarathustra* in a reliable and nuanced manner, making it useful even today (at least to readers of German). Naumann was also highly critical of the machinations of Nietzsche's sister, Elisabeth Förster-Nietzsche, as she enlisted sympathetic editors to manufacture her own image of Nietzsche and her own edition of his works. Historically Naumann's commentary is valuable because it is part of the phenomenal reception of Nietzsche's ideas at the turn of the century, and because it is early enough to be untainted by the negative fall-out of the two world wars and their lingering damage to Nietzsche's reputation. The next comprehensive attempt to explain *Zarathustra* began in the 1930s and took the form of a six-year seminar given by C. G. Jung at the university of Zurich. For decades the unpublished notes of this seminar circulated in photocopy among the Nietzsche underground at various universities until finally they were edited and published by James L. Jarrett as *Nietzsche's "Zarathustra": Notes of the Seminar Given in 1934–1939 by C. G. Jung* (2 vols., Princeton University Press, 1988). This commentary by chapter is unparalleled in revealing the complex creative process behind *Zarathustra*, and though preachy at times, it subjects both Nietzsche and his creation to an anthropological approach that only Jung could present. Jarrett's editing is quite skillful, while the seminar format of the "notes" makes this commentary uniquely discursive.

More recent commentaries devoted exclusively to *Zarathustra* and limited to a single volume are extremely useful as well. Laurence Lampert's *Nietzsche's Teaching: An Interpretation of "Thus Spoke Zarathustra"* (Yale University Press, 1986), establishes the need for a new teaching, the nature of the teaching, and the foundational role it plays in the history of philosophy. Lampert's *Nietzsche and Modern Times: A Study of Bacon, Descartes, and Nietzsche* (Yale University Press, 1993), much broader in scope, goes further in the direction of specifying the ecological, earth-affirming properties of Nietzsche's teaching via Zarathustra. Kathleen Higgin's *Nietzsche's "Zarathustra"* (Temple University Press, 1987), which she prefers to designate not as commentary but "analysis" instead, treats Zarathustra in the context of the teachers Socrates and Christ. She strives to rehabilitate the reputation of *Zarathustra* as a whole, and particularly Part IV. Stanley Rosen, in *The Mask of Enlightenment: Nietzsche's "Zarathustra"* (Cambridge University Press, 1995), comments on most of the chapters while bringing all of Nietzsche's writings to bear on this difficult and, for him, sometimes disturbing book. Rosen is mindful of the contradiction inherent in Nietzsche's attempt to speak simultaneously to the few (esoterically) and to everyone (exoterically). Robert Gooding-Williams, in *Zarathustra's Dionysian Modernism* (Stanford University Press, 2001), has delivered the latest of the *Zarathustra*-commentaries, and perhaps the most powerful in terms of maintaining hermeneutic continuity. The concept of a "Dionysian modernism" is effective in unifying the study and highlighting Zarathustra's mission as a revival of the earth's passions. Joachim Köhler's *Zarathustra's Secret: The Interior Life of Friedrich Nietzsche* (Yale University Press, 2002, translation of *Zarathustras Geheimnis*, 1992), purports to be a biography exposing the gamut of Nietzsche's philosophizing as secret code for the glorification of homosexuality. Köhler reduces all of Nietzsche's motivations and teachings to his alleged homoeroticism, sometimes with breathtaking obtuseness, and he uses it to undermine Nietzsche's philosophical validity.

Articles that address significant aspects of *Zarathustra* include Gary Shapiro, "The Rhetoric of Nietzsche's *Zarathustra*," in *Philosophical Style: An Anthology about the Writing and Reading of Philosophy*, ed. Berel Lang (Chicago: Nelson-Hall, 1980), pp. 347–85; Robert B. Pippin, "Irony and Affirmation in Nietzsche's *Thus Spoke Zarathustra*," in

Nietzsche's New Seas: Explorations in Philosophy, Aesthetics, and Politics, ed. Michael Allen Gillespie and Tracy B. Strong (Chicago and London: University of Chicago Press, 1988), pp. 45–71; Daniel W. Conway, "Solving the Problem of Socrates: Nietzsche's *Zarathustra* as Political Irony," *Political Theory* 16:2 (1998), pp. 257–80; Keith Ansell-Pearson, "Who is the *Übermensch*? Time, Truth, and Woman in Nietzsche," *Journal of the History of Ideas* 53:2 (1992), pp. 309–31; Graham Parkes, "Staying Loyal to the Earth: Nietzsche as an Ecological Thinker" in *Nietzsche's Futures*, ed. John Lippit (St. Martin's Press, 1999), pp. 167–88.

There are also several books that deal substantially with *Zarathustra* while not attempting to provide running commentary on chapter and verse. The first of these is Karl Löwith's *Nietzsche's Philosophy of the Eternal Recurrence of the Same* (University of California Press, 1997; translation of *Nietzsches Philosophie der ewigen Wiederkehr des Gleichen*, 1956), still the most thorough and compelling philosophical treatment to date of the unifying doctrine of *Zarathustra*. Philip Grundlehner's *The Poetry of Friedrich Nietzsche* (Oxford University Press, 1986), sheds light not only on the dithyrambs interspersed throughout Part IV, but on Nietzsche's entire lyrical poetic output, of which *Zarathustra* is in many ways symptomatic. The debate concerning poetry vs. philosophy is given careful treatment in Grundlehner's study. Rudolf Kreis's *Nietzsche, Wagner and die Juden* (Königshausen und Neumann, 1995) is underutilized in the English-speaking world. Kreis's great service lies not in his thesis that Nietzsche opposed Wagner by writing *Zarathustra* as an "anti-*Parsifal*," but in his more broadly juxtaposing the earth-affirming ethos of the ancient Jews with the earth-denying ethos of modern Christian anti-Semitism. Kreis's book traces the fortunes of the earth as ecosystem, casting the encounter between Nietzsche and Wagner as a defining moment. John Richardson's *Nietzsche's System* (Oxford University Press, 1996) represents a highly readable and refined analysis of both the superhuman and the will to power. Richardson makes strides toward an ecumenical Nietzsche when he consistently renders German *Mensch* as "human being," but he fails to follow through by rendering *Übermensch* as superhuman. For the purpose of providing an elegant and readable translation "overman" may well be the preferred expression, but for purposes of scholarship, the English-speaking world should have advanced far enough beyond Shaw's and Marvel's comic book "superman" to speak in terms of the superhuman. Gregory Moore's *Nietzsche, Biology and*

Metaphor (Cambridge University Press, 2002), though disappointing in its failure to recognize the Dionysian as a source of Nietzsche's biologically inclined rhetoric, is nonetheless the best study to date on how Nietzsche responded to the scientific literature of his day in constructing his own views on evolution and degeneration. Adrian Del Caro's *Grounding the Nietzsche Rhetoric of Earth* (Walter de Gruyter, 2004) unpacks Zarathustra's proclamation that "the superhuman is the meaning of the earth," and delivers a multifaceted treatment of the ecological Nietzsche.

Note on the text

The text used for this translation is printed in the now standard edition of Nietzsche's works edited by Giorgio Colli and Mazzino Montinari (Berlin: de Gruyter, 1967–77). Their edition and their *Kritische Studien-ausgabe* in fifteen volumes (Berlin: de Gruyter, 1988) have been used in the preparation of the footnotes to this edition. The spacing and versification of the original are preserved in this edition.

Thus Spoke Zarathustra
A Book for All and None
First Part

Zarathustra's Prologue

1

When Zarathustra was thirty years old he left his home and the lake of his home and went into the mountains. Here he enjoyed his spirit and his solitude and for ten years he did not tire of it. But at last his heart transformed, – one morning he arose with the dawn, stepped before the sun and spoke thus to it:

"You great star! What would your happiness be if you had not those for whom you shine?

For ten years you have come up here to my cave: you would have tired of your light and of this route without me, my eagle and my snake.

But we awaited you every morning, took your overflow from you and blessed you for it.

Behold! I am weary of my wisdom, like a bee that has gathered too much honey. I need hands that reach out.

I want to bestow and distribute until the wise among human beings have once again enjoyed their folly, and the poor once again their wealth.

For this I must descend into the depths, as you do evenings when you go behind the sea and bring light even to the underworld, you super-rich star!

Like you, I must *go down*[1] as the human beings say, to whom I want to descend.

So bless me now, you quiet eye that can look upon even an all too great happiness without envy!

Bless the cup that wants to flow over, such that water flows golden from it and everywhere carries the reflection of your bliss!

Behold! This cup wants to become empty again, and Zarathustra wants to become human again."

– Thus began Zarathustra's going under.

---

[1] German uses *untergehen*, literally "to go under" for the expression the sun "goes down." Nietzsche throughout *Zarathustra* uses wordplay to signify that Zarathustra's "going under" is a "going over" or transition, *übergehen*, from human to superhuman, from man to overman. After Zarathustra draws his first analogy between himself and the sun, I use "going under" for *untergehen* and its noun form *Untergang*. In setting or going down the sun marks a transition. Zarathustra meanwhile has been higher than human in both figurative and literal terms, and so his "going under" has the effect of him transitioning to human again. However, on the ecumenical level, when human beings transition or go under, and when they "overcome" the human, they should achieve the superhuman (overman).

2

Zarathustra climbed down alone from the mountains and encountered no one. But when he came to the woods suddenly an old man stood before him, who had left his saintly hut in search of roots in the woods. And thus spoke the old man to Zarathustra:

"This wanderer is no stranger to me: many years ago he passed by here. Zarathustra he was called; but he is transformed.

Back then you carried your ashes to the mountain: would you now carry your fire into the valley? Do you not fear the arsonist's punishment?

Yes, I recognize Zarathustra. His eyes are pure, and no disgust is visible around his mouth. Does he not stride like a dancer?

Zarathustra is transformed, Zarathustra has become a child, an awakened one is Zarathustra. What do you want now among the sleepers?

You lived in your solitude as if in the sea, and the sea carried you. Alas, you want to climb ashore? Alas, you want to drag your own body again?"

Zarathustra answered: "I love mankind."[2]

"Why," asked the saint, "did I go into the woods and the wilderness in the first place? Was it not because I loved mankind all too much?

Now I love God: human beings I do not love. Human beings are too imperfect a thing for me. Love for human beings would kill me."

Zarathustra replied. "Why did I speak of love? I bring mankind a gift."

"Give them nothing," said the saint. "Rather take something off them and help them to carry it – that will do them the most good, if only it does you good!

And if you want to give to them, then give nothing more than alms, and make them beg for that too!"

"No," answered Zarathustra. "I do not give alms. For that I am not poor enough."

The saint laughed at Zarathustra and spoke thus: "Then see to it that they accept your treasures! They are mistrustful of hermits and do not believe that we come to give gifts.

---

[2] "Ich liebe die Menschen" means literally "I love human beings." Earlier translators ignored the ecological framework in which Nietzsche wrote *Zarathustra* by using expressions like "man." The prologue establishes a prevailing semantic field, a framework in which human beings, animals, nature and earth interact or should interact as never before.

To them our footsteps sound too lonely in the lanes. And if at night lying in their beds they hear a man walking outside, long before the sun rises, they probably ask themselves: where is the thief going?

Do not go to mankind and stay in the woods! Go even to the animals instead! Why do you not want to be like me – a bear among bears, a bird among birds?"

"And what does the saint do in the woods?" asked Zarathustra.

The saint answered: "I make songs and sing them, and when I make songs I laugh, weep and growl: thus I praise God.

With singing, weeping, laughing and growling I praise the god who is my god. But tell me, what do you bring us as a gift?"

When Zarathustra had heard these words he took his leave of the saint and spoke: "What would I have to give you! But let me leave quickly before I take something from you!" – And so they parted, the oldster and the man, laughing like two boys laugh.

But when Zarathustra was alone he spoke thus to his heart: "Could it be possible! This old saint in his woods has not yet heard the news that *God is dead*!" –

3

When Zarathustra came into the nearest town lying on the edge of the forest, he found many people gathered in the market place, for it had been promised that a tightrope walker would perform. And Zarathustra spoke thus to the people:

"*I teach you the overman.*[3] Human being is something that must be overcome. What have you done to overcome him?

All creatures so far created something beyond themselves; and you want to be the ebb of this great flood and would even rather go back to animals than overcome humans?

[3] "Ich lehre euch den Übermenschen." Just as *Mensch* means human, human being, *Übermensch* means superhuman, which I render throughout as overman, though I use human being, mankind, people, and humanity to avoid the gendered and outmoded use of "man." Two things are achieved by using this combination. First, using "human being" and other species-indicating expressions makes it clear that Nietzsche is concerned ecumenically with humans as a species, not merely with males. Secondly, expanding beyond the use of "man" puts humans in an ecological context; for Zarathustra to claim that "the overman shall be the meaning of the earth" is to argue for a new relationship between humans and nature, between humans and the earth. Overman is preferred to superhuman for two basic reasons; first, it preserves the word play Nietzsche intends with his constant references to going under and going over, and secondly, the comic book associations called to mind by "superman" and super-heroes generally tend to reflect negatively, and frivolously, on the term superhuman.

What is the ape to a human? A laughing stock or a painful embarrassment. And that is precisely what the human shall be to the overman: a laughing stock or a painful embarrassment.

You have made your way from worm to human, and much in you is still worm. Once you were apes, and even now a human is still more ape than any ape.

But whoever is wisest among you is also just a conflict and a cross between plant and ghost. But do I implore you to become ghosts or plants?

Behold, I teach you the overman!

The overman is the meaning of the earth. Let your will say: the overman *shall be* the meaning of the earth!

I beseech you, my brothers, *remain faithful to the earth* and do not believe those who speak to you of extraterrestrial hopes! They are mixers of poisons whether they know it or not.

They are despisers of life, dying off and self-poisoned, of whom the earth is weary: so let them fade away!

Once the sacrilege against God was the greatest sacrilege, but God died, and then all these desecrators died. Now to desecrate the earth is the most terrible thing, and to esteem the bowels of the unfathomable higher than the meaning of the earth!

Once the soul gazed contemptuously at the body, and then such contempt was the highest thing: it wanted the body gaunt, ghastly, starved. Thus it intended to escape the body and the earth.

Oh this soul was gaunt, ghastly and starved, and cruelty was the lust of this soul!

But you, too, my brothers, tell me: what does your body proclaim about your soul? Is your soul not poverty and filth and a pitiful contentment?

Truly, mankind is a polluted stream. One has to be a sea to take in a polluted stream without becoming unclean.

Behold, I teach you the overman: he is this sea, in him your great contempt can go under.

What is the greatest thing that you can experience? It is the hour of your great contempt. The hour in which even your happiness turns to nausea and likewise your reason and your virtue.

The hour in which you say: 'What matters my happiness? It is poverty and filth, and a pitiful contentment. But my happiness ought to justify existence itself!'

The hour in which you say: 'What matters my reason? Does it crave knowledge like the lion its food? It is poverty and filth and a pitiful contentment!'

The hour in which you say: 'What matters my virtue? It has not yet made me rage. How weary I am of my good and my evil! That is all poverty and filth and a pitiful contentment!'

The hour in which you say: 'What matters my justice? I do not see that I am ember and coal. But the just person is ember and coal!'

The hour in which you say: 'What matters my pity? Is pity not the cross on which he is nailed who loves humans? But my pity is no crucifixion.'

Have you yet spoken thus? Have you yet cried out thus? Oh that I might have heard you cry out thus!

Not your sin – your modesty cries out to high heaven, your stinginess even in sinning cries out to high heaven!

Where is the lightning that would lick you with its tongue? Where is the madness with which you should be inoculated?

Behold, I teach you the overman: he is this lightning, he is this madness! –"

When Zarathustra had spoken thus someone from the crowd cried out:

"We have heard enough already about the tightrope walker, now let us see him too!" And all the people laughed at Zarathustra. But the tightrope walker, believing that these words concerned him, got down to his work.

4

Now Zarathustra looked at the people and he was amazed. Then he spoke thus:

"Mankind is a rope fastened between animal and overman – a rope over an abyss.

A dangerous crossing, a dangerous on-the-way, a dangerous looking back, a dangerous shuddering and standing still.

What is great about human beings is that they are a bridge and not a purpose: what is lovable about human beings is that they are a *crossing over* and a *going under*.

I love those who do not know how to live unless by going under, for they are the ones who cross over.

I love the great despisers, because they are the great venerators and arrows of longing for the other shore.

I love those who do not first seek behind the stars for a reason to go under and be a sacrifice, who instead sacrifice themselves for the earth, so that the earth may one day become the overman's.

I love the one who lives in order to know, and who wants to know so that one day the overman may live. And so he wants his going under.

I love the one who works and invents in order to build a house for the overman and to prepare earth, animals and plants for him: for thus he wants his going under.

I love the one who loves his virtue: for virtue is the will to going under and an arrow of longing.

I love the one who does not hold back a single drop of spirit for himself, but wants instead to be entirely the spirit of his virtue: thus he strides as spirit over the bridge.

I love the one who makes of his virtue his desire and his doom: thus for the sake of his virtue he wants to live on and to live no more.

I love the one who does not want to have too many virtues. One virtue is more virtue than two, because it is more of a hook on which his doom may hang.

I love the one whose soul squanders itself, who wants no thanks and gives none back: for he always gives and does not want to preserve himself.[4]

I love the one who is ashamed when the dice fall to his fortune and who then asks: am I a cheater? – For he wants to perish.

I love the one who casts golden words before his deeds and always does even more than he promises: for he wants his going under.

I love the one who justifies people of the future and redeems those of the past: for he wants to perish of those in the present.

I love the one who chastises his god, because he loves his god: for he must perish of the wrath of his god.

I love the one whose soul is deep even when wounded, and who can perish of a small experience: thus he goes gladly over the bridge.

I love the one whose soul is overfull, so that he forgets himself, and all things are in him: thus all things become his going under.

---

[4] See Luke 17:33. This is the first of approximately 135 direct allusions to the Bible, in which Nietzsche typically applies Christ's words to Zarathustra's task, or inverts Christ's words in order to achieve a life- and earth-affirming effect. Whenever possible, these passages will be translated using the phrasing of the Bible. For drafts and alternative versions of the various chapters, biblical references, and other references see vol. XIV of the *Kritische Studienausgabe*, which provides commentary to vols. I–XIII and treats TSZ on pp. 279–344.

I love the one who is free of spirit and heart: thus his head is only the entrails of his heart, but his heart drives him to his going under.

I love all those who are like heavy drops falling individually from the dark cloud that hangs over humanity: they herald the coming of the lightning, and as heralds they perish.

Behold, I am a herald of the lightning and a heavy drop from the cloud: but this lightning is called overman. –"

5

When Zarathustra had spoken these words he looked again at the people and fell silent. "There they stand," he said to his heart, "they laugh, they do not understand me, I am not the mouth for these ears.

Must one first smash their ears so that they learn to hear with their eyes? Must one rattle like kettle drums and penitence preachers? Or do they believe only a stutterer?

They have something of which they are proud. And what do they call that which makes them proud? Education they call it, it distinguishes them from goatherds.

For that reason they hate to hear the word 'contempt' applied to them. So I shall address their pride instead.

Thus I shall speak to them of the most contemptible person: but he is *the last human being*."

And thus spoke Zarathustra to the people:

"It is time that mankind set themselves a goal. It is time that mankind plant the seed of their highest hope.

Their soil is still rich enough for this. But one day this soil will be poor and tame, and no tall tree will be able to grow from it anymore.

Beware! The time approaches when human beings no longer launch the arrow of their longing beyond the human, and the string of their bow will have forgotten how to whir!

I say to you: one must still have chaos in oneself in order to give birth to a dancing star. I say to you: you still have chaos in you.

Beware! The time approaches when human beings will no longer give birth to a dancing star. Beware! The time of the most contemptible human is coming, the one who can no longer have contempt for himself.

Behold! I show you *the last human being*.

'What is love? What is creation? What is longing? What is a star?' – thus asks the last human being, blinking.

Then the earth has become small, and on it hops the last human being, who makes everything small. His kind is ineradicable, like the flea beetle; the last human being lives longest.

'We invented happiness' – say the last human beings, blinking.

They abandoned the regions where it was hard to live: for one needs warmth. One still loves one's neighbor and rubs up against him: for one needs warmth.

Becoming ill and being mistrustful are considered sinful by them: one proceeds with caution. A fool who still stumbles over stones or humans!

A bit of poison once in a while; that makes for pleasant dreams. And much poison at the end, for a pleasant death.

One still works, for work is a form of entertainment. But one sees to it that the entertainment is not a strain.

One no longer becomes poor and rich: both are too burdensome. Who wants to rule anymore? Who wants to obey anymore? Both are too burdensome.

No shepherd and one herd! Each wants the same, each is the same, and whoever feels differently goes voluntarily into the insane asylum.

'Formerly the whole world was insane' – the finest ones say, blinking.

One is clever and knows everything that has happened, and so there is no end to their mockery. People still quarrel but they reconcile quickly – otherwise it is bad for the stomach.

One has one's little pleasure for the day and one's little pleasure for the night: but one honors health.

'We invented happiness' say the last human beings, and they blink."

And here ended the first speech of Zarathustra, which is also called "The Prologue," for at this point he was interrupted by the yelling and merriment of the crowd. "Give us this last human being, oh Zarathustra" – thus they cried – "make us into these last human beings! Then we will make you a gift of the overman!" And all the people jubilated and clicked their tongues. But Zarathustra grew sad and said to his heart:

"They do not understand me. I am not the mouth for these ears.

Too long apparently I lived in the mountains, too much I listened to brooks and trees: now I speak to them as to goatherds.

My soul is calm and bright as the morning mountains. But they believe I am cold, that I jeer, that I deal in terrible jests.

And now they look at me and laugh, and in laughing they hate me too. There is ice in their laughter."

6

Then, however, something happened that struck every mouth silent and forced all eyes to stare. For in the meantime the tightrope walker had begun his work; he had emerged from a little door and was walking across the rope stretched between two towers, such that it hung suspended over the market place and the people. Just as he was at the midpoint of his way, the little door opened once again and a colorful fellow resembling a jester leaped forth and hurried after the first man with quick steps. "Forward, sloth, smuggler, pale face! Or I'll tickle you with my heel! What business have you here between the towers? You belong in the tower, you should be locked away in the tower, for you block the way for one who is better than you!" And with each word he came closer and closer to him. But when he was only one step behind him, the terrifying thing occurred that struck every mouth silent and forced all eyes to stare: – he let out a yell like a devil and leaped over the man who was in his way. This man, seeing his rival triumph in this manner, lost his head and the rope. He threw away his pole and plunged into the depths even faster than his pole, like a whirlwind of arms and legs. The market place and the people resembled the sea when a storm charges in: everyone fled apart and into one another, and especially in the spot where the body had to impact.

But Zarathustra stood still and the body landed right beside him, badly beaten and broken, but not yet dead. After a while the shattered man regained consciousness and saw Zarathustra kneeling beside him. "What are you doing here?" he said finally. "I've known for a long time that the devil would trip me up. Now he is going to drag me off to hell: are you going to stop him?"

"By my honor, friend!" answered Zarathustra. "All that you are talking about does not exist. There is no devil and no hell. Your soul will be dead even sooner than your body – fear no more!"

The man looked up mistrustfully. "If you speak the truth," he said, "then I lose nothing when I lose my life. I am not much more than an animal that has been taught to dance by blows and little treats."

"Not at all," said Zarathustra. "You made your vocation out of danger, and there is nothing contemptible about that. Now you perish of your vocation, and for that I will bury you with my own hands."

When Zarathustra said this the dying man answered no more, but he moved his hand as if seeking Zarathustra's hand in gratitude. –

7

Meanwhile evening came and the market place hid in darkness. The people scattered, for even curiosity and terror grow weary. But Zarathustra sat beside the dead man on the ground and was lost in thought, such that he lost track of time. Night came at last and a cold wind blew over the lonely one. Then Zarathustra stood up and said to his heart:

"Indeed, a nice catch of fish Zarathustra has today! No human being did he catch, but a corpse instead.

Uncanny is human existence and still without meaning: a jester can spell its doom.

I want to teach humans the meaning of their being, which is the overman, the lightning from the dark cloud 'human being.'

But I am still far away from them, and I do not make sense to their senses. For mankind I am still a midpoint between a fool and a corpse.

The night is dark, the ways of Zarathustra are dark. Come, my cold and stiff companion! I shall carry you where I will bury you with my own hands."

8

When Zarathustra had said this to his heart, he hoisted the corpse onto his back and started on his way. And he had not yet gone a hundred paces when someone sneaked up on him and whispered in his ear – and behold! The one who spoke was the jester from the tower. "Go away from this town, oh Zarathustra," he said. "Too many here hate you. The good and the just hate you and they call you their enemy and despiser; the believers of the true faith hate you and they call you the danger of the multitude. It was your good fortune that they laughed at you: and really, you spoke like a jester. It was your good fortune that you took up with the dead dog; when you lowered yourself like that, you rescued yourself for today. But go away from this town – or tomorrow I shall leap over you, a living man over a dead one." And when he had said this, the man disappeared, but Zarathustra continued his walk through dark lanes.

At the town gate he met the gravediggers. They shone their torches in his face, recognized Zarathustra and sorely ridiculed him. "Zarathustra is lugging away the dead dog: how nice that he's become a gravedigger! For our hands are too pure for this roast. Would Zarathustra steal this morsel from the devil? So be it then! And good luck with your meal! If only the devil were not a better thief than Zarathustra! – he'll steal them both, he'll devour them both!" And they laughed and huddled together.

Zarathustra did not say a word and went on his way. By the time he had walked for two hours past woods and swamps, he had heard too much of the hungry howling of wolves and he grew hungry himself. And so he stopped at a lonely house in which a light was burning.

"Hunger falls upon me like a robber," said Zarathustra. "In woods and swamps my hunger falls upon me and in the deep night.

My hunger has odd moods. Often it comes to me only after a meal, and today it did not come the whole day: just where was it?"

And so Zarathustra pounded on the door to the house. An old man appeared, bearing a light, and he asked: "Who comes to me and to my bad sleep?"

"A living man and a dead one," replied Zarathustra. "Give me food and drink, I forgot it during the day. Whoever feeds the hungry quickens his own soul – thus speaks wisdom."

The old man went away but returned promptly and offered Zarathustra bread and wine. "This is a bad region for those who hunger," he said. "That is why I live here. Beast and human being come to me, the hermit. But bid your companion eat and drink, he is wearier than you." Zarathustra replied: "My companion is dead, I would have a hard time persuading him." "That does not concern me," snapped the old man. "Whoever knocks at my house must also take what I offer him. Eat and take care!" –

Thereupon Zarathustra walked again for two hours, trusting the path and the light of the stars, for he was a practiced night-walker and loved to look in the face of all sleepers. But as dawn greyed Zarathustra found himself in a deep wood and no more path was visible to him. Then he laid the dead man into a hollow tree – for he wanted to protect him from the wolves – and he laid himself down head first at the tree, upon the earth and the moss. And soon he fell asleep, weary in body but with a calm soul.

9

Long Zarathustra slept, and not only the dawn passed over his face but the morning as well. At last, however, he opened his eyes: amazed Zarathustra looked into the woods and the silence, amazed he looked into himself. Then he stood up quickly, like a seafarer who all at once sees land, and he rejoiced, for he saw a new truth. And thus he spoke to his heart:

"It dawned on me: I need companions, and living ones – not dead companions and corpses that I carry with me wherever I want.

Instead I need living companions who follow me because they want to follow themselves – wherever I want.

It dawned on me: let Zarathustra speak not to the people, but instead to companions! Zarathustra should not become the shepherd and dog of a herd!

To lure many away from the herd – for that I came. The people and herd shall be angry with me: Zarathustra wants to be called a robber by shepherds.

Shepherds I say, but they call themselves the good and the just. Shepherds I say: but they call themselves the faithful of the true faith.

Look at the good and the just! Whom do they hate most? The one who breaks their tablets of values, the breaker, the lawbreaker – but he is the creative one.

Look at the faithful of all faiths! Whom do they hate most? The one who breaks their tablets of values, the breaker, the lawbreaker – but he is the creative one.

Companions the creative one seeks and not corpses, nor herds and believers. Fellow creators the creative one seeks, who will write new values on new tablets.

Companions the creative one seeks, and fellow harvesters; for to him everything stands ready for harvest. But he lacks the hundred scythes, and so he plucks out spikes and is angry.

Companions the creative one seeks, and those who know how to whet their scythes. They shall be called annihilators and despisers of good and evil. But they are the harvesters and the celebrators.

Fellow creators seeks Zarathustra, fellow harvesters and fellow celebrators Zarathustra seeks: what need does he have of herds and shepherds and corpses!

And you, my first companion, take care! I buried you well in your tree, I concealed you well from the wolves.

But I am leaving you, the time is up. Between dawn and dawn a new truth came to me.

I shall not be a shepherd, nor a gravedigger. I do not want to even speak again with the people – for the last time have I spoken to a dead person.

I shall join the creators, the harvesters, the celebrators: I shall show them the rainbow and all the steps to the overman.

I shall sing my song to lonesome and twosome hermits, and for him who still has ears for the unheard of, I shall make his heart heavy with my happiness.

I want to go to my goal, and I go my own way; over the hesitating and dawdling I shall leap. Thus let my going be their going under!"

10

Thus Zarathustra had spoken to his heart when the sun stood at noon, then he gazed at the sky with a questioning look, for above him he heard the sharp cry of a bird. And behold! An eagle cut broad circles through the air, and upon it hung a snake, not as prey but as a friend, for the snake curled itself around the eagle's neck.

"It is my animals!" said Zarathustra, and his heart was delighted.

"The proudest animal under the sun and the wisest animal under the sun – they have gone forth to scout.

They want to determine whether Zarathustra is still alive. Indeed, am I still alive?

I found it more dangerous among human beings than among animals; Zarathustra walks dangerous paths. May my animals guide me!"

When Zarathustra had said this he recalled the words of the saint in the woods, sighed and spoke thus to his heart:

"May I be wiser! May I be wise from the ground up like my snake!

But I ask the impossible, and so I ask instead of my pride that it always walk with my wisdom!

And if some day my wisdom abandons me – oh it loves to fly away! – may my pride then fly away with my folly!"

– Thus began Zarathustra's going under.

The Speeches of Zarathustra

On the Three Metamorphoses

Three metamorphoses of the spirit I name for you: how the spirit becomes a camel, and the camel a lion, and finally the lion a child.

To the spirit there is much that is heavy; to the strong, carrying spirit imbued with reverence. Its strength demands what is heavy and heaviest.

What is heavy? thus asks the carrying spirit. It kneels down like a camel and wants to be well loaded.

What is heaviest, you heroes? thus asks the carrying spirit, so that I might take it upon myself and rejoice in my strength.

Is it not this: lowering oneself in order to hurt one's pride? Letting one's foolishness glow in order to mock one's wisdom?

Or is it this: abandoning our cause when it celebrates victory? Climbing high mountains in order to tempt the tempter?

Or is it this: feeding on the acorns and grass of knowledge and for the sake of truth suffering hunger in one's soul?

Or is it this: being ill and sending the comforters home and making friends with the deaf who never hear what you want?

Or is it this: wading into dirty water when it is the water of truth, and not shrinking away from cold frogs and hot toads?

Or is it this: loving those who despise us, and extending a hand to the ghost when it wants to frighten us?

All of these heaviest things the carrying spirit takes upon itself, like a loaded camel that hurries into the desert, thus it hurries into its desert.

But in the loneliest desert the second metamorphosis occurs. Here the spirit becomes lion, it wants to hunt down its freedom and be master in its own desert.

Here it seeks its last master, and wants to fight him and its last god. For victory it wants to battle the great dragon.

Who is the great dragon whom the spirit no longer wants to call master and god? "Thou shalt" is the name of the great dragon. But the spirit of the lion says "I will."

"Thou shalt" stands in its way, gleaming golden, a scaly animal, and upon every scale "thou shalt!" gleams like gold.

The values of millennia gleam on these scales, and thus speaks the most powerful of all dragons: "the value of all things – it gleams in me.

All value has already been created, and the value of all created things – that am I. Indeed, there shall be no more 'I will!'" Thus speaks the dragon.

My brothers, why is the lion required by the spirit? Why does the beast of burden, renouncing and reverent, not suffice?

To create new values – not even the lion is capable of that: but to create freedom for itself for new creation – that is within the power of the lion.

To create freedom for oneself and also a sacred No to duty: for that, my brothers, the lion is required.

To take the right to new values – that is the most terrible taking for a carrying and reverent spirit. Indeed, it is preying, and the work of a predatory animal.

Once it loved "thou shalt" as its most sacred, now it must find delusion and despotism even in what is most sacred to it, in order to wrest freedom from its love by preying. The lion is required for this preying.

But tell me, my brothers, of what is the child capable that even the lion is not? Why must the preying lion still become a child?

The child is innocence and forgetting, a new beginning, a game, a wheel rolling out of itself, a first movement, a sacred yes-saying.

Yes, for the game of creation my brothers a sacred yes-saying is required. The spirit wants *its* will, the one lost to the world now wins *its own* world.

Three metamorphoses of the spirit I named for you: how the spirit became a camel, and the camel a lion, and finally the lion a child. –

Thus spoke Zarathustra. And then he sojourned in the town which is called The Motley Cow.

On the Teachers of Virtue

A wise man was praised to Zarathustra who could speak well of sleep and of virtue. For this he was much honored and rewarded, and all the youths sat at his feet. Zarathustra went to him and sat at his feet with all the youths. And thus spoke the wise man:

"Have honor and bashfulness for sleep! That is the first thing! And avoid all who sleep badly and remain awake nights!

Even the thief is bashful toward sleep; he constantly steals through the night, silently. But the watchman of the night is shameless, and shamelessly he carries his horn.

Sleeping is no mean art, it is necessary to remain awake the entire day for it.

Ten times a day you must overcome yourself, that makes for a good weariness and is poppy for the soul.

Ten times you must reconcile yourself again with yourself, for overcoming causes bitterness and the unreconciled sleep badly.

Ten truths you must find by day, or else you will still be seeking truth by night and your soul will have remained hungry.

Ten times you must laugh by day and be cheerful, or else your stomach will bother you at night, this father of gloom.

Few know it but one must have all the virtues in order to sleep well. Shall I bear false witness? Shall I commit adultery?

Shall I covet my neighbor's maid? All that would be incompatible with good sleep.

And even when one has all the virtues, one must understand one more thing: how to send the virtues to sleep at the right time.

So that they do not quarrel with each other, the good little women! And quarrel over you, wretch!

At peace with God and neighbor, thus good sleep demands. And at peace too with the neighbor's devil! Otherwise he will be at your house at night.

Honor the authorities and practice obedience, even toward the crooked authorities! Thus good sleep demands. What can I do about it that the powers like to walk on crooked legs? He shall always be the best shepherd in my view who leads his sheep to the greenest pasture; this is compatible with good sleep.

I do not want many honors, nor great treasures – that inflames the spleen. But sleep is bad without a good name and a little treasure.

A little company is more welcome to me than evil company, but they must go and come at the right time, for this is compatible with good sleep.

I also like very much the poor in spirit, they promote sleep. Blessed are they, especially when they are always told they are right.

Thus passes the day for the virtuous one. Now when night comes I am careful not to summon sleep – the master of virtues does not like to be summoned!

Instead I think what I have done and thought throughout the day. Ruminating, I ask myself, patient as a cow; what then were my ten overcomings?

And what were the ten reconciliations and the ten truths and the ten laughters to which my heart treated itself?

In this manner reflecting and rocked by forty thoughts, sleep suddenly falls upon me, the unsummoned, the master of virtues.

Sleep knocks at my eyelids, and they become heavy. Sleeps brushes my mouth, and it stays open.

Truly, on soft soles it comes to me, the dearest of thieves, and steals my thoughts: stupid I stand there like this chair.

But then I am not standing for long, and soon I am lying." –

When Zarathustra heard the wise man speak thus, he laughed inwardly in his heart, for something dawned on him, and he spoke thus to his heart:

"That wise man there with his forty thoughts is just a fool to me, but I believe that he well understands sleep.

Happy the one who lives even near this wise man! Such a sleep is infectious, and it infects even through a thick wall.

In this teacher nothing less than magic resides, and not in vain did youths sit at the feet of this preacher of virtue.

The meaning of his wisdom is: wake in order to sleep well. And truly, if life had no meaning and if I had to choose nonsense, then to me too this would be the worthiest nonsense I could choose.

Now I understand clearly what was once sought before all else when teachers of virtue were sought. Good sleep was sought and poppy-blossomed virtues to boot!

For all these highly praised wise men and teachers wisdom was the sleep without dreams: they knew no better meaning of life.

And still today there are a few like this preacher of virtue, and some not so honest. But their time is up, not for long will they be standing, and soon they'll be lying.

Blessed are these sleepy ones, for they shall soon nod off." –

Thus spoke Zarathustra.

On the Hinterworldly[5]

Once Zarathustra too cast his delusion beyond humans, like all hinter-worldly. At that time the world seemed to me the work of a suffering and tortured god.

Then the world seemed a dream to me and the fiction of a god; colorful smoke before the eyes of a divine dissatisfied being.

Good and evil and joy and suffering and I and you – colorful smoke it seemed to me before creative eyes. The creator wanted to look away from himself and so he created the world.

It is drunken joy to the suffering one to look away from one's suffering and to lose oneself. Drunken joy and losing-oneself the world once seemed to me.

This world, the eternally imperfect, the mirror image and imperfect image of an eternal contradiction – a drunken joy to its imperfect creator: thus the world once seemed to me.

So I too once cast my delusion beyond humans, like all hinterworldly. Beyond humans in truth?

Oh my brothers, this god that I created was of human make and madness, like all gods!

Human he was, and only a poor flake of human and ego. From my own ash and ember it came to me, this ghost, and truly! It did not come to me from beyond!

What happened, my brothers? I overcame myself, my suffering self, I carried my own ashes to the mountain, I invented a brighter flame for myself and behold! The ghost *shrank* from me!

Now it would be suffering and torture for the convalesced one to believe in such ghosts. Now it would be suffering and humiliation. Thus I speak to the hinterworldly.

It was suffering and incapacity that created all hinterworlds, and that brief madness of happiness that only the most suffering person experiences.

---

[5] "Von den Hinterweltlern," literally: on those who are of, or believe in, a world beyond, a hidden or a back-world, a secret world, bears similar connotations to English hinterland, i.e. regions that are remote, far away from the cities. *Hintermann* is a man behind the scenes, a secret advisor; *Hintergedanken* are secret thoughts or ulterior motives. *Hintern* as a noun is the same as English "behind," with behind meaning a person's backside.

Weariness that wants its ultimate with one great leap, with a death leap; a poor unknowing weariness that no longer even wants to will: that created all gods and hinterworlds.

Believe me, my brothers! It was the body that despaired of the body – it probed with the fingers of a befooled spirit on the walls of the ultimate.

Believe me, my brothers! It was the body that despaired of the earth – then it heard the belly of being speaking to it.

And then it wanted to break head first through the ultimate walls, and not only with its head, beyond to "the other world."

But "the other world" is well hidden from humans, that dehumaned, inhuman world that is a heavenly nothing. And the belly of being does not speak at all to humans, unless as a human.

Indeed, all being is hard to prove and hard to coax to speech. Tell me, my brothers, is not the strangest of all things still proven best?

Yes, this ego and the ego's contradiction and confusion still speak most honestly about its being; this creating, willing, valuing ego which is the measure and value of things.

And this most honest being, this ego – it speaks of love and it still wants the body, even when it poetizes and fantasizes and flutters with broken wings.

It learns to speak ever more honestly, this ego. And the more it learns, the more it finds words and honors for the body and the earth.

My ego taught me a new pride, I teach it to mankind: no longer bury your head in the sand of heavenly things, but bear it freely instead, an earthly head that creates a meaning for the earth!

I teach mankind a new will: to *want* the path that human beings have traveled blindly, to pronounce it good and no longer sneak to the side of it like the sick and the dying-out.

It was the sick and the dying-out who despised the body and the earth and invented the heavenly and its redeeming drops of blood. But even these sweet and shadowy poisons they took from the body and the earth!

They wanted to escape their misery and the stars were too distant for them. So they sighed "Oh if only there were heavenly paths on which to sneak into another being and happiness!" – Then they invented their schemes and bloody little drinks!

Now they fancied themselves detached from this earth, these ingrates. But what did they have to thank for the fits and bliss of their detachment? Their body and this earth.

Zarathustra is gentle to the sick. Indeed, he is not angered by their ways of comfort and ingratitude. May they become convalescents and overcomers and create for themselves a higher body!

Nor is he angered by the convalescent when he tenderly gazes upon his delusion and sneaks around the grave of his God at midnight. But to me even his tears remain sickness and sick body.

There were always many sickly people among those who poetize and are addicted to God; with rage they hate the knowing ones and that youngest of virtues which is called honesty.

Backward they look always toward darker times, for then, truly, delusion and faith were another matter. Raving of reason was next to godliness, and doubting was sin.

All too well I know these next-to-godliness types: they want people to believe in them, and that doubting is sin. All too well I know also what they themselves believe in most.

Indeed, not in hinterworlds and redeeming blood drops, but instead they too believe most in the body, and their own body is to them their thing in itself.

But to them it is a sickly thing, and gladly would they jump out of their skin. Hence they listen to the preachers of death and they preach of hinterworlds themselves.

Hear my brothers, hear the voice of the healthy body: a more honest and purer voice is this.

More honestly and more purely speaks the healthy body, the perfect and perpendicular body, and it speaks of the meaning of the earth.

Thus spoke Zarathustra.

On the Despisers of the Body

To the despisers of the body I want to say my words. I do not think they should relearn and teach differently, instead they should bid their own bodies farewell – and thus fall silent.

"Body am I and soul" – so speaks a child. And why should one not speak like children?

But the awakened, the knowing one says: body am I through and through, and nothing besides; and soul is just a word for something on the body.

The body is a great reason, a multiplicity with one sense, a war and a peace, one herd and one shepherd.

Your small reason, what you call "spirit" is also a tool of your body, my brother, a small work- and plaything of your great reason.

"I" you say and are proud of this word. But what is greater is that in which you do not want to believe – your body and its great reason. It does not say I, but *does* I.

What the sense feels, what the spirit knows, in itself that will never have an end. But sense and spirit would like to persuade you that they are the end of all things: so vain are they.

Work- and plaything are sense and spirit, behind them still lies the self. The self also seeks with the eyes of the senses, it listens also with the ears of the spirit.

Always the self listens and seeks: it compares, compels, conquers, destroys. It rules and is also the ruler of the ego.

Behind your thoughts and feelings, my brother, stands a powerful commander, an unknown wise man – he is called self. He lives in your body, he is your body.

There is more reason in your body than in your best wisdom. And who knows then to what end your body requires precisely your best wisdom?

Your self laughs at your ego and its proud leaps. "What are these leaps and flights of thought to me?" it says to itself. "A detour to my purpose. I am the leading strings of the ego and the prompter of its concepts."

The self says to the ego: "Feel pain here!" And then it suffers and reflects on how it might suffer no more – and just for that purpose *it is supposed* to think.

The self says to the ego: "Feel pleasure here!" Then it is pleased and reflects on how it might feel pleased more often – and for that purpose *it is supposed* to think!

To the despisers of the body I want to say a word. That they disrespect is based on their respect. What is it that created respect and disrespect and value and will?

The creative self created respect and disrespect for itself, it created pleasure and pain for itself. The creative body created spirit for itself as the hand of its will.

Even in your folly and your contempt, you despisers of the body, you serve your self. I say to you: your self itself wants to die and turns away from life.

No longer is it capable of that which it wants most: to create beyond itself. This it wants most of all, this is its entire fervor.

But now it is too late for that, and so your self wants to go under, you despisers of the body.

Your self wants to go under, and for this reason you became despisers of the body! For you no longer are capable of creating beyond yourselves.

And that is why you are angry now at life and earth. There is an unknown envy in the looking askance of your contempt.

I will not go your way, you despisers of the body! You are not my bridges to the overman! –

Thus spoke Zarathustra.

On the Passions of Pleasure and Pain

My brother, if you have one virtue, and it is your virtue, then you have it in common with no one.

To be sure, you want to call her by name and caress her; you want to tug at her ear and have fun with her.

And behold! Now you have her name in common with the people and have become the people and the herd with your virtue!

You would do better to say: "Unspeakable and nameless is that which causes my soul agony and sweetness and is even the hunger of my entrails."

Let your virtue be too high for the familiarity of names, and if you must speak of it, then do not be ashamed to stammer about it.

Then speak and stammer: "This is *my* good, I love this, thus I like it entirely, thus alone do I want the good.

I do not want it as a divine law, I do not want is as a human statute and requirement. It shall be no signpost for me to overearths and paradises.

It is an earthly virtue that I love: there is little prudence in it and least of all the reason of the many.

But this bird built its nest in my house, therefore I love and caress it, now it sits next to me on its golden eggs."

Thus you should stammer and praise your virtue.

Once you had passions and named them evil. But now you have only your virtues: they grew out of your passions.

You set your highest goal at the heart of these passions, and then they became your virtues and passions of pleasure.

And whether you stemmed from the clan of the irascible or the lascivious or the fanatic or the vengeful:

Ultimately all your passions became virtues and all your devils became angels.

Once you had wild dogs in your cellar, but ultimately they transformed into birds and lovely singers.

Out of your poisons you brewed your balsam; your cow, melancholy, you milked – now you drink the sweet milk of its udder.

And now nothing evil grows anymore out of you, unless it is the evil that grows from the struggle among your virtues.

My brother, if you are lucky then you have one virtue and no more: thus will you go more easily over the bridge.

It is distinguishing to have many virtues, but it is a hard lot. And many went into the desert and killed themselves because they were weary of being the battle and battlefield of virtues. My brother, are war and battle evil? But this evil is necessary, envy and mistrust and slander among your virtues are necessary.

Look, how each of your virtues is greedy for the highest. It wants your entire spirit, to be *its* herald; it wants your entire strength in rage, hatred and love.

Each virtue is jealous of the other, and jealousy is a terrible thing. Even virtues can perish of jealousy.

Whoever is ringed by the flame of jealousy in the end will turn his poisonous stinger upon himself, like the scorpion.

Oh my brother, have you never seen a virtue slander and stab itself?

Human being is something that must be overcome, and therefore you should love your virtues – for of them you will perish. –

Thus spoke Zarathustra.

On the Pale Criminal

You do want to kill, you judges and sacrificers, until the animal has nodded? Behold, the pale criminal has nodded: from his eyes speaks the great contempt.

"My ego is something that shall be overcome: my ego is to me the great contempt for mankind," so speak these eyes.

That he condemned himself was his highest moment: do not allow the sublime one to return to his baseness!

There is no redemption for one who suffers so from himself, unless it were the quick death.

Your killing, you judges, should be pity and not revenge. And insofar as you kill, see to it that you yourselves justify life!

It is not enough that you reconcile yourself with the one you kill. Let your sadness be love for the overman – thus you justify that you still live!

"Enemy" you should say, but not "villain"; "sick man" you should say, but not "scoundrel"; "fool" you should say, but not "sinner."

And you, red judge, if you were to speak aloud all the things you have already done in your thoughts, then everyone would cry: "Away with this filth and poisonous worm!"

But thought is one thing, and deed another, and the image of a deed yet another. The wheel of motive does not roll between them.

An image made this pale human pale. He was equal to his deed when he committed it, but he could not bear its image once he had done it.

From then on he always saw himself as the doer of one deed. I call this madness: the exception reversed itself to the essence.

A streak in the dirt stops a hen cold; the stroke he executed stopped his poor reason cold – madness *after* the deed I call this.

Listen, you judges! There is still another madness, and it is before the deed. Oh, you did not crawl deeply enough into this soul!

Thus speaks the red judge: "Why did this criminal kill? He wanted to rob." But I say to you: his soul wanted blood, not robbery. He thirsted for the bliss of the knife!

But his poor reason did not comprehend this madness and it persuaded him. "What does blood matter?" it said. "Don't you at least want to commit robbery in the process? Take revenge?"

And so he listened to his poor reason, like lead its speech lay upon him – and he robbed as he murdered. He did not want to be ashamed of his madness.

And now the lead of his guilt lies on him again, and again his poor reason is so stiff, so paralyzed, so heavy.

If only he could shake his head, then his burden would roll off – but who could shake this head?

What is this human being? A pile of illnesses that reach out into the world through his spirit: there they seek their prey.

What is this human being? A ball of wild snakes that seldom have peace from each other – so they go forth for themselves and seek prey in the world.

Behold this poor body! What it suffered and craved this poor soul interpreted for itself – it interpreted it as murderous lust and greed for the bliss of the knife.

Whoever grows ill now is befallen by the evil that is evil now; he wants to hurt with that which makes him hurt. But there have been other ages and another evil and good.

Once doubt was evil and the will to self. Back then sick people became heretics and witches: as heretics and witches they suffered and wanted to cause suffering.

But this does not want to get to your ears: it harms your good people, you say to me. But what matter your good people to me!

There is much about your good people that makes me disgusted, and verily not their evil. I wish they had a madness from which they would perish, like this pale criminal!

Indeed, I wish their madness were called truth or loyalty or justice – but they have their virtue in order to live long and in pitiful contentment.

I am a railing by the torrent: grasp me whoever is able to grasp me! But your crutch I am not. –

Thus spoke Zarathustra.

On Reading and Writing

Of all that is written I love only that which one writes with his blood. Write with blood, and you will experience that blood is spirit.

It is not easily possible to understand the blood of another: I hate the reading idlers.

Whoever knows the reader will do nothing more for the reader. One more century of readers – and the spirit itself will stink.

That everyone is allowed to learn to read ruins not only writing in the long run, but thinking too.

Once the spirit was God, then it became human and now it is even becoming rabble.

Whoever writes in blood and proverbs does not want to be read, but to be learned by heart.

In the mountains the shortest way is from peak to peak, but for that one must have long legs. Proverbs should be peaks, and those who are addressed should be great and tall.

The air thin and pure, danger near and the spirit full of cheerful spite: these fit together well.

I want to have goblins around me, for I am courageous. Courage that scares off ghosts creates its own goblins – courage wants to laugh.

I no longer sympathize with you; this cloud beneath me, this black and heavy thing at which I laugh – precisely this is your thundercloud.

You look upward when you long for elevation. And I look down because I am elevated.

Who among you can laugh and be elevated at the same time?

Whoever climbs the highest mountain laughs at all tragic plays and tragic realities.

Courageous, unconcerned, sarcastic, violent – thus wisdom wants us: she is a woman and always loves only a warrior.

You say to me: "Life is hard to bear." But why would you have your pride in the morning and your resignation in the evening?

Life is hard to bear: but then do not carry on so tenderly! We are all of us handsome, load bearing jack- and jillasses.

What have we in common with the rosebud that trembles because a drop of dew lies on its body?

It is true: we love life not because we are accustomed to life but because we are accustomed to love.

There is always some madness in love. But there is also always some reason in madness.

And even to me, one who likes life, it seems butterflies and soap bubbles and whatever is of their kind among human beings know most about happiness.

To see these light, foolish, delicate, sensitive little souls fluttering – that seduces Zarathustra to tears and songs.

I would only believe in a god who knew how to dance.

And when I saw my devil, there I found him earnest, thorough, deep, somber: it was the spirit of gravity – through him all things fall.

Not by wrath does one kill, but by laughing. Up, let us kill the spirit of gravity!

I learned to walk, since then I let myself run. I learned to fly, since then I do not wait to be pushed to move from the spot.

Now I am light, now I fly, now I see myself beneath me, now a god dances through me.

Thus spoke Zarathustra.

On the Tree on the Mountain

Zarathustra's eyes had discerned that a young man avoided him. As he walked one evening alone through the mountains surrounding the town, which is called The Motley Cow, behold, there while walking he found this young man leaning against a tree, gazing wearily into the valley. Zarathustra grasped the tree at which the young man sat, and spoke thus:

"If I wanted to shake this tree here with my hands, I would not be able to.

But the wind that we do not see torments and bends it wherever it wants. We are bent and tormented worst by invisible hands."

Then the young man stood up, perplexed, and said: "I hear Zarathustra and I was just thinking about him." Zarathustra responded:

"Why are you startled by this? – But it is with human beings as it is with this tree.

The more they aspire to the heights and the light, the more strongly their roots strive earthward, downward, into darkness, depths – into evil."

"Yes, into evil!" cried the young man. "How is it possible that you discovered my soul?"

Zarathustra smiled and said: "Some souls will never be discovered, unless they are first invented."

"Yes, into evil!" cried the young man again.

"You speak the truth, Zarathustra. I no longer trust myself since aspiring to the heights, and no one trusts me anymore – how did this happen?

I'm changing too fast. My today contradicts my yesterday. I often skip steps when I climb – no step forgives me that.

If I am at the top then I always find myself alone. No one speaks with me, the frost of loneliness makes me shiver. What do I want in the heights?

My contempt and my longing grow together; the higher I climb, the more I despise the one who climbs. What does he want in the heights?

How ashamed I am of my climbing and stumbling! How I mock my violent panting! How I hate the flying one! How weary I am in the heights!"

Here the young man fell silent. And Zarathustra regarded the tree at which they stood and spoke thus:

"This tree stands here lonely on the mountain; it grew high beyond humans and animals.

And if it wanted to speak, it would have no one who understood it: so high it grew.

Now it waits and waits – but for what does it wait? It lives too near the clouds' abode: it waits for the first lightning bolt?"

When Zarathustra had said this the young man cried out, gesturing agitatedly: "Yes, Zarathustra, you speak the truth. I longed for my destruction when I aspired to the heights, and you are the lightning for which I waited! Look, what am I anymore, now that you have appeared among us! It is my *envy* of you that has destroyed me!" – Thus spoke the young man and he wept bitterly. But Zarathustra put his arm around him and led him away.

And after they had walked together for a while Zarathustra started speaking thus:

"It tears my heart apart. Better than your words can say, your eyes tell me all your danger.

You are still not free, you *seek* freedom. Your seeking made you sleep-deprived and over-awake.

You aspire to the free heights, your soul thirsts for the stars. But your wicked instincts also thirst for freedom.

Your wild dogs want to get free; they bark with joy in their cellar when your spirit contrives to liberate all prisons.

To me you are still a prisoner who plots his freedom. Alas, the soul of such prisoners grows clever, but also deceptive and rotten.

The one who is free of spirit must still purify himself. Much prison and mold is left in him: his eyes must still become pure.

Yes, I know your danger. But by my love and hope I beseech you: do not throw away your love and hope!

30

You still feel noble, and the others who grudge you and give you the evil eye, they still feel your nobility too. Know that a noble person stands in everyone's way.

A noble person also stands in the way of the good: and even when they call him a good man, they do so in order to get rid of him.

The noble person wants to create new things and a new virtue. The good person wants old things, and for old things to be preserved.

But it is not the danger of the noble one that he will become a good person, but a churl, a mocker, an annihilator.

Oh, I knew noble people who lost their highest hope. And then they slandered all high hopes.

Then they lived churlishly in brief pleasures, scarcely casting their goals beyond the day.

'Spirit is lust too' – so they spoke. Then the wings of their spirit broke, and now it crawls around and soils what it gnaws.

Once they thought of becoming heroes: now they are libertines. To them the hero is grief and ghastliness.

But by my love and hope I beseech you: do not throw away the hero in your soul! Hold holy your highest hope!" –

Thus spoke Zarathustra.

On the Preachers of Death

There are preachers of death, and the earth is full of people to whom departure from life must be preached.

The earth is full of the superfluous, life is spoiled by the all too many. May they be lured from this life with the "eternal life!"

"Yellow ones," so the preachers of death are called, or "black ones." But I want to show them to you in still different colors.

There are the terrible ones, who carry the predator about in themselves and have no choice but lust or self-laceration. And even their lusting is self-laceration.

They have not even become human beings, these terrible ones: may they preach departure from life and pass away themselves!

There are the consumptive of the soul: scarcely are they born when they begin to die and long for the teachings of weariness and resignation.

They would like to be dead and we shall honor their will! Let us beware of waking these dead and disturbing these living coffins!

They encounter a sick or a very old person or a corpse, and right away they say "life is refuted!"

But only they are refuted and their eyes, which see only the one face of existence.

Cloaked in thick melancholy and greedy for the small accidents that bring death, thus they wait and clench their teeth.

Or again: they reach for candy while mocking their childishness; they cling to their straw of life and mock the fact that they cling to a straw.

Their wisdom says: "A fool who goes on living, but we are such fools! And precisely that is the most foolish thing about life!"

"Life is only suffering," so speak others, and do not lie; then see to it that *you* cease. Then see to it that the life that is only suffering ceases!

And let the doctrine of your virtue speak thus: "Thou shalt kill thyself! Thou shalt steal thyself away!"

"Sex is sin," say the ones who preach death – "let us step aside and not beget children!"

"Giving birth is strenuous," – say the others – "why continue to give birth? One bears only the unhappy!" And they too are preachers of death.

"Pity is needed," – so say the third kind. "Take what I have! Take what I am! All the less does life bind me!"

If they were the pitying kind through and through, they would ruin the lives of their neighbors. Being evil – that would be their proper goodness.

But they want to get free of life; what do they care that they bind others still tighter with their chains and gifts!

And you too, for whom life is hectic work and unrest: are you not very weary of life? Are you not very ripe for the sermon of death?

All of you who are in love with hectic work and whatever is fast, new, strange – you find it hard to bear yourselves, your diligence is escape and the will to forget yourself.

If you believed more in life, you would hurl yourself less into the moment. But you do not have enough content in yourselves for waiting – not even for laziness!

Everywhere sounds the voice of those who preach death: and the earth is full of people to whom departure from life must be preached.

Or "the eternal life." It's all the same to me – if only they pass away quickly!

Thus spoke Zarathustra.

On War and Warriors

We do not want to be spared by our best enemies, nor by those whom we love thoroughly. So let me tell you the truth now!

My brothers in war! I love you thoroughly, I am and I was like you. And I am also your best enemy. So let me tell you the truth now!

I know of the hate and envy of your heart. You are not great enough to not know hate and envy. So at least be great enough to not be ashamed of them!

And if you cannot be saints of knowledge, then at least be its warriors. They are the companions and forerunners of such saintliness.

I see many soldiers: if only I saw many warriors! "Uni-form" one calls what they wear: if only what they conceal with it were not uni-form!

You should be the kind of men whose eyes always seek an enemy – *your* enemy. And with some of you there is a hate at first sight.

You should seek your enemy, wage your war and for your thoughts! And when your thought is defeated, then your honesty should cry out in triumph even for that!

You should love peace as the means to new wars. And the short peace more than the long one.

I do not recommend work to you, but struggle instead. I do not recommend peace to you, but victory instead. Your work shall be a struggle, your peace shall be a victory!

One can be silent and sit still only when one has a bow and arrow; otherwise there is blabbering and quarreling. Your peace shall be a victory!

You say it is the good cause that hallows even war? I tell you: it is the good war that hallows any cause.

War and courage have done more great things than love of one's neighbor. Not your pity but your bravery has rescued the casualties so far.

What is good? you ask. Being brave is good. Let little girls say: "Being good is what is pretty and stirring at the same time."

You are called heartless, but your heart is genuine and I love the shame of your heartiness. You are ashamed of your flood, and others are ashamed of their ebb.

You are ugly? Well so be it, my brothers! Then don the sublime, the mantle of the ugly!

And when your soul grows big it becomes mischievous, and there is sarcasm in your sublimity. I know you.

In sarcasm the mischievous one and the weakling meet. But they misunderstand one another. I know you.

You may have only those enemies whom you can hate, but not enemies to despise. You must be proud of your enemy: then the successes of your enemy are your successes too.

Rebellion – that is the nobility of slaves. Let your nobility be obedience! Your commanding itself shall be obeying!

To a good warrior "thou shalt" sounds nicer than "I will." And everything you hold dear you should first have commanded to you.

Let your love for life be love for your highest hope, and let your highest hope be the highest thought of life!

But you shall have your highest thought commanded by me – and it says: human being is something that shall be overcome.

So live your life of obedience and war! What matters living long! Which warrior wants to be spared!

I spare you not, I love you thoroughly, my brothers in war! –

Thus spoke Zarathustra.

On the New Idol

Somewhere still there are peoples and herds, but not where we live, my brothers: here there are states.

State? What is that? Well then, lend me your ears now, for I shall say my words about the death of peoples.

State is the name of the coldest of all cold monsters. It even lies coldly, and this lie crawls out of its mouth: "I, the state, am the people."

This is a lie! The ones who created the peoples were the creators, they hung a faith and a love over them, and thus they served life.

The ones who set traps for the many and call them "state" are annihilators, they hang a sword and a hundred cravings over them.

Where there are still peoples the state is not understood, and it is hated as the evil eye and the sin against customs and rights.

This sign I give you: every people speaks its own tongue of good and evil – which the neighbor does not understand. It invented its own language through customs and rights.

But the state lies in all the tongues of good and evil, and whatever it may tell you, it lies – and whatever it has, it has stolen.

Everything about it is false; it bites with stolen teeth, this biting dog. Even its entrails are false.

Language confusion of good and evil: this sign I give you as the sign of the state. Indeed, this sign signifies the will to death! Indeed, it beckons the preachers of death!

Far too many are born: the state was invented for the superfluous!

Just look at how it lures them, the far-too-many! How it gulps and chews and ruminates them!

"On earth there is nothing greater than I: the ordaining finger of God am I" – thus roars the monster. And not only the long-eared and the shortsighted sink to their knees!

Oh, even to you, you great souls, it whispers its dark lies! Unfortunately it detects the rich hearts who gladly squander themselves!

Yes, it also detects you, you vanquishers of the old God! You grew weary in battle and now your weariness still serves the new idol!

It wants to gather heroes and honorable men around itself, this new idol! Gladly it suns itself in the sunshine of your good consciences – the cold monster!

It wants to give *you* everything, if *you* worship it, the new idol. Thus it buys the shining of your virtue and the look in your proud eyes.

It wants to use you as bait for the far-too-many! Indeed, a hellish piece of work was thus invented, a death-horse clattering in the regalia of divine honors!

Indeed, a dying for the many was invented here, one that touts itself as living; truly, a hearty service to all preachers of death!

State I call it, where all are drinkers of poison, the good and the bad; state, where all lose themselves, the good and the bad; state, where the slow suicide of everyone is called – "life."

Just look at these superfluous! They steal for themselves the works of the inventors and the treasures of the wise: education they call their thievery – and everything turns to sickness and hardship for them!

Just look at these superfluous! They are always sick, they vomit their gall and call it the newspaper. They devour one another and are not even able to digest themselves.

Just look at these superfluous! They acquire riches and yet they become poorer. They want power and first of all the crowbar of power, much money – these impotent, impoverished ones!

Watch them scramble, these swift monkeys! They scramble all over each other and thus drag one another down into the mud and depths.

They all want to get to the throne, it is their madness – as if happiness sat on the throne! Often mud sits on the throne – and often too the throne on mud.

Mad all of them seem to me, and scrambling monkeys and overly aroused. Their idol smells foul to me, the cold monster: together they all smell foul to me, these idol worshipers.

My brothers, do you want to choke in the reek of their snouts and cravings? Smash the windows instead and leap into the open!

Get out of the way of the bad smell! Go away from the idol worship of the superfluous!

Get out of the way of the bad smell! Get away from the steam of these human sacrifices!

Even now the earth stands open for great souls. Many seats are still empty for the lonesome and twosome, fanned by the fragrance of silent seas.

An open life still stands open for great souls. Indeed, whoever possesses little is possessed all the less: praised be a small poverty!

There, where the state ends, only there begins the human being who is not superfluous; there begins the song of necessity, the unique and irreplaceable melody.

There, where the state *ends* – look there, my brothers! Do you not see it, the rainbow and the bridges of the overman? –

Thus spoke Zarathustra.

On the Flies of the Market Place

Flee, my friend, into your solitude! I see you dazed by the noise of the great men and stung by the stings of the little.

Wood and cliff know worthily how to keep silent with you. Be once more like the tree that you love, the broad-branching one: silent and listening it hangs over the sea.

Where solitude ends, there begins the market place; and where the market place begins, there begins too the noise of the great actors and the buzzing of poisonous flies.

In the world even the best things are still worthless without the one person who first performs them: the people call these great men performers.

The people little understand what is great, that is: the creator. But they have a sense for all performers and actors of great things.

The world revolves around the inventors of new values: – it revolves invisibly. But the people and fame revolve around actors: thus is the course of the world.

Spirit the actor has, but little conscience of spirit. He always believes in whatever makes people believe most strongly – believe in *him*!

Tomorrow he will have a new belief and the day after tomorrow an even newer one. He has hasty senses, like the people, and a fickle ability to scent.

To overthrow – to him that means: to prove. To drive insane – to him that means: to convince. And blood to him is the best of all possible grounds.

A truth that slips into only the finer ears he calls a lie and nothing. Indeed, he only believes in gods that make great noise in the world!

The market place is full of pompous jesters – and the people are proud of their great men! They are the men of the hour.

But the hour presses them, and so they press you. And from you too they want a Yes or a No. Alas, do you want to set your chair between pro and contra?

Be without envy on account of these unconditional and pressing types, you lover of truth! Never before has truth hung on the arm of an absolutist.

Return to your safety on account of these precipitous types: only in the market place is one assaulted with Yes? or No?

For all deep wells experience is slow; they must wait long before they know *what* fell into their depth.

Away from the market place and fame all greatness takes place; away from the market place and fame the inventors of new values have lived all along.

Flee, my friend, into your solitude: I see you stung by poisonous flies. Flee where raw, strong air blows!

Flee into your solitude! You have lived too long near the small and the pitiful. Flee their invisible revenge! Against you they are nothing but revenge.

Do not raise your arm against them anymore! They are innumerable, and it is not your lot to be a shoo-fly.

Innumerable are these small and pitiful ones; and rain drops and weeds have sufficed to bring down many a proud structure.

You are no stone, but already you have become hollow from many drops. You will shatter and burst still from many drops.

I see you weary from poisonous flies, torn bloody in a hundred places, and yet your pride does not even become angered.

They want blood from you in all innocence, their bloodless souls demand blood – and so they sting away in all innocence.

But you, deep one, you suffer too deeply even from small wounds; and before you could even heal yourself, the same poisonous worm crawled across your hand.

You are too proud to slay these sweet-toothed creatures. But beware, or it will become your doom to bear all their poisonous injustice!

They also buzz around you with their praise; importunity is their praising! They want the closeness of your skin and your blood.

They flatter you like a god or devil; they snivel before you as before a god or devil. What's the use! They are sycophants and snivelers and nothing more.

Often too they give themselves charming airs. But that has always been the cleverness of cowards; yes, cowards are clever!

They think about you much with their narrow souls – you always give them pause! Everything that is thought about much gives pause.

They punish you for all your virtues. What they forgive you thoroughly are only – your mistakes.

Because you are mild and of just temperament, you say: "They are not guilty of their petty existence." But their narrow souls think: "All great existence is guilty."

Even when you are mild toward them they still feel despised by you; and they repay your benefaction with hidden malefactions.

Your wordless pride always contradicts their taste; they jubilate if only you are modest enough to be vain.

That which we recognize in a person we also inflame in him – therefore beware of the petty!

They feel small before you, and their baseness glimmers and glows at you in invisible revenge.

Haven't you noticed how often they fall silent when you approach them, and how their strength abandoned them like the smoke of a dying fire?

Yes my friend, you are the bad conscience of your neighbors, for they are unworthy of you. Therefore they hate you and would like much to suck your blood.

Your neighbors will always be poisonous flies; that which is great in you – that itself must make them more poisonous and ever more fly-like.

Flee, my friend, into your solitude and where raw, strong air blows! It is not your lot to be a shoo-fly. –

Thus spoke Zarathustra.

On Chastity

I love the forest. It is bad to live in the cities; there too many are in heat.

Is it not better to fall into the hands of a murderer than into the dreams of a woman in heat?

And just look at these men: their eyes say it – they know nothing better on earth than to lie with a woman.

There is mud at the bottom of their souls; and watch out if their mud has spirit too!

If only you were perfect at least as animals! But to animals belongs innocence.

Do I advise you to kill your senses? I advise you on the innocence of your senses.

Do I advise you to chastity? In some people chastity is a virtue, but in many it is almost a vice.

They abstain, to be sure: but the bitch, sensuality, leers with envy out of everything they do.

Even into the heights of their virtue and all the way into their cold spirit this beast follows them with its unrest.

And how sweetly the bitch, sensuality, knows how to beg for a piece of spirit when she is denied a piece of meat!

You love tragedies and everything that makes the heart break? But I am mistrustful of your bitch.

Your eyes are too cruel for me and they gaze with lust in search of sufferers. Has your lust not simply disguised itself, and now calls itself pity?

And this parable too I give to you: not a few who wanted to drive out their devil went into swine themselves.

Those for whom chastity is difficult should be advised against it, or else it could become their road to hell – that is, the mud and the heat of the soul.

Do I speak of dirty things? That is not the worst of it to me.

Not when truth is dirty, but when it is shallow the seeker of knowledge steps reluctantly into its water.

Indeed, there are chaste people through and through; they are milder of heart, they laugh more gladly and more richly than you.

They laugh at chastity too and ask: "what is chastity?

Is chastity not folly? But this folly came to us, and not we to it.

We offered this guest hostel and heart: now it dwells with us – may it stay as long as it wants!"

Thus spoke Zarathustra.

On the Friend

"One is always too many around me" – thus thinks the hermit. "Always one times one – in the long run that makes two!"

I and me are always too eager in conversation: how could I stand it if there were no friend?

For the hermit the friend is always a third: the third is the cork that prevents the conversation of the two from sinking into the depths.

Oh, there are too many depths for all hermits. That is why they long so for a friend and his height.

Our faith in others betrays the areas in which we would like to have faith in ourselves. Our longing for a friend is our betrayer.

And often one uses love merely to leap over envy. And often one attacks and makes an enemy in order to conceal that one is open to attack.

"At least be my enemy!" – Thus speaks true respect that does not dare to ask for friendship.

If one wants a friend, then one must also want to wage war for him: and in order to wage war, one must *be able* to be an enemy.

One should honor the enemy even in one's friend. Can you step up to your friend without stepping over to him?

In one's friend one should have one's best enemy. You should be closest to him in heart when you resist him.

You want to wear no garb before your friend? Is it supposed to be to your friend's honor that you give yourself to him as you are? But for that he curses you to the devil!

Whoever makes no secret of himself outrages others; so much reason do you have to fear nakedness! Indeed, if you were gods then you could be ashamed of your clothing!

For your friend you cannot groom yourself beautifully enough, for you should be his arrow and longing for the overman.

Have you ever seen your friend sleeping – so that you discover how he really looks? What after all is the face of your friend? It is your own face, in a rough and imperfect mirror.

Have you ever seen your friend sleeping? Weren't you startled that your friend looks as he does? Oh my friend, human being is something that must be overcome.

The friend should be a master of guessing and keeping silent: you must not want to see everything. Your dream should reveal to you what your friend does while waking.

Let your compassion be a guessing, so that you might first know whether your friend wants compassion. Perhaps what he loves in you is your unbroken eye and the look of eternity.

Let compassion for your friend conceal itself beneath a hard shell, so that in biting on it you lose a tooth! That way it will have its delicacy and sweetness.

Are you pure air and solitude and bread and medicine to your friend? Many cannot loosen their own chains and yet they are a redeemer for the friend.

Are you a slave? Then you cannot be a friend. Are you a tyrant? Then you cannot have friends.

All too long a slave and a tyrant have been concealed in woman. That is why woman is not yet capable of friendship: she knows only love.

In the love of a woman are injustice and blindness toward everything that she does not love. And even in the knowing love of a woman there is everywhere still assault and lightning and night next to light.

Woman is not yet capable of friendship: women are still cats, and birds. Or, at best, cows.[6]

---

[6] Nietzsche's bitterness toward women, and especially his view that women are incapable of friendship, were no doubt influenced by his traumatic experience with Lou Salomé, with whom he had

Woman is not yet capable of friendship. But tell me, you men, who then among you is capable of friendship?

Oh how repulsive is your poverty, you men, and the stinginess of your souls! As much as you give your friend I will give even to my enemy, and would not be poorer for it.

There is comradeship: may there be friendship!

Thus spoke Zarathustra.

On a Thousand and One Goals

Many lands Zarathustra saw and many peoples; thus he discovered many peoples' good and evil. No greater power on earth did Zarathustra find than good and evil.

No people could live that did not first esteem; but if they want to preserve themselves, then they must not esteem as their neighbor esteems.

Much that was called good by this people was called scorn and disgrace by another: thus I found. Much I found that was called evil here and decked in purple honors there.

Never did one neighbor understand the other: always his soul was amazed at his neighbor's delusion and malice.

A tablet of the good hangs over every people. Observe, it is the tablet of their overcomings; observe, it is the voice of their will to power.

Praiseworthy to them is whatever they consider difficult; what is indispensable and difficult, is called good, and whatever stems from the highest need and still liberates, the rarest, the most difficult – that is praised as holy.

Whatever lets them rule and triumph and shine, to the dread and envy of their neighbor, that they consider as the high, the first, the measuring, the meaning of all things.

Truly, my brother, once you discover a people's need and land and sky and neighbor, you guess as well the law of their overcomings, and why they climb on this ladder to their hope.

been in love. The writing of the first two parts of TSZ coincides with and chronicles Nietzsche's coming to terms with the profound betrayal he felt at the hands of both Salomé and his friend Paul Rée. See Adrian Del Caro, "Andreas-Salomé and Nietzsche: New Perspectives," *Seminar* 36:1 (2000), pp. 79–96.

"Always you shall be the first and tower above others: no one shall your jealous soul love, unless it is the friend" – this is what made the soul of a Greek tremble: with this he walked the path of greatness.

"Speak the truth and be skilled with the bow and arrow" – this seemed both dear and difficult to the people from whom my name derives – the name that is both dear and difficult to me.[7]

"Honor father and mother and comply with their will down to the roots of one's soul" – this tablet of overcoming a different people hung over themselves and became powerful and eternal thereby.

"Practice loyalty and for loyalty's sake risk honor and blood even on evil and dangerous things" – teaching themselves thus another people conquered themselves, and thus conquering themselves they became pregnant and heavy with great hopes.

Indeed, humans gave themselves all of their good and evil. Indeed, they did not take it, they did not find it, it did not fall to them as a voice from heaven.

Humans first placed values into things, in order to preserve themselves – they first created meaning for things, a human meaning!

That is why they call themselves "human," that is: the esteemer.

Esteeming is creating: hear me, you creators! Esteeming itself is the treasure and jewel of all esteemed things.

Only through esteeming is there value, and without esteeming the nut of existence would be hollow. Hear me, you creators!

Change of values – that is the change of creators. Whoever must be a creator always annihilates.

First peoples were creators and only later individuals; indeed, the individual himself is still the youngest creation.

Peoples once hung a tablet of the good over themselves. Love that wants to rule and love that wants to obey such tablets created together.

---

[7] This is a direct allusion to Zoroaster, Zarathustra's namesake. The ancient religion of Zoroastrianism is still practiced by some in Iran, formerly called Persia. Nietzsche explains the significance of using the German name of Zoroaster for his modern-day prophet in *Ecce Homo*, ch. 14, section 3, where he writes: "Zarathustra is more truthful than any other thinker. His teaching and it alone has truthfulness as the supreme virtue – that is, the opposite of the *cowardice* of the 'idealist' who flees from reality; Zarathustra has more courage in his body than all thinkers put together. Speak the truth and *be skilled with the bow and arrow*, that is Persian virtue." In this passage Nietzsche's three peoples are the Persians, the Jews, and the Germans.

Delight in the herd is older than delight in the ego, and as long as good conscience is synonymous with herd, only bad conscience says: ego.

Truly, the sly ego, loveless, wanting its benefit in the benefit of the many: that is not the origin of the herd, but instead its going under.

It was always lovers and creators who created good and evil. The fire of love glows in the names of all virtues and the fire of wrath.

Zarathustra saw many lands and many peoples: no greater power did Zarathustra find on earth than the works of the lovers: "good" and "evil" are their names.

Truly, a behemoth is the power of this praising and blaming. Tell me, who will conquer it for me, you brothers? Tell me, who will throw the fetters over the thousand necks of this beast?

A thousand goals there have been until now, for there have been a thousand peoples. Only the fetters for the thousand necks are still missing, the one goal is missing. Humanity still has no goal.

But tell me, my brothers: if humanity still lacks a goal, does it not also still lack – humanity itself? –

Thus spoke Zarathustra.

On Love of the Neighbor

You crowd around your neighbor and you have pretty words for it. But I say to you: your love of the neighbor is your bad love of yourselves.

You flee to your neighbor to escape yourself and you want to make a virtue of it: but I see through your "selflessness."

The You is older than the I; the You is pronounced sacred, but not yet the I: and so humans crowd around their neighbors.

Do I recommend love of the neighbor to you? I prefer instead to recommend flight from the neighbor and love of the farthest!

Higher than love of the neighbor is love of the farthest and the future; higher still than love of human beings is love of things and ghosts.

This ghost that runs before you, my brother, is more beautiful than you; why do you not give it your flesh and your bones? But you are afraid and run to your neighbor.

You cannot stand yourselves and do not love yourselves enough: now you want to seduce your neighbor to love and gild yourselves with his error.

I wish you were unable to stand all these neighbors and their neighbors; then you would have to create your friend and his overflowing heart out of yourself.

You invite a witness when you want someone to speak well of you; and when you have seduced him into thinking well of you, you then think well of yourselves.

Not only he lies who speaks though he knows better, but the real liar is the one who speaks though he knows nothing. And so you visit each other and speak of yourselves and deceive your neighbor with yourselves.

Thus speaks the fool: "The company of people ruins one's character, especially when one has none."

One person goes to his neighbor because he seeks himself, and the other because he would like to lose himself. Your bad love of yourselves makes your loneliness into a prison.

Those farther away pay for your love of the neighbor; and even when you are together five at a time, always a sixth one must die.

Nor do I love your festivals: too many actors I found there, and even the spectators behaved often like actors.

I do not teach you the neighbor, but the friend. The friend shall be your festival of the earth and an anticipation of the overman.

I teach you the friend and his overflowing heart. But one must understand how to be a sponge, if one wants to be loved by overflowing hearts.

I teach you the friend in whom the world stands complete, a bowl of goodness – the creating friend who always has a complete world to bestow.

And just as the world rolled apart for him, so it rolled together again in rings, as the becoming of good through evil, as the becoming of purpose out of accident.

Let the future and the farthest be the cause of your today: in your friend you shall love the overman as your cause.

My brothers, I do not recommend love of the neighbor to you: I recommend love of the farthest to you.

Thus spoke Zarathustra.

On the Way of the Creator

Do you want to go into isolation, my brother? Do you want to seek the way to yourself? Linger a bit longer and listen to me.

"Whoever seeks easily gets lost himself. All isolation is guilt," thus speaks the herd. And long have you belonged to the herd.

The voice of the herd will still resonate in you too. And when you will say "I no longer am of one conscience with you," then it will be a lament and a pain.

Behold, this pain itself bore the one conscience, and the last shimmer of this conscience still glows on your misery.

But you want to go the way of your misery, which is the way to yourself? Then show me your right and your strength to it!

Are you a new strength and a new right? A first movement? A wheel rolling out of itself? Can you compel even the stars to revolve around you?

Oh, there is so much lust for the heights! There are so many spasms of the ambitious! Show me that you are not one of the lustful and the ambitious!

Oh, there are so many great thoughts that do nothing more than a bellows: they puff up and make emptier.

You call yourself free? Your dominating thought I want to hear, and not that you escaped from a yoke.[8]

Are you the kind of person who had the *right* to escape from a yoke? There are some who threw away their last value when they threw away their servitude.

Free from what? What does Zarathustra care! But brightly your eyes should signal to me: free *for what*?

Can you give yourself your own evil and good and hang your will above yourself like a law? Can you be your own judge and the avenger of your law?

It is terrible to be alone with the judge and avenger of one's own law. Thus does a star get thrown out into desolate space and into the icy breath of solitary being.

Today you suffer still from the many, you lonely one: for today you still have your courage and your hopes intact.

---

[8] *Joche*, yoke, is the same word in German and English. Here Nietzsche specifically has a yoke in mind because he is addressing the possibility of freedom among those who are yoked. In "On a Thousand and One Goals," Nietzsche uses the word *Fesseln* (fetters) in connection with the beast with a thousand necks, not yoke as indicated in the Kaufmann translation.

But one day solitude will make you weary, one day your pride will cringe and your courage will gnash its teeth. One day you will cry "I am alone!"

One day will you will no longer see your high, and your low will be all too near; your sublimity itself will frighten you like a ghost. One day you will cry: "Everything is false!"

There are feelings that want to kill the lonely one; if they do not succeed, well, then they must die themselves! But are you capable of being a murderer?

Do you know the word "contempt" yet, my brother? And the agony of your justice, namely to be just to those who despise you?

You compel many to relearn about you; they weigh that heavily against you. You came near to them and yet passed by: they will never forgive you that.

You pass over and beyond them, but the higher you climb the smaller you are to the eyes of envy. But the ones who fly they hate most.

"How would you be just toward me?" – you must say – "I choose your injustice as my fair share."

Injustice and filth they throw at the lonely one. But my brother, if you want to be a star then you must shine through for them all the more!

And beware of the good and the just! They like to crucify those who invent their own virtue – they hate the lonely one.

Beware too of holy simplicity! Everything is unholy to it that is not simple; it also likes to play with fire – the stake.

And beware of the attacks of your love! Too quickly the lonely one extends his hand to those he encounters.

To some people you should not give your hand, but instead only your paw: and I want that your paw also has claws.

But the worst enemy whom you can encounter will always be yourself; you ambush yourself in caves and woods.

Lonely one, you go the way to yourself! And past you yourself leads your way and past your seven devils!

To your own self you will be heretic and witch and soothsayer and fool and doubter and unholy man and villain.

You must want to burn yourself up in your own flame: how could you become new if you did not first become ashes!

Lonely one, you go the way of the creator: you will create yourself a god out of your seven devils!

Lonely one, you go the way of the lover: you love yourself and that is why you despise yourself as only lovers despise.

The lover wants to create because he despises! What does he know of love who did not have to despise precisely what he loved!

With your love go into your isolation and with your creativity, my brother; and only later will justice limp after you.

With my tears go into your isolation, my brother. I love him who wants to create over and beyond himself and thus perishes. –

Thus spoke Zarathustra.

On Little Women Old and Young

"Why do you creep about so timidly in the twilight, Zarathustra? And what do you conceal so cautiously beneath your coat?

Is it a treasure that was given to you? Or a child that was born to you? Or do you yourself now walk the paths of thieves, you friend of the evil?" –

"Indeed, my brother!" spoke Zarathustra. "It is a treasure that was given to me: it is a little truth, which I carry.

But it is unruly like a young child, and if I do not hold its mouth shut, then it cries out too loudly.

As I went my way alone today, at the hour when the sun sets, I met a little old woman and she spoke thus to my soul:

'Much has Zarathustra spoken also to us women, and yet he has never spoken to us about woman.'

And I replied to her: 'About woman one should speak only to men.'

'Speak to me too about woman,' she said. 'I am old enough to forget it right away.'

And I humored the little old woman and spoke thus to her:

Everything about woman is a riddle, and everything about woman has one solution: it is called pregnancy.

A man is for woman a means: the end is always the child. But what is woman for a man?

Two things the real man wants: danger and play. That is why he wants woman as the most dangerous plaything.

A man should be raised for war and woman for the recreation of the warrior: everything else is folly.

Fruits that are all too sweet – these the warrior does not like. Therefore he likes woman; even the sweetest woman is still bitter.

Better than a man, woman understands children, but a man is more childish than a woman.

In the real man a child is concealed: it wants to play. Up now, you women, go discover the child in the man!

Let woman be a plaything, pure and fine, like a gemstone radiated by the virtues of a world that does not yet exist.

Let the ray of a star shine in your love! Let your hope be called: 'May I give birth to the overman!'

Let courage be in your love! With your love you should throw yourself at him who makes you afraid!

Let your honor be in your love! Otherwise woman understands little about honor. But let this be your honor: always to love more than you are loved, and never to be second.

Let a man be afraid of a woman when she loves; then she makes any sacrifice, and every other thing is without value to her.

Let a man be afraid of a woman when she hates; for at the bottom of his soul a man is merely evil, but woman is bad there.

Whom does a woman hate most? – Thus spoke the iron to the magnet: 'I hate you most because you attract, but are not strong enough to attract me to you.'

The happiness of a man says: I will. The happiness of a woman says: he wills.

'Behold, just now the world became perfect!' – Thus thinks every woman when she obeys out of total love.

And a woman must obey and find a depth for her surface. Surface is a woman's disposition, a flexible, stormy skin over shallow water. But a man's disposition is deep, his stream roars in underground caves; woman intuits his strength but does not comprehend it." –

Then the little old woman replied to me: "Much that is sweet Zarathustra has said, and especially for those who are young enough for it.

Peculiar, though, that Zarathustra knows women only little, and yet he is right about them! Does this happen because with women nothing is impossible?

And now, by way of thanks, accept a little truth! Surely I am old enough for it!

Bundle it up and hold its mouth shut, or else it will cry out too loudly, this little truth."

"Give me your little truth, woman!" I said. And thus spoke the little old woman:

"You go to women? Do not forget the whip!"[9] –

Thus spoke Zarathustra.

On the Adder's Bite

One day Zarathustra had fallen asleep beneath a fig tree, since it was hot, and he had laid his arm over his face. Then an adder came along and bit him in the neck, so that Zarathustra cried out in pain. When he had taken his arm from his face he looked at the snake; it recognized the eyes of Zarathustra, turned around awkwardly and tried to get away. "Not so fast," spoke Zarathustra. "You have not yet accepted my thanks! You waked me in time, my way is still long." "Your way is still short," said the adder sadly: "My poison kills." Zarathustra smiled. "Since when did a dragon ever die of snake poison?" he said. "But take back your poison! You are not rich enough to give it to me." Then the snake fell upon his neck once again and licked his wound.

When Zarathustra once told this to his disciples they asked: "And what, oh Zarathustra, is the moral of your story?" To which Zarathustra responded thus:

"The annihilator of morals the good and just call me: my story is immoral.

If you should have an enemy, then do not requite him evil with good, for that would shame him. Instead prove that he has does you some good.

And be angry rather than shaming someone! And if you are cursed at, I do not like it that you want to bless. Better to curse along a bit!

And if a great wrong befell you, then quickly add five small ones to it! Ghastly to behold is a person who suffers a wrong all by himself.

Did you know this already? A wrong shared is half a right. And the one who should take a wrong upon himself is the one who can bear it!

[9] Recent scholarship on Nietzsche's view of women reveals a deeper appreciation of women than the one suggested here, which is seductively misleading. In the 1882 photo of Nietzsche, Paul Rée, and Lou Salomé, the two men are "in harness" in front of a tiny cart, while Lou Salomé holds a toy whip. See Adrian Del Caro, "Nietzsche, Sacher-Masoch, and the Whip," *German Studies Review* 21:2 (1998), pp. 241–61.

A small revenge is more humane than no revenge at all. And if the punishment is not also a right and an honor for the transgressor, then I do not like your punishing either.

It is more noble to pronounce oneself wrong than to remain right, especially if one is right. Only one has to be rich enough for that.

I do not like your cold justice; and from the eyes of your judges gazes always the executioner and his cold steel.

Tell me, where is the justice found that is love with seeing eyes?

Then invent me the kind of love that not only bears all punishment but also all guilt!

Then invent me the kind of justice that pardons everyone, except the one who judges!

And do you want to hear this too? In the person who would be thoroughly just, even lies become philanthropy.

But how could I want to be thoroughly just! How can I give to each his own! Let this be enough for me: I give to each *my* own.

Finally, my brothers, beware of doing wrong to any hermits! How could a hermit forget? How could he requite?

A hermit is like a deep well. It is easy to throw in a stone; but once it has sunk to the bottom, tell me: who would fetch it up again?

Beware of offending the hermit! But if you've already done so, well then, kill him too!"

Thus spoke Zarathustra.

On Child and Marriage

I have a question for you alone, my brother: like a plumb bob I cast this question into your soul, in order to know how deep it is.

You are young and wish for a child and marriage for yourself. But I ask you: are you a person who has a *right* to wish for a child?

Are you the victor, the self conqueror, the master of your senses, the ruler of your virtues? Thus I ask you.

Or do the animal and neediness speak out of your wish? Or loneliness? Or discord with yourself?

I want your victory and your freedom to long for a child. You should build living monuments to your victory and your liberation.

Your should build over and beyond yourself. But first I want you built yourselves, square in body and soul.

You should not only reproduce, but surproduce! May the garden of marriage help you to that!

You should create a higher body, a first movement, a wheel rolling out of itself – a creator you should create.

Marriage: that is what I call the will by two for creating the one who is more than those who created it. Respect for one another I call marriage, and respect for the one who wills such a willing.

Let this be the meaning and the truth of your marriage. But that which the far-too-many call marriage, these superfluous ones – oh, what do I call that?

Oh, this poverty of the soul by two! Oh, this filth of the soul by two! Oh, this pitiful contentment by two!

Marriage they call all this; and they say their marriages are made in heaven.

Well, I do not like it, this heaven of the superfluous! No, I do not like them, these animals tangled in the heavenly net!

And may the God stay away from me who limps up to bless what he has not joined together!

Do not laugh at such marriages! Which child would not have reason to weep about its parents?

Worthy this man seemed to me, and ripe for the meaning of the earth; but when I saw his woman, the earth seemed to me a house for the senseless.

Indeed, I wish the earth would quake in convulsions whenever a saint and a goose mate.

This one went forth like a hero seeking truths, and finally he bagged himself a little dressed up lie. He calls it his marriage.

That one was socially reserved and a choosy chooser. But all at once he ruined his company once and for all: he calls it his marriage.

That one sought a maid with the virtues of an angel. But all at once he became the maid of a woman and now he even has to turn himself into an angel.

Cautious I found all buyers now, and all have cunning eyes. But even the cunning man still buys his wife in a poke.

Many brief follies – that is what you call love. And your marriage makes an end of many brief follies, as one long stupidity.

Your love of woman and woman's love of man, oh! If only it were compassion for suffering and for disguised gods! But mostly it is two animals discovering each other.

But even your best love is merely an ecstatic parable and a painful smolder. It is a torch that should light you to higher ways.

Over and beyond yourselves you must someday love! Thus *learn* first to love! And therefore you must drink the bitter cup of your love.

There is bitterness in the cup of even the best love: thus it causes longing for the overman, thus it causes your thirst, you creator!

Thirst for the creator, arrow and longing for the overman: speak, my brother, is this your will to marriage?

Holy I pronounce such a will and such a marriage. –

Thus spoke Zarathustra.

On Free Death[10]

Many die too late, and some die too early. The doctrine still sounds strange: "Die at the right time!"

Die at the right time: thus Zarathustra teaches it.

To be sure, how could the person who never lives at the right time ever die at the right time? Would that he were never born! – Thus I advise the superfluous.

But even the superfluous boast about their dying, and even the hollowest nut still wants to be cracked.

Everyone regards dying as important; but death is not yet a festival. As of yet people have not learned how to consecrate the most beautiful festivals.

I show you the consummating death that becomes a goad and a promise to the living.

The consummated one dies *his* death, victorious, surrounded by those who hope and promise.

Thus one should learn to die; and there should be no festival where such a dying person does not swear oaths to the living!

To die thus is best; second best, however, is to die fighting and to squander a great soul.

But your grinning death, the one that creeps up like a thief and yet comes as master – it is hated as much by the fighter as by the victor.

---

[10] "Vom freien Tode" – on free death – suggests *der Freitod*, suicide (death entered into freely). As usual Nietzsche's emphasis is on the quality of one's life, here juxtaposed with the symbolism of one's death.

My death I praise to you, the free death that comes to me because *I* want.

And when will I want it? – Whoever has a goal and an heir wants death at the right time for his goal and heir.

And out of reverence for his goal and heir he will no longer hang withered wreaths in the sanctuary of life.

Indeed, I do not want to be like the rope makers: they stretch out their threads and in doing so always walk backwards.

Some become too old even for their truths and victories; a toothless mouth no longer has the right to every truth.

And everyone who wants to have fame must take leave of honor from time to time and practice the difficult art of leaving – at the right time.

One must stop letting oneself be eaten when one tastes best; this is known by those who want to be loved for a long time.

There are sour apples, to be sure, whose lot demands that they wait for the last day of autumn; and immediately they become ripe, yellow and wrinkled.

With some the heart ages first and with others the mind. A few are hoary in their youth, but the late young stay long young.

For some life fails: a poisonous worm eats its way to their heart. Let them see to it that their dying succeeds all the more.

Some never become sweet, they rot already in summer. It is cowardice that keeps them clinging to the branch.

Far too many live and far too long they hang on their branches. Would that a storm came to shake all this rot and worm-food from the tree!

Would that preachers of the *quick* death came! They would be the right storms and shakers of the trees of life for me! But I hear only preaching of the slow death and patience with all things "earthly."

Indeed, you preach patience with earthly things? It is the earthly things that have too much patience with you, you slanderers!

Truly, too early did that Hebrew die, the one who is honored by the preachers of slow death; and for many it has since become their doom that he died too early.

He still knew only tears and the melancholy of the Hebrews, together with the hatred of the good and just – the Hebrew Jesus; then longing for death overcame him.

If only he had remained in the desert and far away from the good and the just! Perhaps he would have learned to live and to love the earth – and even to laugh!

Believe me, my brothers! He died too early; he himself would have recanted his teaching if he had reached my age! He was noble enough for recanting!

But he had not yet matured. A youth loves immaturely, and immaturely too he hates mankind and earth. Still tethered and heavy to him are his mind and the wings of his spirit.

But in a man there is more child than in a youth, and less melancholy; he knows more about death and life.

Free for death and free in death, a sacred nay-sayer when it is no longer time for yes: thus he knows about death and life.

Do not allow your death to be a slander against mankind and earth, my friends: that I beseech of the honey of your soul.

In your dying your spirit and your virtue should still glow, like a sunset around the earth; or else your dying has failed you.

Thus I myself want to die, so that you my friends love the earth more for my sake; and I want to become earth again, so that I may have peace in the one who bore me.

Truly, Zarathustra had a goal, he threw his ball. Now you my friends are the heirs of my goal, to you I throw the golden ball.

More than anything I like to see you, my friends, throwing the golden ball! And so I linger yet a bit on earth: forgive me that!

Thus spoke Zarathustra.

On the Bestowing Virtue[11]

I

When Zarathustra had taken leave of the city, which was dear to his heart and whose name was The Motley Cow, many who called themselves his disciples followed him, and they provided him escort. Thus they came to a crossroads; then Zarathustra told them he wanted to walk alone now, for he was a friend of walking alone. In parting, however, his disciples

---

[11] "Von der schenkenden Tugend," with *schenken* meaning "to bestow" rather than merely "to give." German uses *schenken* to connote the special kind of giving as a gift, a present, a grant, or a donation. "Giving" captures some of this, but German uses *geben* (to give) just as English does.

presented him with a staff upon whose golden knob a snake encircled the sun. Zarathustra was delighted with the staff and leaned on it; then he spoke thus to his disciples.

Tell me now: how did gold come to have the highest value? Because it is uncommon and useless and gleaming and mild in its luster; it bestows itself always.

Only as the image of the highest virtue did gold come to have the highest value. Goldlike gleams the gaze of the bestower. Golden luster makes peace between moon and sun.

Uncommon is the highest virtue and useless, it is gleaming and mild in its luster: a bestowing virtue is the highest virtue.

Truly, I guess you well, my disciples: like me you strive for the bestowing virtue. What would you have in common with cats or wolves?

This is your thirst: to become sacrifices and gifts yourselves, and therefore you thirst to amass all riches in your soul.

Insatiably your soul strives for treasures and gems, because your virtue is insatiable in wanting to bestow.

You compel all things to and into yourselves, so that they may gush back from your well as the gifts of your love.

Indeed, such a bestowing love must become a robber of all values, but hale and holy I call this selfishness.

There is another selfishness, one all too poor, a hungering one that always wants to steal; that selfishness of the sick, the sick selfishness.

With the eye of the thief it looks at all that gleams; with the greed of hunger it eyes those with ample food; and always it creeps around the table of the bestowers.

Sickness speaks out of such craving and invisible degeneration; the thieving greed of this selfishness speaks of a diseased body.

Tell me, my brothers: what do we regard as bad and worst? Is it not *degeneration*? – And we always diagnose degeneration where the bestowing soul is absent.

Upward goes our way, over from genus to super-genus.[12] But a horror to us is the degenerating sense which speaks: "Everything for me."

---

[12] Degeneration (*Entartung*) is based on genus, just as *Entartung* is based on *Art*, meaning genus, species, type, or kind. Nietzsche's concern is with the human species, which he sees threatened by degeneration. Those humans who possess a superabundance of the bestowing virtue are transitioning from human (the species or *Art*) to superhuman (*Über-Art*). In Part IV Zarathustra will again refer specifically to a new "beautiful species."

Upward flies our sense; thus it is a parable of our body, a parable of elevation. Such elevation parables are the names of the virtues.

Thus the body goes through history, becoming and fighting. And the spirit – what is it to the body? The herald of its fights and victories, companion and echo.

Parables are all names of good and evil: they do not express, they only hint. A fool who wants to know of them!

Pay attention, my brothers, to every hour where your spirit wants to speak in parables: there is the origin of your virtue.

There your body is elevated and resurrected; with its bliss it delights the spirit, which becomes creator and esteemer and lover and benefactor of all things.

When your heart flows broad and full like a river, a blessing and a danger to adjacent dwellers: there is the origin of your virtue.

When you are sublimely above praise and blame, and your will wants to command all things, as the will of a lover: there is the origin of your virtue.

When you despise pleasantness and the soft bed, and cannot bed down far enough away from the softies: there is the origin of your virtue.

When you are the ones who will with a single will, and this turning point of all need points to your necessity: there is the origin of your virtue.

Indeed, it is a new good and evil! Indeed, a new, deep rushing and the voice of a new spring!

It is power, this new virtue; it is a ruling thought and around it a wise soul: a golden sun and around it the snake of knowledge.

2

Here Zarathustra was silent for a while and looked with love at his disciples. Then he continued to speak thus – and his voice had transformed.

Remain faithful to the earth, my brothers, with the power of your virtue! Let your bestowing love and your knowledge serve the meaning of the earth! Thus I beg and beseech you.

Do not let it fly away from earthly things and beat against eternal walls with its wings! Oh, there has always been so much virtue that flew away!

Like me, guide the virtue that has flown away back to the earth – yes, back to the body and life: so that it may give the earth its meaning, a human meaning!

In a hundred ways thus far the spirit as well as virtue has flown away and failed. Oh, in our body now all this delusion and failure dwells: there they have become body and will.

In a hundred ways thus far spirit as well as virtue has essayed and erred. Indeed, human beings were an experiment. Alas, much ignorance and error have become embodied in us!

Not only the reason of millennia – their madness too breaks out in us. It is dangerous to be an heir.

Still we struggle step by step with the giant called accident, and over all humanity thus far nonsense has ruled, the sense-less.

Let your spirit and your virtue serve the meaning of the earth, my brothers: and the value of all things will be posited newly by you! Therefore you shall be fighters! Therefore you shall be creators!

Knowingly the body purifies itself; experimenting with knowledge it elevates itself; all instincts become sacred in the seeker of knowledge; the soul of the elevated one becomes gay.

Physician, help yourself: thus also you help your sick. Let that be his best help, that he sees with his own eyes the one who heals himself.

There are a thousand paths that have never yet been walked; a thousand healths and hidden islands of life. Human being and human earth are still unexhausted and undiscovered.

Wake and listen, you lonely ones! From the future come winds with secretive wingbeats; good tidings are issued to delicate ears.

You lonely of today, you withdrawing ones, one day you shall be a people: from you who have chosen yourselves a chosen people shall grow – and from them the overman.

Indeed, the earth shall yet become a site of recovery! And already a new fragrance lies about it, salubrious – and a new hope!

3

When Zarathustra had said these words, he grew silent like one who has not spoken his last word. Long he weighed the staff in his hand, doubtfully. Finally he spoke thus, and his voice had transformed.

"Alone I go now, my disciples! You also should go now, and alone! Thus I want it.

Indeed, I counsel you to go away from me and guard yourselves against Zarathustra! And even better: be ashamed of him! Perhaps he deceived you.

The person of knowledge must not only be able to love his enemies, but to hate his friends too.

One repays a teacher badly if one always remains a pupil only. And why would you not want to pluck at my wreath?

You revere me, but what if your reverence falls down some day? Beware that you are not killed by a statue!

You say you believe in Zarathustra? But what matters Zarathustra! You are my believers, but what matter all believers!

You had not yet sought yourselves, then you found me. All believers do this; that's why all faith amounts to so little.

Now I bid you lose me and find yourselves; and only when you have all denied me will I return to you.

Indeed, with different eyes, my brothers, will I then seek my lost ones; with a different love will I love you then.

And one day again you shall become my friends and children of a single hope; then I shall be with you a third time, to celebrate the great noon with you.

And that is the great noon, where human beings stand at the midpoint of their course between animal and overman and celebrate their way to evening as their highest hope: for it is the way to a new morning.

Then the one who goes under will bless himself, that he is one who crosses over; and the sun of his knowledge will stand at noon for him.

'*Dead are all gods: now we want the overman to live.*' – Let this be our last will at the great noon!" –

Thus spoke Zarathustra.

Second Part

. . . and only when you have all denied me will I return to you. Indeed, with different eyes, my brothers, will I then seek my lost ones; with a different love will I love you then.

Zarathustra, "On the Bestowing Virtue" (I, p. 59).

The Child with the Mirror

At this time Zarathustra returned again to the mountains and to the solitude of his cave and withdrew from mankind, waiting like a sower who has cast his seeds. But his soul grew full of impatience and desire for those whom he loved, because he still had much to give them. For this is the hardest thing: to close the open hand out of love, and to preserve a sense of shame as a bestower.

Thus moons and years passed for the lonely one; but his wisdom grew and its fullness caused him pain.

But one morning he woke already before dawn, reflected for a long time on his bed and at last spoke to his heart:

What frightened me so in my dream that it waked me? Did not a child approach me carrying a mirror?

"Oh Zarathustra" – spoke the child to me – "look at yourself in the mirror!"

But when I looked into the mirror I cried out, and my heart was shaken; for I did not see myself there, but a devil's grimace and scornful laughter.

Indeed, all too well I understand the dream's sign and warning: my *teaching* is in danger, weeds want to be wheat!

My enemies have become powerful and have distorted the image of my teaching, so that those dearest to me must be ashamed of the gifts I gave them.

My friends are lost to me; the hour has arrived to seek my lost ones! –

With these words Zarathustra leaped to his feet, but not like a frightened person fighting for air, but instead more like a seer and a singer on whom the spirit has descended. In amazement his eagle and his snake looked at him, for like the dawn an impending happiness lay upon his face.

What just happened to me, my animals? – said Zarathustra. Am I not transformed? Did bliss not come to me like a storm wind?

Foolish is my happiness and it will speak foolish things: it is still too young – so have patience with it!

I am wounded by my happiness: all sufferers shall be physicians to me!

Once again I may descend to my friends and also to my enemies! Zarathustra may speak again and bestow and do what he loves best for loved ones!

My impatient love floods over in torrents, downward, toward sunrise and sunset. From silent mountains and thunderheads of pain my soul roars into the valleys.

Too long have I longed and gazed into the distance. Too long I belonged to solitude – thus I forgot how to be silent.

I have become mouth through and through, and a brook's bounding from high boulders: I want to plunge my speech down into the valleys.

And may my torrent of love plunge into impasses! How could a torrent not finally make its way to the sea!

Truly, there is a lake in me, a hermit-like and self-sufficient lake; but my torrent of love tears it along – down to the sea!

New ways I go, a new speech comes to me; I became weary, like all creators, of old tongues. My spirit no longer wants to wander on worn soles.

All speech runs too slowly for me: – I leap into your chariot, storm! And I shall whip even you with the whip of my malice!

Like a shout and a jubilation I want to journey over broad seas until I find the blessed isles where my friends dwell –

And my enemies among them! How I love everyone now, with whom I may simply speak! Even my enemies belong to my bliss.

And when I want to mount my wildest horse, then my spear always helps me up best: it is the ever-ready servant of my foot –

The spear I hurl against my enemies! How I thank my enemies that at last I may hurl it!

Too great was the tension of my cloud: between lightning peals of laughter I shall throw hail showers into the depths.

Violently my chest will heave then, violently it will blow its storm over mountains: thus relief comes to it.

Indeed, my happiness and my freedom come like a storm! But my enemies should believe *the evil one* is raging over their heads.

Indeed, you too will be frightened, my friends, because of my wild wisdom; and perhaps you will flee from it together with my enemies.

Oh, if only I understood how to lure you back with shepherds' flutes! Oh, if only my lioness-wisdom could learn to roar tenderly! And much we have already learned with each other!

My wild wisdom wound up pregnant on lonely mountains; on naked stones she bore her young, her youngest.

Now she runs foolishly through harsh desert and seeks and seeks gentle turf – my old wild wisdom!

Upon the gentle turf of your hearts, my friends! – upon your love she would like to bed her most beloved!

Thus spoke Zarathustra.

On the Blessed Isles

The figs fall from the trees, they are good and sweet; and as they fall, their red skin ruptures. I am a north wind to ripe figs.

Thus, like figs, these teachings fall to you, my friends: now drink their juice and their sweet flesh! It is autumn all around and pure sky and afternoon.

See what fullness is around us! And from such superabundance it is beautiful to look out upon distant seas.

Once people said God when they gazed upon distant seas; but now I have taught you to say: overman.

God is a conjecture, but I want that your conjecturing not reach further than your creating will.

Could you *create* a god? – Then be silent about any gods! But you could well create the overman.

Not you yourselves perhaps, my brothers! But you could recreate your-selves into fathers and forefathers of the overman: and this shall be your best creating! –

God is a conjecture: but I want your conjecturing to be limited to what is thinkable.

Could you *think* a God? – But let this mean will to truth to you; that everything be transformed into what is humanly thinkable, humanly visible, humanly feelable! You should think your own senses to their conclusion!

And what you called world, that should first be created by you: your reason, your image, your will, your love itself it should become! And truly, for your own bliss, you seekers of knowledge!

And how would you bear life without this hope, you seekers of knowledge? Neither into the incomprehensible nor into the irrational could you have been born.

But to reveal my entire heart to you, my friends: *if* there were gods, how could I stand not to be a god! *Therefore* there are no gods.

I drew this conclusion to be sure; but now it draws me. –

God is a conjecture: but who could drink all the agony of this conjecture without dying? Should the creating person's faith be taken, and from the eagle its soaring in eagle heights?

God is a thought that makes crooked everything that is straight, and causes everything that stands to turn. What? Should time be gone, and all that is not everlasting be merely a lie?

To think this causes whirling and dizziness to human bones and even vomiting to the stomach: indeed, the turning disease I call it, to conjecture such things.

Evil I call it and misanthropic: all this teaching of the one and the plenum and the unmoved and the sated and the everlasting!

All that is everlasting – that is merely a parable! And the poets lie too much.

But the best parables should speak about time and becoming: they should be praise and justification of all that is not everlasting!

Creating – that is the great redemption from suffering, and life's becoming light. But in order for the creator to be, suffering is needed and much transformation.

Indeed, much bitter dying must be in your life, you creators! Therefore you are advocates and justifiers of all that is not everlasting.

In order for the creator himself to be the child who is newly born, he must also want to be the birth-giver and the pain of giving birth.

Indeed, through a hundred souls I went my way and through a hundred cradles and pangs of birth. Many a farewell have I taken already; I know the heartbreaking final hours.

But thus my creating will wills it, my destiny. Or, to tell it more honestly to you: just such a destiny – my will wills.

Everything that feels, suffers in me and is in prison; but my will always comes to me as my liberator and bringer of joy.

Willing liberates: that is the true teaching of will and liberty – thus Zarathustra teaches it.

No more willing and no more esteeming and no more creating! Oh, if only this great weariness would always keep away from me!

Even in knowing I feel only my will's lust to beget and to become; and if there is innocence in my knowledge, then this happens because the will to beget is in it.

Away from God and gods this will lured me; what would there be to create, after all, if there were gods?

But I am always driven anew to human beings by my ardent will to create; thus the hammer is driven toward the stone.

Oh you human beings, in the stone sleeps an image, the image of my images! A shame it must sleep in the hardest, ugliest stone!

Now my hammer rages cruelly against its prison. Shards shower from the stone: what do I care?

I want to perfect it, for a shadow came to me – the stillest and lightest of all things once came to me!

The overman's beauty came to me as a shadow. Oh, my brothers! Of what concern to me anymore – are gods! –

Thus spoke Zarathustra.

On the Pitying

My friends, a gibe was told to your friend: "Just look at Zarathustra! Does he not wander among us like we were animals?"

But it is better said this way: "The seeker of knowledge wanders among human beings *as* among animals."

Human beings themselves, however, the seeker of knowledge calls: the animal that has red cheeks.

How did this happen? Is it not because they have had to be ashamed so often?

Oh my friends! Thus speaks the seeker of knowledge: Shame, shame, shame – that is the history of human beings!

And that is why the noble person commands himself not to shame; shame he demands of himself before all sufferers.

Indeed, I do not like them, the merciful who are blissful in their pitying: they lack too much in shame.

If I must be pitying, then I certainly do not want to be called such; and if I am, then preferably from a distance.

Gladly would I cover my head and flee before I am recognized, and thus I bid you do as well, my friends!

May my destiny always lead those like you, who do not suffer, across my path, and those with whom I *may* share hope and meal and honey!

Indeed, I probably did this and that for sufferers, but I always seemed to do myself better when I learned to enjoy myself better.

Ever since there have been humans, the human being has enjoyed himself too little: That alone, my brothers, is our original sin!

And if we learn to enjoy ourselves better, then we forget best how to hurt others and plot hurt for them.

Therefore I wash the hand that helped the sufferer, therefore too I wipe even my soul.

For inasmuch as I saw the sufferer suffering, I was ashamed for the sake of his shame; and when I helped him I severely violated his pride.

Great indebtedness does not make people thankful, but vengeful instead; and if the small kindness is not forgotten then it will become a gnawing worm.

"Be cold in accepting! Let your accepting serve to distinguish!" – Thus I counsel those who have nothing to give away.

I, however, am a bestower. Gladly I bestow as friend to friends. But strangers and poor people may pluck the fruit from my tree themselves: that way there is less shame.

But beggars should be abolished completely! Indeed, one is angered in giving and angered in not giving to them.

And the same for sinners and bad consciences! Believe me, my friends, bites of conscience teach people to bite.

Worst, however, are petty thoughts. Indeed, better to do evil than to think small!

You say, to be sure: "Pleasure in small mischief saves us many a great evil deed." But here one should not want to save.

An evil deed is like a sore: it itches and scratches and ruptures – it speaks honestly.

"Behold, I am sickness" – thus speaks the evil deed, that is its honesty.

But a petty thought is like a fungus; it creeps and crouches and does not want to be anywhere – until the whole body is rotten and wilted with little fungi.

To the one who is possessed by the devil, however, I whisper these words in his ear: "Better to raise your devil until it is big! Even for you there is still a way to greatness!" –

Oh my brothers! One knows a bit too much about everyone! And though some become transparent to us, we can by no means pass through them on that account.

It is difficult to live with people because remaining silent is so difficult.

And we are not most unfair toward those who are repugnant to us, but toward those who do not at all concern us.

But if you have a suffering friend, then be a resting place to his suffering, yet at the same time a hard bed, a camp bed: thus you will be most useful to him.

And if a friend does evil to you, then say: "I forgive you what you have done to me; but that you did it to *yourself* – how could I forgive that!"

Thus speaks all great love; it overcomes even forgiveness and pitying.

One should hold on firmly to one's heart, for if one lets it go, how quickly one then loses one's head!

Oh, where in the world has greater folly occurred than among the pitying? And what in the world causes more suffering than the folly of the pitying?

Woe to all lovers who do not yet have an elevation that is above their pitying!

Thus the devil once spoke to me: "Even God has his hell: it is his love for mankind."

And recently I heard him say these words: "God is dead; God died of his pity for mankind."

Thus I warn you against pity: *from it* a heavy cloud is coming to mankind! Indeed, I understand weather forecasting!

But note these words too: all great love is above even all its pitying, for it still wants to create the beloved!

"I offer myself to my love, *and my neighbor as myself*" – thus it is said of all creators.

But all creators are hard. –

Thus spoke Zarathustra.

On Priests

And once Zarathustra gave a sign to his disciples and spoke these words to them:

"Here are priests, and though they are my enemies, go quietly past them and with sleeping swords!

Among them too there are heroes; many of them suffered too much, so they want to make others suffer.

69

They are evil enemies: nothing is more vengeful than their humility. And whoever attacks them is easily besmirched.

But my blood is related to theirs, and I want to know that my blood is honored even in theirs."

And when they had passed by Zarathustra was seized by pain; and not long had he wrestled with his pain when he rose and began to speak thus:

"I feel for these priests. And though I also find them distasteful, that is the least of my concerns since I have been among human beings.

But I suffer and suffered with them; to me they are prisoners and marked men. The one they call redeemer clapped them in irons: –

In irons of false values and words of delusion! Oh that someone would yet redeem them from their redeemer!

Once they believed they landed on an island as the sea tossed them around; but see, it was a sleeping monster!

False values and words of delusion: these are the worst monsters for mortals – long does doom sleep and wait in them.

But at last it comes and wakes and devours and gulps whatever built itself huts upon it.

Oh look at these huts that the priests built themselves! Churches they call their sweet smelling caves.

Oh how repulsive is this falsified light, this stale air! Here, where the soul to its height – is denied flight!

Instead their faith commands: 'Up the stairs on your knees, you sinners!'

Indeed, I would rather see the shameless than the rolled back eyes of their shame and devotion!

Who created such caves and stairs of penitence? Were they not those who wanted to hide and were ashamed beneath the pure sky?

And only when the pure sky peeks again through broken ceilings and down upon grass and red poppy and broken walls – only then will I turn my heart again to the sites of this God.

They called God what contradicted and hurt them, and truly, there was much heroics in their adoration!

And they knew no other way to love their God than to nail the human being to a cross!

They intended to live as corpses, they decked out their corpse in black; from their speeches I still smell the rotten spice of death chambers.

And whoever lives near them lives near black ponds, out of which the toad sings its song with sweet melancholy.

Better songs they will have to sing for me before I learn to believe in their redeemer; more redeemed his disciples would have to look!

I would like to see them naked, for beauty alone should preach penitence. But who is persuaded anyway by this masked gloom!

Indeed, their redeemers themselves did not come from freedom and the freedom of seventh heaven! Indeed, they themselves never walked on the carpets of knowledge!

The spirit of these redeemers consisted of gaps; but into every gap they had plugged a delusion, their stopgap, whom they named God.

Their spirit drowned in their pitying, and when they swelled and overswelled with pity, always a great folly floated on top.

Zealously and with shouting they drove their herd along their path, as if there were only one path to the future! Indeed, these shepherds, too, still belonged among the sheep!

Small spirits and roomy souls these shepherds had, but my brothers; what small countries even the roomiest souls have been so far!

Blood-signs they wrote along the way that they walked, and their folly taught that one proves the truth with blood.

But blood is the worst witness of truth; blood poisons even the purest teaching into delusion and hatred of the heart.

And if someone goes through fire for his teaching – what does this prove? Indeed, it means more when one's own teaching comes out of one's own fire!

A sultry heart and a cold head: where these come together the howling wind originates, the 'redeemer.'

There have been greater ones, to be sure, and higher born than those whom the people call redeemers, these sweeping howling winds!

And you must be redeemed even from those greater than all redeemers, my brothers, if you want to find your way to freedom!

Never yet has there been an overman. Naked I saw both, the greatest and the smallest human being –

All too similar they are to one another. Truly, even the greatest I found – all too human!"

Thus spoke Zarathustra.

On the Virtuous

With thunder and heavenly fireworks one must speak to slack and sleeping senses.

But the voice of beauty speaks softly; it creeps only into the most awakened souls.

Softly today my shield trembled and laughed; it is the holy laughter and trembling of beauty.

At you, virtuous ones, my beauty laughed today. And thus its voice came to me: "They still want – to be paid!"

You still want to be paid, you virtuous! Want to have reward for virtue, and heaven for earth, and eternity for your today?

And now you're angry with me for teaching that there is no reward and paymaster? And truly, I do not even teach that virtue is its own reward.

Oh, this is my sorrow; reward and punishment have been lied into the ground of things – and now even into the ground of your souls, you virtuous!

But like the snout of a boar my words shall tear open the ground of your souls; a plowshare I shall be to you.

All the secrets of your ground shall be brought to light; and when you lie uprooted and broken in the sun, your lie also will be separated from your truth.

For this is your truth: you are too *pure* for the filth of the words revenge, punishment, reward, retribution.

You love your virtue as the mother her child; but when did anyone ever hear that a mother wanted to be paid for her love?

Your virtue is your dearest self. The ring's thirst is in you; every ring struggles and turns to reach itself again.

And each work of your virtue is like the star that dies out; always its light is still on its way and wandering – and when will it no longer be on its way?

Thus the light of your virtue is still underway, even when the work is done. And even if now forgotten and dead, its ray of light still lives and wanders.

Your virtue should be your self and not a foreign thing, a skin, a cloaking: that is the truth from the ground of your soul, you virtuous! –

But surely there are those who equate virtue with spasm under a whip, and you have listened too much to their cries!

And there are others who call it virtue when their vices grow lazy; and when their hatred and their jealousy stretch their limbs for once, their "justice" perks up and rubs its sleepy eyes.

And there are others who are pulled down, their devil pulls them. But the more they sink the more ardently glow their eyes and the craving for their god.

Oh, their cries too penetrated your ears, you virtuous: "What I am *not*, that, that is God and virtue to me!"

And there are others who come along heavy and creaking like wagons carting stones downhill: they speak much of dignity and virtue – they call their brake virtue!

And there are others who are like run of the mill clocks that have been wound up: they go tick-tock and want to have their tic called virtue.

Indeed, I have my fun with these; wherever I find such clocks I will wind them up with my mockery, and make them whir for me!

And others are proud of their handful of justice, and for its sake they commit outrage against all things, such that the world is drowned in their injustice.

Oh, how foul the word "virtue" sounds coming from their mouths! And when they say: "I am just," then it sounds always like: "I am just avenged!"

With their virtue they want to scratch out the eyes of their enemies; and they elevate themselves only to degrade others.

And then again there are those who sit in their swamp and speak thus from out of the reeds: "Virtue – that means sitting quietly in the swamp.

We bite no one and avoid anyone who wants to bite; and in all matters we have that opinion that is given us."

And then again there are those who love gestures and think: virtue is a kind of gesture.

Their knees always adore and their hands are extolments of virtue, but their hearts know nothing of it.

And then again there are those who consider it virtue to say: "Virtue is necessity"; but at bottom they believe only that the police are a necessity.

And some who cannot see the high in people call it virtue that they see the low all too near, thus they call their evil eye virtue.

And a few want to be edified and built up and call that virtue; and others want to be toppled – and call that virtue too.

And in this manner almost all believe they have a share of virtue; and at the very least each person wants to be an expert on "good" and "evil."

But Zarathustra has not come to say to all these liars and fools: "What do *you* know about virtue! What *could* you know about virtue!" –

Instead, my friends, I wish you would grow weary of the old words you have learned from the fools and liars:

Grow weary of the words "reward," "retribution," "punishment," "revenge in justice" –

Grow weary of saying: "What makes a deed good is that it is selfless."

Oh my friends! I wish *your* self were in the deed like the mother is in the child: let that be *your* word on virtue!

Indeed, I may have taken from you a hundred words and your virtue's favorite toys; and now you are angry with me as children become angry.

They played by the sea – then the wave came and tore their toys into the deep: now they weep.

But the same wave shall bring them new toys and lavish new colorful shells before them!

Thus will they be consoled; and like them you, too, my friends shall have your consolations – and new colorful shells! –

Thus spoke Zarathustra.

On the Rabble

Life is a well of joy; but where the rabble also drinks, there all wells are poisoned.

I appreciate all that is clean; but I do not like to see the grinning snouts and the thirst of the unclean.

They cast their eyes down into the well; now their disgusting smile reflects back up to me from the well.

They have poisoned the holy water with their lustfulness; and when they called their filthy dreams joy, they poisoned even words.

The flame shrinks when they put their dank hearts on the fire; the spirit itself seethes and smokes wherever the rabble approaches the fire.

In their hands fruits becomes sickly sweet and overripe; their gaze makes fruit trees prone to windfall and withered at the crown.

And some who turned away from life only turned away from the rabble, not wanting to share well and flame and fruit with the rabble.

And some who went into the wilderness and suffered thirst with beasts of prey simply did not want to sit around the cistern with filthy camel drivers.

And some who came along like annihilators and like a hailstorm to all orchards merely wanted to plant their foot into the maw of the rabble to stuff its throat.

And the bite I gagged on most was not the knowledge that life itself requires hostility and dying and torture crosses –

Instead I once asked, and almost choked on my question: What? Does life also *require* the rabble?

Are poisoned wells and stinking fires and soiled dreams and maggots required in life's bread?

Not my hatred but my nausea fed hungrily on my life! Oh, I often grew weary of the spirit when I found even the rabble had wit!

And I turned my back on the rulers when I saw what they call ruling today: haggling and bartering for power – with the rabble!

Among peoples of foreign tongues I lived, with my ears closed, so that the haggling of their tongue and their bartering for power would remain foreign to me. And holding my nose I walked annoyed through all yesterday and today; truly, all yesterday and today smell foul of the writing rabble!

Like a cripple who became deaf and blind and dumb; thus I lived for a long time, so as not to live with the power-, the scribble-, the pleasure-rabble.

Laboriously my spirit climbed steps, and cautiously; alms of joy were its refreshment; for the blind man life crept by as if on a cane.

But what happened to me? How did I redeem myself from nausea? Who rejuvenated my eyes? How did I manage to fly to the height where no more rabble sits at the well?

Did my nausea itself create wings for me and water-divining powers? Truly, into the highest regions I had to fly in order to rediscover the wellspring of joy!

Oh I found it, my brothers! Here in the highest regions the wellspring of joy gushes for me! And there is a life from which no rabble drinks!

Almost too forcefully you flow, well of joy! And often you empty the cup again in wanting to fill it!

And I must still learn to approach you more modestly; all too forcefully my heart still streams toward you –

My heart, upon which my summer burns, the brief, hot, melancholy, superblissful summer; how my summer heart yearns for your coolness!

Gone the hesitating gloom of my spring! Gone the malice of my snowflakes in June! I have become summer and summer noon entirely!

A summer in the highest regions with cold springs and blissful silence: Oh come, my friends, and let the silence become even more blissful!

For it is *our* height and our homeland; too high and steep we live here for all the unclean and their thirst.

Cast your pure eyes into the wellspring of my joy, you friends! How could it become murky from that! It shall laugh back at you with *its* purity.

We build our nest in the tree called future; eagles shall bring us solitary ones food in their beaks!

Truly, no food in which the unclean are allowed to share! They would think they were devouring fire and burn their snouts!

Truly, we keep no homesteads ready here for the unclean! To their bodies and to their minds our happiness would seem a cave of ice!

And like strong winds we want to live above them, neighbors to eagles, neighbors to snow, neighbors to the sun: thus live strong winds.

And some day I want to blow among them like a wind and steal their breath away with my spirit: thus my future wills it.

Indeed, Zarathustra is a strong wind to all lowlands; and this counsel he gives to his enemies and to everything that spits and spews: "Beware of spitting *against* the wind!"

Thus spoke Zarathustra.

On the Tarantulas

Look here, this is the hole of the tarantula! Do you want to see the tarantula itself? Its web hangs here; touch it, make it tremble.

Here it comes, willingly – welcome, tarantula! On your back your triangle and mark sits in black; and I know too what sits in your soul.

Revenge sits in your soul: wherever you bite, there black scabs grow; your poison makes the soul whirl with revenge!

So I speak to you in parables, you who cause the souls to whirl, you preachers of *equality*! Tarantulas you are to me and hidden avengers!

But I want to expose your hiding places to the light; therefore I laugh into your face my laughter of the heights.

Therefore I tear at your web, so that your rage might lure you from your lie-hole lair, and your revenge might spring forth from behind your word "justice." For *that mankind be redeemed from revenge*: that to me is the bridge to the highest hope and a rainbow after long thunderstorms.

But the tarantulas want it otherwise, to be sure. "That the world become full of the thunderstorms of our revenge, precisely that we would regard as justice," – thus they speak with one another.

"We want to exact revenge and heap insult on all whose equals we are not" – thus vow the tarantula hearts.

"And 'will to equality' – that itself from now on shall be the name for virtue; and against everything that has power we shall raise our clamor!"

You preachers of equality, the tyrant's madness of impotence cries thus out of you for "equality": your secret tyrant's cravings mask themselves thus in your words of virtue!

Aggrieved conceit, repressed envy, perhaps the conceit and envy of your fathers: it erupts from you like a flame and the madness of revenge.

What is silent in the father learns to speak in the son; and often I found the son to be the father's exposed secret.

They resemble the inspired, but it is not the heart that inspires them – but revenge. And when they are refined and cold, it is not the spirit but envy that makes them refined and cold.

Their jealousy even leads them along the thinkers' path; and this is the mark of their jealousy – they always go too far, such that their exhaustion must ultimately lay itself to sleep in snow.

From each of their laments revenge sounds, in each of their praisings there is harm, and being the judge is bliss to them.

But thus I counsel you my friends: mistrust all in whom the drive to punish is strong!

Those are people of bad kind and kin; in their faces the hangman and the bloodhound are visible.

Mistrust all those who speak much of their justice! Indeed, their souls are lacking not only honey.

And when they call themselves "the good and the just," then do not forget that all they lack to be pharisees is – power!

My friends, I do not want not be mixed in with and mistaken for others.

There are those who preach my doctrine of life, and at the same time they are preachers of equality and tarantulas.

They speak in favor of life, these poisonous spiders, even though they are sitting in their holes and have turned against life, because they want to do harm.

They want to harm those who hold power today, for among them the sermon on death is still most at home.

If it were otherwise, then the tarantulas would teach otherwise; and they after all were formerly the best world slanderers and burners of heretics.

I do not want to be mixed in with and mistaken for these preachers of equality. For thus justice speaks *to me*: "humans are not equal."

And they shouldn't become so either! What would my love for the overman be if I spoke otherwise?

On a thousand bridges and paths they shall throng to the future, and ever more war and inequality shall be set between them: thus my great love commands me to speak!

Inventors of images and ghosts shall they become in their hostility, and with their images and ghosts they shall yet fight the highest fight against each other!

Good and evil, and rich and poor, and high and trifling, and all the names of values: they shall be weapons and clanging signs that life must overcome itself again and again!

Life itself wants to build itself into the heights with pillars and steps; it wants to gaze into vast distances and out upon halcyon beauties – *therefore* it needs height!

And because it needs height, it needs steps and contradiction between steps and climbers! Life wants to climb and to overcome itself by climbing.

And look here, my friends! Here, where the tarantula's hole is, the ruins of an ancient temple are rising – look here now with enlightened eyes!

Indeed, the one who once heaped his thoughts skyward here in stone – he knew the secret of all life like the most wise!

That struggle and inequality and war for power and supremacy are found even in beauty: he teaches us that here in the clearest parable.

How divinely the vault and the arch bend and break each other as they wrestle; how they struggle against each other with light and shadow, these divinely struggling ones –

In this manner sure and beautiful let us also be enemies, my friends! Divinely let us struggle *against* each other!

Alas! Then the tarantula bit me, my old enemy! Divinely sure and beautiful it bit me on the finger!

"Punishment and justice must be" – thus it thinks. "Not for nothing shall he sing his songs in honor of hostility here!"

Yes, it has avenged itself! And alas! Now it will also make my soul whirl with revenge!

But so that I do *not* whirl, my friends, bind me fast to this pillar here! I would rather be a stylite than a whirlwind of revenge!

Indeed, Zarathustra is no tornado or whirlwind; and if he is a dancer, nevermore a tarantella dancer! –

Thus spoke Zarathustra.

On the Famous Wise Men

The people you have served and the people's superstition, all you famous wise men! – and *not* the truth! And precisely on that account you were accorded respect.

And for this reason too they tolerated your lack of faith, because it was a joke and a jog to the people. Thus does the master allow his slaves to have their way, delighting all the while in their frolicking.

But whoever is despised by the people like a wolf by dogs; this is the free spirit, the foe of fetters, the non-adorer, the one who houses in the woods.

Hunting him out of his lair – to the people this has always meant "a sense of what is right." On him the people have always sicced their dogs with the sharpest teeth.

"For the truth is here if only the people are here! Woe, woe to the seekers!" – Thus it has echoed for all time.

You wanted to justify your people's reverence; that is what you called "will to truth," you famous wise men!

And your heart always said to itself: "From the people I came: from there too God's voice came to me."

As advocates of the people you were always stiff-necked and clever, like asses.

And many a powerful one who wanted to travel well with the people harnessed a little ass in front of his horses, a famous wise man.

And now, you famous wise men, I wish you would finally throw off the lion skin completely!

The mottled skin of the predator, and the mane of the explorer, the searcher, the conqueror!

Oh, before I would learn to believe in your "truthfulness" you would first have to break your revering will.

Truthful – thus I call the one who goes into godless deserts and has broken his revering heart.

In the yellow sand and burned by the sun he may squint thirstily at islands rich with springs, where living things rest beneath dark trees.

But his thirst does not persuade him to become the same as these comfortable ones; for where there are oases, there are idols as well.

Hungry, violent, lonely, godless; thus the lion-will wants itself.

Free from the happiness of the servant, redeemed of gods and adorations, fearless and fearsome, great and lonely; thus is the will of the truthful.

In the desert the truthful have always dwelled, the free spirits, as the rulers of the desert; but in the cities dwell the well-fed, famous wise men – the draft animals.

For they, as asses, always pull – the *people's* cart!

Not that I am angry with them for it; but to me they remain servants and harnessed, even if they gleam in golden harnesses.

And often they were good servants and praiseworthy. For virtue speaks thus: "If you must serve, then seek the one who benefits most from your service!

The spirit and virtue of your master shall grow from your being his servant; thus you yourself grow with his spirit and his virtue!"

And truly, you famous wise men, you servants of the people! You yourselves grew with the people's spirit and virtue – and the people through you! I say this in your honor!

But to me you remain the people even in your virtues, the people with stupid eyes – the people who don't know what *spirit* is!

Spirit is life that itself cuts into life; by its own agony it increases its own knowledge – did you know that?

And the happiness of spirit is this: to be anointed and consecrated by tears to serve as a sacrificial animal – did you know that?

And the blindness of the blind, and his seeking and probing shall yet testify to the power of the sun into which he gazed – did you know that?

And the seeker of knowledge shall learn *to build* with mountains! It means little that the spirit moves mountains – did you know that?

You know only the spark of the spirit, but you do not see the anvil that it is, nor the cruelty of its hammer!

Indeed, you do not know the pride of the spirit! But even less would you be able to bear the spirit's modesty, if it ever wanted to speak!

And never yet have you been permitted to throw your spirit into a pit of snow; you are not hot enough for that! And so you do not know the thrills of its coldness.

But in all things you act too familiarly with the spirit, and wisdom you often make into a poorhouse and hospital for bad poets.

You are no eagles, thus you have not experienced the happiness in the terror of the spirit. And whoever is not a bird should not build nests over abysses.

To me you are lukewarm, but every deep knowledge flows cold. Ice-cold are the innermost wells of the spirit, invigorating for hot hands and human doers.

Honorable you stand there, and stiff with ramrod backs, you famous wise men! – You are not driven by strong wind and will.

Have you never seen a sail go over the sea, rounded and billowed and trembling with the vehemence of the wind?

Like the sail, trembling with the vehemence of the spirit, my wisdom goes over the sea – my wild wisdom!

But you servants of the people, you famous wise men – how *could* you go with me! –

Thus spoke Zarathustra.

The Night Song

It is night: now all fountains speak more loudly. And my soul too is a fountain.

It is night: only now all the songs of the lovers awaken. And my soul too is the song of a lover.

An unstilled, an unstillable something is in me; it wants to be heard. A craving for love is in me, which itself speaks the language of love.

I am light; oh that I were night! But this is my loneliness, that I am girded by light.

Oh that I were dark and nocturnal! How I would suck at the breasts of light!

And even you I would bless, you little twinkling stars and glowworms up there! – And be blissful for your gift of light.

But I live in my own light, I drink back into myself the flames that break out of me.

I do not the know the happiness of receiving; and often I dreamed that stealing must be more blessed than receiving.

This is my poverty, that my hand never rests from bestowing; this is my envy, that I see waiting eyes and the illuminated nights of longing.

Oh misery of all bestowers! Oh darkening of my sun! Oh craving to crave! Oh ravenous hunger in satiety!

They receive from me, but do I still touch their souls? There is a cleft between giving and receiving; and the closest cleft is the last to be bridged.

A hunger grows out of my beauty; I wish to harm those for whom I shine, I wish to rob those on whom I have bestowed: – thus I hunger for malice.

Withdrawing my hand when a hand already reaches for it; hesitating like the waterfall that hesitates even while plunging – thus I hunger for malice.

My fullness plots such vengeance; such trickery gushes from my loneliness.

My happiness in bestowing died in bestowing, my virtue wearied of itself in its superabundance!

For one who always bestows, the danger is loss of shame; whoever dispenses always has calloused hands and heart from sheer dispensing.

My eye no longer wells up at the shame of those who beg; my hand became too hard for the trembling of filled hands.

Where have the tears of my eye and the down of my heart gone? Oh loneliness of all bestowers! Oh muteness of all who shine!

Many suns revolve in desolate space. To everything that is dark they speak with their light – to me they are mute.

Oh this is the enmity of light toward that which shines; mercilessly it goes its orbit.

Unjust in its deepest heart toward that which shines: cold toward suns – thus every sun goes.

Like a storm the suns fly their orbit, that is their motion. They follow their inexorable will; that is their coldness.

Oh it is you only, you dark ones, you nocturnal ones, who create warmth out of that which shines! Oh it is you only who drink milk and refreshment from the udders of light!

Alas, ice surrounds me, my hand burns itself on iciness! Alas, there is thirst in me that yearns for your thirst!

It is night: alas that I must be light! And thirst for the nocturnal! And loneliness!

It is night: now my longing breaks out of me like a well – I long to speak.

It is night: now all fountains speak more loudly. And my soul too is a fountain.

It is night: only now all the songs of the lovers awaken. And my soul too is the song of a lover.

Thus sang Zarathustra.

The Dance Song

One evening Zarathustra walked through the woods with his disciples, and as he searched for a well, behold, he then came upon a green meadow that was silently bordered by trees and shrubs; upon it girls danced with each other. As soon as the girls recognized Zarathustra, they stopped dancing; but Zarathustra approached them with a friendly gesture and spoke these words:

"Do not stop dancing, you lovely girls! No spoil sport has come to you with his evil eye, no enemy of girls.

God's advocate before the devil am I; but the devil is the spirit of gravity. How could I be hostile toward godlike dancing, you light ones? Or toward girls' feet with pretty ankles?

I may well be a wood and a night of dark trees, yet whoever does not shrink from my darkness will also find rose slopes under my cypresses.

And he will also find the little god, surely, who is the favorite of girls; he lies next to the well, still, with closed eyes.

Indeed, he fell asleep in broad daylight, the loafer! Did he chase too much after butterflies?

Do not be angry with me, you beautiful dancing girls, if I chastise the little god a bit! He will probably yell and weep – but he is comical even when weeping!

And with tears in his eyes he shall ask you for a dance, and I myself will sing a song to his dance:

A dance and a mocking song to the spirit of gravity, my supreme highest and most powerful devil, of whom it is said that he is 'the ruler of the world.' " –

And this is the song that Zarathustra sang as Cupid and the girls danced together.

Into your eye I gazed recently, oh life! And then into the unfathomable I seemed to sink.

But you pulled me out with your golden fishing rod; you laughed mockingly when I called you unfathomable.

"Thus sounds the speech of all fish," you said. "What *they* do not fathom, is unfathomable.

But I am merely fickle and wild and in all things a woman, and no virtuous one:

Whether to you men I am called 'profundity' or 'fidelity,' 'eternity' or 'secrecy.'

But you men always bestow on us your own virtues – oh, you virtuous men!"

Thus she laughed, the incredible one, but I never believe her and her laughing when she speaks ill of herself.

And when I spoke in confidence with my wild wisdom, she said to me angrily: "You will, you covet, you love, and only therefore do you *praise* life!"

Then I almost answered maliciously and told the angry woman the truth; and one can not answer more maliciously than when one "tells the truth" to one's wisdom.

Thus matters stand between the three of us. At bottom I love only life – and verily, most when I hate it!

But that I am fond of wisdom and often too fond; that is because she reminds me so much of life!

She has her eyes, her laugh and even her little golden fishing rod – is it my fault that the two look so much alike?

And when life once asked me: "Who is this wisdom anyway?"– I hastened to reply: "Oh yes! Wisdom!

One thirsts for her and does not become sated, one peeks through veils, one snatches through nets.

Is she beautiful? What do I know! But even the oldest carps are baited by her.

She is fickle and stubborn; often I saw her bite her lip and comb her hair against the grain.

Perhaps she is evil and false, and in all things a female; but when she speaks ill of herself, precisely then she seduces the most."

When I had said this to life she laughed sarcastically and closed her eyes: "Whom are you talking about?" she said. "Surely about me?

And even if you are right – does one say *that* to my face? But now speak too of your own wisdom!"

Oh, and now you opened your eyes again, oh beloved life! And again I seemed to sink into the unfathomable. –

Thus sang Zarathustra. But when the dance had ended and the girls departed, he became sad.

"The sun set long ago," he remarked at last. "The meadow is moist, coolness emanates from the woods.

Something unknown is around me and it gazes pensively. What – you are still alive, Zarathustra?

Why? Wherefore? Whereby? Whither? Where? How? Is it not folly to continue living? –

Alas, my friends, it is the evening whose questions emerge from me. Forgive me my sadness!

Evening came: forgive me that evening came!"

Thus spoke Zarathustra.

The Grave Song

"There is the island of graves, the silent one; there too are the graves of my youth. There I shall carry an evergreen wreath of life."

Resolving thus in my heart I crossed the sea. –

Oh you visions and apparitions of my youth! Oh all you glances of love, you godlike glancing moments! How quickly you died! I remember you today like my dead.

From you, from my dearest departed, comes a sweet fragrance, releasing my tears and my heart. Indeed, it shakes and releases the heart of this lonely seafarer.

I am still the richest and the one to be envied most – I the loneliest one! For I *had* you once, and you have me still: tell me, for whom did such rosy apples fall from the tree as for me?

I am still the heir and earth of your love, blossoming in remembrance of you with colorful, wild-growing virtues, oh you most beloved!

Indeed, we were made to stay close to each other, you noble, strange wonders; and not like skittish birds did you come to me and to my desire – no, as trusting ones to a trusting one!

Yes, made for loyalty, like me, and for tender eternities; I must now refer to you by your disloyalty, you godlike glances and glancing moments, for I've learned no other name yet.

Indeed, you died too soon for me, you fugitives. Yet you did not flee me, nor did I flee you: we are mutually innocent in our disloyalty.

To kill *me* they strangled you, you songbirds of my hopes! Yes, at you, my dearest ones, malice always shot its arrows – to strike my heart!

And it struck! For you were always closest to my heart, my possession and what possessed me: *for that* you had to die young and all too early!

The arrow was shot at the most vulnerable thing that I possessed; that was you, whose skin is like down and even more like a smile that dies of a glance!

But these words I shall speak to my enemies: what is all murder of human beings compared to what you did to me!

More evil you did to me than all murder of human beings. You took from me what was irretrievable – thus I speak to you, my enemies!

For you murdered my youth's visions and dearest wonders! You took my playmates from me, the blessed spirits! In remembrance of them I lay down this wreath and this curse.

This curse against you, my enemies! For you cut my eternity short, like a sound breaks off in cold night! It barely reached me as the flash of godlike eyes – as a glancing moment!

Thus at a good hour my purity once spoke to me: "Godlike shall all beings be to me."

Then you fell upon me with filthy ghosts; alas, where now has that good hour fled? "All days shall be holy to me" – so spoke the wisdom of my youth, once; truly, the speech of a gay wisdom!

But then you enemies stole my nights and sold them into sleepless agony; alas, where now has my gay wisdom fled?

Once I yearned for happy signs from birds; then you led an owl abomination across my path, a repulsive one. Alas, where then did my tender yearning flee?

Once I pledged to renounce all nausea; then you transformed those near and nearest me into boils of pus. Alas, where then did my noblest pledge flee?

As a blind man I once walked blessed paths; then you tossed filth onto the path of the blind man, and now he is repulsed by the old blind man's footpath.

And when I did what was hardest for me and celebrated the victory of my overcomings; then you made those who loved me cry out that I hurt them most.

Indeed, that was always your doing; you turned to gall my best honey and the hard work of my best bees.

You always dispatched the most impudent beggars to my charity; you always crowded the incurably shameless around my pity. Thus you wounded my virtue in its faith.

And when I laid down even what was holiest to me as a sacrifice; instantly your "piety" placed its fatter gifts on top, such that what was holiest to me choked in the smoke of your fat.

And once I wanted to dance as I had never danced before; over and beyond all heavens I wanted to dance. Then you swayed my favorite singer.

And then he struck up a horrid, dreadful tune; indeed, he tooted in my ears like a mournful horn!

Murderous singer, tool of malice, most innocent one! Already I stood poised for my best dance; then you murdered my enchantment with your tones!

Only in dance do I know how to speak the parables of the highest things – and now my highest parable remained unspoken in my limbs!

My highest hope remained unspoken and unredeemed! And all the visions and comforts of my youth died.

How did I bear it? How did I overturn and overcome such wounds? How did my soul rise again from these graves?

Yes, there is something invulnerable, unburiable in me, something that explodes boulders: it is called *my will*. Silently and unchanged it strides through the years.

It wants to walk its course on my feet, my old will; its mind is heart-hardened and invulnerable.

Invulnerable am I only in the heel. You still live and are the same, most patient one! You have always broken through all graves!

In you what is unredeemed of my youth lives on; and as life and youth you sit here hoping upon greying ruins of graves.

Yes, to me you are still the shatterer of all graves: Hail to you, my will! And only where there are graves are there resurrections. –

Thus sang Zarathustra. –

On Self-Overcoming

"Will to truth" you call that which drives you and makes you lustful, you wisest ones?

Will to thinkability of all being, that's what *I* call your will!

You first want to *make* all being thinkable, because you doubt, with proper suspicion, whether it is even thinkable.

But for you it shall behave and bend! Thus your will wants it. It shall become smooth and subservient to the spirit, as its mirror and reflection.

That is your entire will, you wisest ones, as a will to power; and even when you speak of good and evil and of valuations.

You still want to create the world before which you could kneel: this is your ultimate hope and intoxication.

The unwise, to be sure, the people – they are like a river on which a skiff floats; valuations are seated in the skiff, solemn and cloaked.

Your will and your values you set upon the river of becoming; what the people believe to be good and evil reveals to me an ancient will to power.

It was you, you wisest ones, who placed such guests into the skiff and gave them pomp and proud names – you and your dominating will!

Now the river carries your skiff along: it *has to* carry it. It matters little whether the breaking wave foams and angrily opposes the keel!

The river is not your danger and the end of your good and evil, you wisest ones; but this will itself, the will to power – the unexhausted begetting will of life.

But in order that you understand my words on good and evil, I also want to tell you my words on life and on the nature of all that lives.

I pursued the living, I walked the greatest and the smallest paths in order to know its nature.

With a hundredfold mirror I captured even its glance, when its mouth was closed, so that its eyes could speak to me. And its eyes spoke to me.

However, wherever I found the living, there too I heard the speech on obedience. All living is an obeying.

And this is the second thing that I heard: the one who cannot obey himself is commanded. Such is the nature of the living.

This however is the third thing that I heard: that commanding is harder than obeying. And not only that the commander bears the burden of all obeyers, and that this burden easily crushes him: –

In all commanding it seemed to me there is an experiment and a risk; and always when it commands, the living risks itself in doing so.

Indeed, even when it commands itself, even then it must pay for its commanding. It must become the judge and avenger and victim of its own law.

How does this happen? I asked myself. What persuades the living to obey and command, and to still practice obedience while commanding?

Hear my words, you wisest ones! Check seriously to see whether I crept into the very heart of life and into the roots of its heart!

Wherever I found the living, there I found the will to power; and even in the will of the serving I found the will to be master.

The weaker is persuaded by its own will to serve the stronger, because it wants to be master over what is still weaker: this is the only pleasure it is incapable of renouncing.

And as the smaller gives way to the greater, in order for it to have its pleasure and power over the smallest, so too the greatest gives way, and for the sake of power it risks – life itself.

That is the giving-way of the greatest, that it is a risk and a danger and a tossing of dice unto death.

And where there are sacrificing and favors and love-looks, there too is the will to be master. Along secret passages the weaker sneaks into the fortress and straight to the heart of the more powerful – and there it steals power.

And this secret life itself spoke to me: "Behold," it said, "I am that *which must always overcome itself.*

To be sure, you call it will to beget or drive to a purpose, to something higher, more distant, more manifold: but all this is one, and one secret.

I would rather perish than renounce this one thing; and truly, wherever there is decline and the falling of leaves, behold, there life sacrifices itself – for power!

That I must be struggle and becoming and purpose and the contradiction of purposes – alas, whoever guesses my will guesses also on what *crooked* paths it must walk!

Whatever I may create and however I may love it – soon I must oppose it and my love, thus my will wants it.

And even you, seeker of knowledge, are only a path and footstep of my will; indeed, my will to power follows also on the heels of your will to truth!

Indeed, the one who shot at truth with the words 'will to existence' did not hit it: this will – does not exist!

For, what *is* not can not will; but what is in existence, how could this still will to exist!

Only where life is, is there also will; but not will to life, instead – thus I teach you – will to power!

Much is esteemed more highly by life than life itself; yet out of esteeming itself speaks – the will to power!" –

Thus life once taught me, and from this I shall yet solve the riddle of your heart, you wisest ones.

Truly, I say to you: good and evil that would be everlasting – there is no such thing! They must overcome themselves out of themselves again and again.

You do violence with your values and words of good and evil, you valuators; and this is your hidden love and the gleaming, trembling and flowing-over of your souls.

But a stronger force grows out of your values and a new overcoming; upon it egg and eggshell break.

And whoever must be a creator in good and evil – truly, he must first be an annihilator and break values.

Thus the highest evil belongs to the highest goodness, but this is the creative one. –

Let us speak of this, you wisest ones, even if it is bad to do so. Keeping silent is worse; all truths that are kept silent become poisonous.

And may everything break that can possibly be broken by our truths! Many a house has yet to be built!

Thus spoke Zarathustra.

On the Sublime Ones

The bottom of my sea is calm – who would guess that it conceals playful monsters?

My depth is unfathomable, but it gleams with swimming riddles and laughters.

I saw a sublime one today, a solemn one, an ascetic of the spirit; oh how my soul laughed at his ugliness!

With his chest sticking out like those who hold their breath he stood there, the sublime one, silently:

Adorned with ugly truths, his hunter's spoils, and rich in tattered clothing; many thorns clung to him also – but I saw nary a rose.

He had not yet learned laughing and beauty. Gloomy this hunter returned from the woods of knowledge.

He returned home from his battle with wild animals; but from his earnestness too a wild animal gazes – an unconquered one!

And he stands there like a tiger that wants to spring; but I don't like these tense souls, my taste is hostile to all these retiring types.

And you tell me, friends, that taste and tasting are nothing to be disputed? But all life is disputing of taste and tasting!

Taste: that is simultaneously weight and scale and weigher, and woe to all that would live without disputing weight and scale and weighers!

If he would tire of his sublimity, this sublime one; only then would his beauty arise – and only then shall I taste him and find him tasteful.

And only when he turns away from himself will he leap over his own shadow – and truly! into *his own* sun.

All too long he sat in the shadows, and the cheeks of this ascetic of the spirit grew pale; he nearly starved on his expectations.

There is still contempt in his eyes, and nausea lingers on his lips. He is peaceful now, to be sure, but his peace has not yet laid itself in the sun.

He should act like a bull; and his happiness should smell of earth and not of contempt for the earth.

I want to see him as a white bull, snorting and bellowing ahead of the plow – and his bellowing should praise everything earthly!

His face is still dark; the shadow of the hand still plays upon him. His sense of sight is still overshadowed.

His deed itself is still the shadow on him; the hand darkens the doer. He has not yet overcome his deed.

I do love the bull's neck on him, but now I also want to see the angel's eyes.

He must also unlearn his hero's will; he shall be elevated, not merely sublime – the ether itself shall elevate him, the will-less one!

He subdued monsters, he solved riddles, but he should also solve his own monsters and riddles; he should transform them into heavenly children.

As of yet his knowledge has not learned to smile and to be without jealousy; his torrential passion has not yet become calm in its beauty.

Indeed, not in satiety shall his yearning keep silent and submerge, but in beauty! Grace belongs to the graciousness of the great-minded.

With his arm laid across his head – thus the hero should rest, thus too he should overcome even his resting.

But precisely for the hero *beauty* is the most difficult of all things. Beauty is not be wrested by any violent willing.

A little more, a little less: right here this means much, here this means the most.

To stand with muscles relaxed and with an unharnessed will: this is most difficult for all of you sublime ones!

When power becomes gracious and descends into view: beauty I call such descending.

And from no one do I want beauty as I do from just you, you powerful one: let your kindness be your ultimate self-conquest.

I know you capable of all evil – therefore from you I want the good.

Indeed, I often laughed at the weaklings who believe themselves good because their paws are lame!

You shall strive to emulate the virtue of a column; ever more beautiful and delicate it becomes, the higher it rises, but inwardly harder and more resistant.

Yes, you sublime one, one day you shall be beautiful and shall hold the mirror up to your own beauty.

Then your soul will shudder with divine desires, and even in your vanity there will be adoration!

For this is the secret of the soul: only when the hero abandons her, she is approached in dream by – the over-hero.[1]

---

[1] This allusion to the myth of Ariadne and Theseus foreshadows the "magician's song" in Part IV, which became one of the *Dionysus Dithyrambs*. Nietzsche was preparing the manuscript of the *Dithyrambs* for publication when he became incapacitated after a series of nervous breakdowns in late 1888 and early 1889. According to the myth, Ariadne is abandoned by her lover Theseus,

Thus spoke Zarathustra.

On the Land of Education

Too far into the future did I fly; dread fell upon me.

And when I looked around, behold! Then time was my only contemporary.

Then I fled backward, homeward – with ever greater haste. Thus I came to you, you of the present, and into the land of education.

For the first time I brought along eyes for you, and a strong desire; indeed, I came with longing in my heart.

But what happened to me? As frightened as I was – I had to laugh! Never had my eyes seen anything so splattered with colors!

I laughed and laughed, while my foot still trembled and my heart as well: "This must be the home of all paint pots!" I said.

With fifty blotches painted on your face and limbs, thus you sat there to my amazement, you people of the present!

And with fifty mirrors around you, flattering and echoing your play of colors!

Indeed, you couldn't wear a better mask, you people of today, than that of your own face! Who could *recognize* you!

Written full with the characters of the past, and even these characters painted over with new characters: thus you have hidden yourselves well from all interpreters of characters!

And even if one were to give you a physical examination, who would even believe you have a body? You seem to be baked from colors and paper slips glued together.

Motley, all ages and peoples peek from your veils; motley, all customs and beliefs speak from your gestures.

and only Dionysus, the demi-god, comes to her ultimate rescue. Nietzsche elevated Ariadne to the symbol of the human soul, Theseus to the symbol of male vanity and all too human (limited) conceptions of the hero, and Dionysus to the role of super-hero (*Über-Held*). See Adrian Del Caro, "Symbolizing Philosophy: Ariadne and the Labyrinth," in *Nietzsche: Critical Assessments* (4 vols.), ed. Daniel W. Conway (London: Routledge, 1998), vol. I, pp. 58–88; and "Nietzschean self-transformation and the transformation of the Dionysian," in *Nietzsche, Philosophy and the Arts*, ed. Salim Kemal, Ivan Gaskell, and Daniel Conway (Cambridge: Cambridge University Press, 1998), pp. 70–91.

If one were to pull away veil and wrap and color and gesture from you, there would be just enough left over to scare away the crows.

Indeed, I myself am the scared crow who once saw you naked and without color; and I flew away when the skeleton beckoned amorously.

I would rather be a day laborer in the underworld and among the shades of yore! – Even the underworldly are fatter and fuller than you!

This, oh this is bitterness for my bowels, that I can stand you neither naked nor clothed, you people of the present!

All uncanniness of the future, and whatever caused flown birds to shudder, is truly homelier and more familiar than your "reality."

For you speak thus: "We are real entirely, and without beliefs and superstition." Thus you stick out your chests – alas, even without chests!

Indeed, how should you be *capable* of believing, you color-splattered ones – you who are paintings of everything that has ever been believed!

Rambling refutations of belief itself are you, and the limb-fracturing of every thought. *Unbelievable* is what *I* call you, you so-called real ones!

All ages prattle against each other in your minds; and the dreams and prattling of all ages were more real than even your waking is!

You are sterile: *therefore* you lack beliefs. But whoever had to create also always had his prophetic dreams and astrological signs – and believed in believing! –

You are half-open gates, at which the gravediggers wait. And this is *your* reality: "Everything deserves to perish."

Oh how you stand there, you sterile ones, how skinny in the ribs! And some one of you probably realized this on his own.

And he spoke: "Surely some god secretly removed something from me while I slept? Indeed, enough to form himself a little woman from it!

Wondrous is the poverty of my ribs!" Thus spoke many a person of the present.

Indeed, you make me laugh, you people of the present! And especially when you are amazed at yourselves!

And woe to me if I couldn't laugh at your amazement, and had to drink down all the repugnant contents of your bowls!

So I shall take you more lightly, as I have a *heavy* burden; and what does it matter to me if beetles and winged worms still land on my bundle?

Indeed, it will not become any heavier for that! And not from you, you people of the present, shall my great weariness come. –

Alas, where shall I climb now with my longing! From all mountains I look out for father- and motherlands.

But nowhere did I find home; I am unsettled in every settlement, and a departure at every gate.

Foreign to me and a mockery are these people of the present to whom my heart recently drove me; and I am driven out of father- and motherlands.

Thus I love only my *children's land*, the undiscovered land in the furthest sea: for it I command my sails to seek and seek.

I want to make it up to my children for being the child of my fathers; and to all the future – for the existence of *this* present!

Thus spoke Zarathustra.

On Immaculate Perception

When the moon rose yesterday I imagined that it wanted to give birth to a sun, so broad and pregnant it lay there on the horizon.

But it lied to me with its pregnancy; and sooner would I believe in the man in the moon than in the woman.

Indeed, he is not much of a man either, this timid nocturnal rhapsodist. Truly, with a bad conscience he wanders over the rooftops.

For he is lecherous and jealous, this monk in the moon, lecherous for the earth and for all the joys of lovers.

No, I do not like him, this tomcat on the rooftops! I am disgusted by all who creep around half-closed windows!

Pious and silent he wanders his way on starry carpets – but I do not like any soft-stepping man's foot on which a spur does not jingle too.

Every honest step speaks; but a cat steals away across the ground. Observe, catlike the moon approaches, and dishonestly. –

This parable I give to you sentimental hypocrites, you "pure perceivers!" *I* call you – lechers!

You too love the earth and the earthly; I found you out! – But there is shame in your love and bad conscience – you resemble the moon!

Your spirit was persuaded to despise the earthly, but not your entrails; and *they* are the strongest part of you!

And now your spirit is ashamed to do the bidding of your entrails, and out of its own shame it takes the paths that sneak and lie.

"For me what is highest" – thus speaks your lying spirit to itself – "would be to look upon life without desire and not like a dog with its tongue hanging out:

To be content in viewing, with dead will, without the grasp and greed of selfishness – cold and ashen grey in my whole body, but with drunken mooning eyes!

To me the dearest thing would be" – thus the seducer seduces himself – "to love the earth as the moon loves it, and to touch its beauty only with the eyes.

And to me the *immaculate* perception of all things would be that I desire nothing from things, except that I might lie there before them like a mirror with a hundred eyes." –

Oh you sentimental hypocrites, you lechers! Your desire lacks innocence, and now therefore you slander all desiring!

Indeed, you do not love the earth as creators, begetters, and enjoyers of becoming!

Where is innocence? Where there is will to beget. And whoever wants to create over and beyond himself, he has the purest will.

Where is beauty? Where I *must will* with my entire will; where I want to love and perish so that an image does not remain merely an image.

Loving and perishing: these have gone together since the beginning of time. Will to love: that means being willing also for death. Thus I speak to you cowards!

But now your emasculated leering wants to be called "contemplation!" And whatever allows itself to be touched by cowardly eyes is supposed to be christened "beautiful!" Oh you besmirchers of noble names!

But that shall be your curse, you immaculate, you pure-perceiving ones, that you shall never give birth; and even if you lie broad and pregnant on the horizon!

Indeed, you take a mouthful of noble words, and we are supposed to believe that your heart is overflowing, you liars?

But *my* words are meager, despised, crooked words; gladly do I pick up what falls beneath the table during your meal.

For with them I can still – tell hypocrites the truth! Yes, my fish bones, mussel shells and thorny leaves shall tickle the noses of hypocrites!

There is always foul air around you and your meals; after all, your lecherous thoughts, your lies and secrets are in the air!

Dare for once to believe yourselves – yourselves and your entrails! Whoever cannot believe himself always lies.

A god's mask you don before yourselves, you "pure ones." Into a god's mask your horrid worm has crawled.

Indeed, you deceive, you "contemplative ones!" Zarathustra too was once the fool of your godlike skins; he had not discovered the coils of snakes with which they were stuffed.

I once imagined seeing a god's soul playing in your play, you pure perceivers! Once I imagined no better art than your arts!

The distance concealed snake-filth and foul odor from me, and that the guile of a lizard lecherously crawled around here.

But I came *near* you: then daylight came to me – and now it comes to you – the moon's fling is at an end!

Look there! Chagrined and pale he stands there – before the dawn!

For she is coming already, the glowing one – *her* love for the earth is coming! Innocence and the creator's desire is all solar love!

Look there, how she glides impatiently across the sea! Do you not feel her thirst and the hot breath of her love?

She would suck at the sea and drink its depths into herself in the heights; now the sea's desire rises with a thousand breasts.

It *wants* to be kissed and sucked by the thirst of the sun; it *wants* to become air and height and footpath of light and light itself!

Indeed, like the sun I love life and all deep seas.

And this *I* call perception: all that is deep shall rise – to my height!

Thus spoke Zarathustra.

On Scholars

As I lay sleeping a sheep munched at the ivy wreath on my head – munched and spoke: "Zarathustra is no longer a scholar."

Spoke it and walked away, reproving and proud. A child told it to me.

I like to lie here where the children play, by the crumbling wall, beneath thistles and red poppies.

I am still a scholar to the children and also to the thistles and the red poppies. They are innocent, even in their spite.

But to the sheep I am no longer a scholar, thus my fate wants it – blessed be it!

For this is the truth: I have moved out of the house of the scholars, and I slammed the door on my way out.

Too long my soul sat hungry at their table; unlike them, I am not trained to approach knowledge as if cracking nuts.

I love freedom and the air over fresh earth; and I would rather sleep on ox hides than on their honors and reputations.

I am too hot and burned up by my own thoughts; often it steals my breath away. Then I have to go out into the open and away from all dusty chambers.

But they sit cool in their cool shade; in all things they want to be mere spectators and they take care not to sit where the sun burns on the steps.

Just like those who stand in the street and gape at the people who pass by; thus too they wait and gape at thoughts that others have thought.

When grasped they puff out clouds of dust like sacks of flour, involuntarily; but who would guess that their dust comes from grain and from the yellow bliss of summer fields?

When they pose as wise, I am chilled by their little proverbs and truths; often there is an odor to their wisdom, as if it came from the swamp, and truly, I have already heard the frog croaking out of it!

They are skilled, they have clever fingers; why would *my* simplicity want to be near their multiplicity? Their fingers know how to do all manner of threading and knotting and weaving, and thus they knit the stockings of the spirit!

They are good clockworks, only one has to see to it that they are properly wound! Then they indicate the hour faithfully and make only a modest noise.

Like mills and stamps they work; one need only toss them one's grain – they know how to grind down kernels and make white dust out of them!

They are good at spying on, and are not the best at trusting one another. Inventive in petty cleverness they lie in wait for those whose knowledge walks on lame feet – they lie in wait like spiders.

I have always seen them prepare poison with caution, and always they donned gloves of glass for their fingers.

And they also know how to play with loaded dice; and I found them so ardent in their play that they sweated.

We are strangers to one another, and their virtues are even more repugnant to me than their falseness and false dice.

And when I dwelled among them, I dwelled over them. For this they bore a grudge against me.

They will hear nothing of it that someone strolls over their heads; and so they placed wood and earth and filth between me and their heads.

Thus they muffled the sound of my steps; and up till now the ones to hear me least have been the most scholarly.

All that is substandard and weakness in humans they laid between themselves and me – "sub-floor" they call it in their houses.

But despite this I stroll with my thoughts *over* their heads; and even if I wanted to stroll atop my own mistakes, I would still be over them and their heads.

For human beings are *not* equal: thus speaks justice. And what I want, *they* would not be permitted to want!

Thus spoke Zarathustra.

On Poets

"Since I have come to know the body better" – Zarathustra said to one of his disciples – "the spirit is only a hypothetical spirit to me; and all that is 'everlasting' – that too is only a parable."

"Thus I heard you speak once before," answered the disciple, "and at that time you added: 'But the poets lie too much.' Why then did you say that the poets lie too much?"

"Why?" said Zarathustra. "You ask why? I do not belong to those whose Why may be questioned.

Is my experience of yesterday? It has been a long time since I experienced the reasons of my opinions.

Would I not have to be a keg of memory if I were also to have my reasons with me?

It is already too much for me to keep my own opinions, and many a bird flies away.

And occasionally I find in my dovecot an animal that has flown to me, a strange one that trembles when I lay my hand upon it.

Yet what did Zarathustra once say to you? That the poets lie too much? – But Zarathustra too is a poet.

Do you believe now that he speaks the truth here? Why do you believe that?"

The disciple answered: "I believe in Zarathustra." But Zarathustra shook his head and smiled.

"Faith does not make me blessed," he said. "Especially not faith in me.

But supposing that someone said in all earnestness that the poets lie too much: he is right – *we* lie too much.

We also know too little and are bad learners, thus we simply have to lie.

And who of us poets has not watered down his wine? Many a poisonous hodgepodge took place in our cellars, much that is indescribable was enacted there.

And because we know little, we take a hearty liking to the spiritually impoverished, especially when they are little young women!

And we are even keen for those things that little old women tell each other evenings. Within ourselves we call that 'the eternal feminine.'[2]

And as if there were a special, secret portal to knowledge that becomes *blocked* to those who learn something, thus we believe in the people and their 'wisdom.'

But this is what all poets believe: that whoever pricks up his ears while lying in the grass or on a lonely slope will divine something about the things that are situated between heaven and earth.

And if tender stirrings come to them, then the poets always think that nature herself is in love with them:

And she creeps up to their ears to tell them secrets and enamored flatteries, the like of which makes them boastful and bloated before all mortals!

Indeed, there are so many things between heaven and earth of which only the poets have dreamed!

And especially *above* the heavens, for all gods are poets' parable, poets' cock and bull!

Indeed, always it lifts us up – namely to the kingdom of the clouds; atop these we set our motley bastards and then call them gods and overmen –

And they are just light enough for these chairs – all these gods and overmen!

---

[2] This chapter takes issue with Goethe and elevates him to the status of supreme poet, but it simultaneously decries the poetic fictions that throughout history sometimes pose as truth. "The eternal feminine" refers to the conclusion of *Faust*, where the Chorus Mysticus announces that Faust is saved, he is lifted up to heaven by the eternal feminine ("Das Ewig-Weibliche/ Zieht uns hinan"), which here also includes the blessed Margarete (Gretchen). See also Part IV, "The Song of Melancholy," where truth and poetizing (fiction) are at odds.

Oh how I am weary of all this imperfection that is supposed to become an event at any cost![3] Oh, how I am weary of poets!"

When Zarathustra had spoken thus, his disciple was angry with him, but he remained silent. And Zarathustra too remained silent, and his gaze had turned inward, as if he were gazing into vast distances. At last he sighed and took a breath.

"I am of today and of the past," he said then. "But there is something in me that is of tomorrow and the day after tomorrow and of days to come.

I became weary of the poets, the old and the new; superficial they all are to me and shallow seas.

They did not think sufficiently to the depths, therefore their feeling did not get to the bottom.

A bit of lust and a bit of boredom – that so far has been their best contemplation.

Ghost whispers and whisking I consider all their harp jingle jangle; what have they ever known of the ardor of tones! –

Nor are they clean enough for me; they all muddy their water to make it seem deep.

And though they gladly pose as reconcilers, to me they remain middle-men mixers and half-and-halfs and unclean! –

Indeed, I cast my net into their seas and wanted to catch good fish; but always I hauled in an ancient god's head.

Thus the sea gave a stone to the hungry. And the poets themselves may well come from the sea.

To be sure, one finds pearls in them, and they are all the more similar to hard shellfish. And instead of a soul I often found salty slime in them.

They also learned vanity from the sea; isn't the sea the peacock of peacocks?

Even before the ugliest of all buffaloes it fans its tail, it never tires of its silver and silky fans of lace.

Defiantly the buffalo looks on, in his soul close to the sand, still closer to the thicket, but closest to the swamp.

---

[3] The references to parable, imperfection, and event are all based on the words of the Chorus Mysticus (see n. 2), consisting of only eight lines, in which Goethe argues that (1) everything not everlasting is merely a parable; (2) what is imperfect becomes an event here (on earth); (3) what is indescribable gets done here; and (4) the eternal feminine lifts us up. Zarathustra expresses his impatience with the glibness of the poets; but observe that he includes the overman among these airy creations.

What does he care of beauty and sea and peacock's finery? This parable I say to the poets.

Truly, their spirit itself is this peacock of peacocks and a sea of vanity!

The spirit of the poet wants spectators: even if they have to be buffaloes! –

But I became weary of this spirit, and I foresee that it will become weary of itself.

Transformed I have already seen the poets, and turning their gaze against themselves.

I saw ascetics of the spirit approaching; they grew out of the poets."

Thus spoke Zarathustra.

On Great Events

There is an island in the sea – not far from the blessed isles of Zarathustra – on which a fiery mountain smokes continually; the people say of it, and especially the little old women among the people say of it, that it was placed like a huge boulder before the gate to the underworld: but through the fiery mountain itself leads the narrow path that winds downward to this gate of the underworld.

Now it was around the time that Zarathustra sojourned on the blessed isles that a ship dropped anchor at the island on which the smoking mountain stands, and its crew went ashore to shoot rabbits. Toward the hour of noon, however, as the captain and his people were together again, they suddenly saw a man approaching them through the air, and a voice clearly said: "It is time! It is high time!" As the figure came closest to them – and it flew past quickly like a shadow in the direction of the fiery mountain – they recognized with the greatest dismay that it was Zarathustra; for all of them had seen him before, except for the captain himself, and they loved him as the people love, with equal parts of love and awe.[4]

---

[4] This story Nietzsche did not make up himself, but as C. G. Jung pointed out in his dissertation of 1902, "On the Psychology and Pathology of So-called Occult Phenomena," Nietzsche inadvertently remembered it from his childhood reading of *Blätter aus Prevorst*, an "antiquated collection of simple-minded Swabian ghost stories." The recollection was triggered by Nietzsche's thought process relating to Zarathustra's trip to hell. "Cryptoamnesia" or "hidden memory" is to be distinguished from simple plagiarism because it is caused by the unconscious. See C. G. Jung, *Psychiatric Studies* in *The Collected Works of C. G. Jung*, vol. I, ed. Sir Herbert Read, Michael Fordham, and Gerhard Adler (2nd edn., Princeton University Press, 1957), pp. vi, 82–3, 101–3, 105.

"Just look!" said the old helmsman, "there goes Zarathustra off to hell!" –

Around the same time that these sailors landed on the fiery island the rumor was circulating that Zarathustra had disappeared; and when people asked his friends, they related how he had departed by ship at night, without saying where he would be traveling.

Thus a restlessness arose, but three days later this restlessness was increased by the sailors' story – and now all the people were saying that the devil had fetched Zarathustra. His disciples laughed at this news, to be sure, and one of them even said: "I would sooner believe that Zarathustra fetched himself the devil." But at the bottom of their souls all of them were filled with worry and longing, and so their joy was great when on the fifth day Zarathustra appeared among them.

And this is the story of Zarathustra's conversation with the fire hound.[5]

"The earth," he said, "has a skin; and this skin has diseases. One of these diseases for example is called: 'Human being.'

And another of these diseases is called 'fire hound'; about him people have told each other many lies and allowed themselves to be lied to much.

To fathom this mystery I went over the sea, and I saw the naked truth, indeed, barefoot up to its throat!

Now I know what the fire hound is all about, and likewise all the underhanded and overthrowing scum-devils of whom not only little old women are afraid.

'Out with you, fire hound, out of your depth!' I cried, 'and confess how deep is this depth! Where did you get what you are snorting there?

You drink deeply from the sea; your salty eloquence betrays that! Really, for a hound of the depths you take your nourishment too much from the surface!

At best I could regard you as the ventriloquist of the earth; and always when I heard overthrowing and underhanded scum-devils speaking, I found them to be the same as you: salty, lying and superficial.

You know how to bellow and to darken with ashes! You are the best big mouths, and you've learned more than enough about bringing mud to a boil.

---

5 The "fire hound" (*Feuerhund*) is Nietzsche's invention, an unflattering portrait of a fire-breathing, revolutionary spirit of the kind who believes in and foments "great events" of a political nature. The rabble apparently believe in the existence of this fire hound, and are impressed by its hellish noise.

Wherever you are, there mud always has to be close by, and much that is spongy, pitted, squeezed, and wants to break free.

"Freedom" the lot of you are best at bellowing, but I lose faith in "great events" as soon as they are surrounded by much bellowing and smoke.

And just believe me, friend Infernal Racket! The greatest events – these are not our loudest, but our stillest hours.

Not around the inventors of new noise does the world revolve, but around the inventors of new values; *inaudibly* it revolves.

And just confess! When your noise and smoke cleared, it was always very little that had happened. What does it matter that a town becomes a mummy and a statue lies in the mud!

And these words I say to all overthrowers of statues. Surely it is the greatest folly to throw salt into the sea and statues into the mud.

In the mud of your contempt lay the statue, but precisely this is its law, that out of contempt life and living beauty grow back to it!

It stands up again with even more godlike features, seductive in its suffering, and truly! It will yet thank you for overthrowing it, you overthrowers!

But this advice I give to kings and churches and to all that is feeble with age and feeble in virtue – just let yourselves be overthrown! So that you might come to life again, and to you – virtue!' –

Thus I spoke before the fire hound, then it interrupted me sullenly and asked: 'Church? What is that?'

'Church?' I answered, 'that is a kind of state, and in fact the most lying kind. But be silent, you hypocrite hound! You already know your kind best!

Like you yourself the state is a hypocrite hound; like you it likes to speak with smoke and bellowing – to make believe, like you, that it speaks from the belly of things.

For it wants absolutely to be the most important animal on earth, this state; and people believe it, too.' –

When I finished saying this the fire hound behaved as though out of his mind with envy. 'What?' it shouted, 'the most important animal on earth? And they believe it too?' And then so much steam and so many horrid voices emanated from his throat that I thought he would choke to death from anger and envy.

At last he grew calmer and his panting let up; but as soon as he was calm I said laughing:

'You are angry, fire hound, therefore I am right about you!

And so that I also remain right, hear now about another fire hound: one who really speaks from the heart of the earth.

His breath exhales gold and golden rain – thus his heart wants it. What are ash and smoke and hot slime to him!

Laughter flutters out of him like a colorful cloud; he is ill disposed toward your gurgling and spitting and the growling of your bowels!

But gold and laughter – that he takes from the heart of the earth; for you should know – *the heart of the earth is made of gold.*'

When the fire hound heard this he could no longer stand to listen to me. Ashamed, he tucked in his tail and barked a feeble 'bow-wow,' then he crawled down into his cave." –

Thus recounted Zarathustra. But his disciples scarcely listened to him, so great was their desire to tell him about the sailors, the rabbits and the flying man.

"What am I supposed to think of that?" he said. "Am I some kind of ghost?

But it must have been my shadow. You must have heard something before about a wanderer and his shadow?[6]

What is certain, however, is that I must keep him shorter – otherwise he will ruin my reputation."

And once again Zarathustra shook his head and wondered. "What am I supposed to think of that?" he said once more.

"Why did the ghost shout: 'It is time! It is high time!'

For what then is it – high time?" –

Thus spoke Zarathustra.

The Soothsayer

"– and I saw a great sadness descend over humanity. The best became weary of their works.

A doctrine circulated, a belief accompanied it: 'Everything is empty, everything is the same, everything was!'

And from every hilltop it rang out: 'Everything is empty, everything is the same, everything was!'

---

[6] *The Wanderer and His Shadow* is the last volume of *Human, All Too Human*, published by Nietzsche in 1880. The wanderer appears in TSZ Part IV as one of the "higher human beings."

We harvested well, but why did all our fruits turn foul and brown? What fell down from the evil moon last night?

All work was for naught, our wine has become poison, the evil eye seared yellow our fields and hearts.

All of us became dry, and if fire were to touch us, then we would turn to dust like ashes – yes, fire itself we have made weary.

All our wells dried up, even the sea retreated. All firm ground wants to crack, but the depths do not want to devour!

'Oh where is there still a sea in which one could drown?' – thus rings our lament – out across the shallow swamps.

Indeed, we have already become too weary to die; now we continue to wake and we live on – in burial chambers!" –

Thus Zarathustra heard a soothsayer speaking; and his prophecy went straight to his heart and transformed him. Sadly he went about and weary; and he became like those of whom the soothsayer had spoken.

"Indeed," thus he spoke to his disciples, "it lacks but little and this long twilight will come. Alas, how shall I rescue my light to the other side!

It must not suffocate in this sadness! It shall be light to more distant worlds and most distant nights!"

Grieving thus in his heart Zarathustra walked about; and for three days he took no drink and no food, had no rest and lost his speech. At last it came to pass that he fell into a deep sleep. But his disciplines sat around him on long night watches and they waited anxiously for him to wake and speak again, and recover from his melancholy.

This, however, is the speech that Zarathustra spoke when he awoke; but his voice came to his disciples as if from far away.

"Hear this dream that I dreamed, my friends, and help me to understand its meaning!

It is still an enigma to me, this dream; its meaning is hidden in it and locked away and it does not yet fly above it on free wings.

I had renounced all life, thus I dreamed. I had become a night watchman and guardian of graves, there on the lonely mountain fortress of death.

Up there I guarded his coffins; the musty vaults stood full of such symbols of conquest. From glass coffins, conquered life looked out at me.

I breathed the odor of eternities turned to dust; my soul lay clammy and dusty, and who could have aired his soul in such a place!

The brightness of midnight was about me always, loneliness crouched beside her, and thirdly, death-rattle silence, the worst of my three lady friends.

I carried keys, the rustiest of all keys; and with them I knew how to open the creakiest of all gates.

Like a bitterly evil croaking the sound penetrated through the long corridors as the gate's wings swung open; hideously this bird screeched, defiant in being awakened.

But even more terrible and heart-constricting was the silence that set in around me when the gate fell quiet, and I sat alone in this treacherous silence.

Thus the time passed and crept by me, if time existed anymore – what do I know! But at last something happened that awakened me.

Three times there were blows at the door, like thundering, and the vaults echoed and howled three times in return; then I went to the gate.

'Alpa!' I cried. 'Who bears his ashes to the mountain? Alpa! Alpa! Who bears his ashes to the mountain?'[7]

And I pressed the key and lifted on the gate and strained. But it would not open even the width of a finger:

Then a roaring wind tore its wings apart; whistling, shrilling and whipping it threw down a black coffin before me:

And amidst the roaring and whistling and shrilling the coffin burst open and spewed forth thousandfold laughter.

And it laughed and mocked and roared against me from a thousand grimaces of children, angels, owls, fools and butterflies the size of children.

I was horribly frightened; it threw me to the ground. And I cried out in terror as I have never cried before.

But my own cries awakened me – and I came to. –"

Thus Zarathustra related his dream and then he was silent, for he did not yet know the interpretation of his dream. But the disciple whom he loved most quickly stood up, took hold of Zarathustra's hand and said:

---

[7] Nietzsche is here using material from a dream he had. He explained the dream to his friend Reinhart von Seydlitz in 1877, and mention of "Alpa" shows up in the unpublished notes of summer 1877. See *Kritische Studienausgabe* XIV: 306. In his dream, Nietzsche was nearing the top of a seemingly endless mountain path when he passed a cave, out of which a mysterious voice cried: "Alpa, Alpa – who carries his ashes to the mountains?" German *Alptraum*, or nightmare, is based on *der Alp*, which according to superstition is a ghost that crouches on the chest of the dreamer and causes bad dreams by pressuring or suffocating.

"Your life itself interprets this dream for us, oh Zarathustra!

Are you yourself not the wind with its shrill whistling, that tears open the gates of the fortresses of death?

Are you yourself not the coffin full of colorful sarcasms and the angelic grimaces of life?

Indeed, like thousandfold children's laughter Zarathustra comes into all burial chambers, laughing at these night watchmen and grave guardians, and whoever else rattles about with dingy keys.

You will frighten and lay them low with your laughter; your power over them will be proven by their swooning and awakening.

And even if the long twilight comes and the weariness unto death, you will not set in our sky, you advocate of life!

You allowed us to see new stars and new splendors of the night; indeed, you spanned laughter itself above us like a colorful tent.

Children's laughter will well up from coffins from now on; a strong wind will come triumphantly to all weariness unto death from now on: of this you yourself are our guarantor and soothsayer!

Indeed, *you yourself dreamed them*, your enemies: that was your hardest dream!

But as you awakened from them and came to yourself, thus shall they awaken from themselves – and come to you!" –

Thus spoke the disciple, and all the others now crowded around Zarathustra and took him by the hands and wanted to persuade him to abandon his bed and his sadness and to return to them. But Zarathustra sat upright on his bed and with a strange look. Like someone who returns home from long sojourns abroad, he gazed at his disciples and examined their faces; and still he did not recognize them. But as they lifted him and helped him to his feet, behold, all at once his eyes transformed; he comprehended all that had happened, stroked his beard and said in a strong voice:

"Well then! This has its time; but for now see to it, my disciples, that we prepare a good meal, and quickly! Thus I plan to do penance for bad dreams!

But the soothsayer shall eat and drink beside me; and truly, I will yet show him a sea in which he can drown!"

Thus spoke Zarathustra. Then, however, he gazed long into the face of the disciple who had served as the dream interpreter, and he shook his head. –

On Redemption

As Zarathustra crossed over the great bridge one day, the cripples and the beggars surrounded him and a hunchback spoke thus to him:

"Behold, Zarathustra! The people too learn from you and are gaining faith in your teaching; but in order to believe you completely, they need one more thing – you must first persuade us cripples! Here you have a fine selection and truly, an opportunity with more than one scruff! You can heal the blind and make the lame walk; and for the one who has too much behind him, you could surely take a bit away – that, I believe, would be the right way to make the cripples believe in Zarathustra!"

Zarathustra, however, responded to the speaker thus: "If one takes the hump from the hunchback, then one takes his spirit too – thus teach the people. And if one gives the blind man his eyesight, then he sees too many bad things on earth, such that he curses the one who healed him. But the one who makes the lame walk causes him the greatest harm, for scarcely does he begin to walk when his vices run away with him – thus teach the people about cripples. And why should Zarathustra not learn also from the people, if the people learn from Zarathustra?

But it is the least thing to me, since I have been among human beings, when I see 'This one is missing an eye and That one an ear and the Third one a leg, and there are Others who lost their tongue or their nose or their head.'

I see and have seen worse, and some of it so hideous that I do not want to speak of everything, and of a few things I do not even want to remain silent; namely human beings who were missing everything except the one thing they have too much of – human beings who are nothing more than one big eye, or one big maw or one big belly or some other big thing – inverse cripples I call such types.

And as I came out of my solitude and crossed over this bridge the first time, then I didn't believe my eyes and I looked and I looked again and said at last: 'That is an ear! An ear as big as a person!' And I looked more closely, and really, beneath the ear something was moving that was pitifully small and pathetic and thin. And, in truth, the gigantic ear sat upon a little slender stalk – but the stalk was a human being! If one used a magnifying glass one could even recognize a tiny, envious miniature face; even a bloated little soul dangling on the stalk. But the people told me that the big ear was not only a human being, but a great human being, a genius. But I have never believed the people when they speak of great human beings – and I maintained my belief that it was an inverse cripple who had too little of everything and too much of one thing."

When Zarathustra had spoken thus to the hunchback and to those for whom he had served as mouthpiece and advocate, he turned deeply upset to his disciples and said:

"Truly, my friends, I walk among human beings as among the fragments and limbs of human beings!

This is what is most frightening to my eyes, that I find mankind in ruins and scattered about as if on a battle field or a butcher field.

And if my gaze flees from the now to the past; it always finds the same: fragments and limbs and grisly accidents – but no human beings!

The now and the past on earth – alas, my friends – that is what is most unbearable to *me*. And I would not know how to live if I were not also a seer of that which must come.

A seer, a willer, a creator, a future himself and a bridge to the future – and alas, at the same time a cripple at this bridge: all that is Zarathustra.

And you too asked yourselves often: 'Who is Zarathustra to us? How shall he be known to us?' And like me you gave yourselves questions for answers.

Is he a promiser? Or a fulfiller? A conqueror? Or an inheritor? An autumn? Or a plow? A physician? Or a convalescent?

Is he a poet? Or a truthful man? A liberator? Or a tamer? A good man? Or an evil man?

I walk among human beings as among the fragments of the future; that future that I see.

And all my creating and striving amounts to this, that I create and piece together into one, what is now fragment and riddle and grisly accident.

And how could I bear to be a human being if mankind were not also creator and solver of riddles and redeemer of accident?

To redeem those who are the past and to recreate all 'it was' into 'thus I willed it!' – only that would I call redemption!

Will – thus the liberator and joy bringer is called; thus I taught you, my friends! And now learn this in addition: the will itself is still a prisoner.

Willing liberates, but what is that called, which claps even the liberator in chains?

'It was': thus is called the will's gnashing of teeth and loneliest misery. Impotent against that which has been – it is an angry spectator of everything past.

The will cannot will backward; that it cannot break time and time's greed – that is the will's loneliest misery.

Willing liberates; what does willing plan in order to rid itself of its misery and mock its dungeon?

Alas, every prisoner becomes a fool! Foolishly as well the imprisoned will redeems itself.

That time does not run backward, that is its wrath. 'That which was' – thus the stone is called, which it cannot roll aside.

And so it rolls stones around out of wrath and annoyance, and wreaks revenge on that which does not feel wrath and annoyance as it does.

Thus the will, the liberator, became a doer of harm; and on everything that is capable of suffering it avenges itself for not being able to go back.

This, yes this alone is *revenge* itself: the will's unwillingness toward time and time's 'it was.'

Indeed, a great folly lives in our will; and it became the curse of all humankind that this folly acquired spirit!

The spirit of revenge: my friends, that so far has been what mankind contemplate best; and wherever there was suffering, punishment was always supposed to be there as well.

For 'punishment' is what revenge calls itself; with a lying word it hypocritically asserts its good conscience.

And because in willing itself there is suffering, based on its inability to will backward – thus all willing itself and all living is supposed to be – punishment!

And now cloud upon cloud rolled in over the spirit, until at last madness preached: 'Everything passes away, therefore everything deserves to pass away!

And this itself is justice, this law of time that it must devour its own children' – thus preached madness.

'All things are ordained ethically according to justice and punishment. Alas, where is redemption from the flux of things and from the punishment called existence?' Thus preached madness.

'Can there be redemption, if there is eternal justice? Alas, the stone "it was" is unmoveable; all punishments too must be eternal!' Thus preached madness.

'No deed can be annihilated; how could it be undone through punishment? This, this is what is eternal about the punishment called existence, that existence must also eternally be deed and guilt again!

Unless the will were to finally redeem itself and willing became not-willing – '; but my brothers, you know this fable song of madness!

Away from these fable songs I steered you when I taught you: 'The will is a creator.'

All 'it was' is a fragment, a riddle, a grisly accident – until the creating will says to it: 'But I will it thus! I shall will it thus!'

But has it ever spoken thus? And when will this happen? Is the will already unharnessed from its own folly?

Has the will already become its own redeemer and joy bringer? Has it unlearned the spirit of revenge and all gnashing of teeth?

And who taught it reconciliation with time, and what is higher than any reconciliation?

That will which is the will to power must will something higher than any reconciliation –

but how shall this happen? Who would teach it to also will backward?"

– But at this point in his speech Zarathustra suddenly broke off and looked entirely like one who is appalled in the extreme. Appalled he looked at his disciples, his eyes penetrated their thoughts and their secret thoughts as if with arrows. But after a little while he laughed again and said, more calmly:

"It's difficult to live with people because keeping silent is so hard. Especially for someone who is talkative." –

Thus spoke Zarathustra. The hunchback meanwhile had listened to the conversation with his face covered, but when he heard Zarathustra laugh he looked up inquisitively and slowly said:

"But why does Zarathustra speak otherwise to us than to his disciples?"

Zarathustra answered: "What's to wonder about in that! One is allowed to speak hunched with hunchbacks!"

"Good," said the hunchback, "and with pupils one may tell tales out of school.

But why does Zarathustra speak otherwise to his pupils – than to himself?" –

On Human Prudence

Not the height: the precipice is what is terrible!

The precipice, where one's gaze plunges *downward* and one's hand grasps *upward*. There the heart is dizzy from its double will.

Oh my friends, can you guess even my heart's double will?

This, this is *my* precipice and my danger, that my gaze plunges into the heights and that my hand must hold to and support itself – on the depths!

My will clings to mankind, I bind myself with chains to mankind because I am drawn upward to the overman; for there my other will wills me.

And *for this* I live blind among people, just as if I did not know them: so that my hand does not entirely lose its faith in the firm.

I do not know you human beings; this darkness and solace are often spread around me.

I sit at the gateway for every rogue and ask: who wants to deceive me?

That is my first human prudence, that I allow myself to be deceived, in order to not be on the lookout for deceivers.

Indeed, if I were on the lookout for mankind, how could mankind be an anchor to my ball? Too easily I would be swept up and away!

This providence lies over my destiny, that I cannot be provident.

And whoever would not die of thirst among human beings must learn to drink from all glasses; and whoever would remain clean among human beings must understand how to wash himself even with dirty water.

And thus I often spoke to comfort myself: "Well then! Cheer up, old heart! One misfortune failed you; enjoy this as your – fortune!"

But this is my other human prudence: I spare the *vain* more than the proud.

Is wounded vanity not the mother of all tragedies? But where pride is wounded, there something even better than pride grows.

For life to be a proper spectacle, its play must be well-played; but for this good play actors are needed.

I found all vain people to be good actors; they play and want to be spectacular – all their spirit is focused in this willing.

They perform themselves, they invent themselves; in their proximity I love to be a spectator of life – it heals me of my melancholy.

Therefore I spare the vain, because they are physicians for my melancholy and keep me riveted to people as if to a play.

And then: who could measure the full depth of the vain man's modesty! I mean him well and pity him his modesty.

From you he wants to acquire his faith in himself; he nourishes himself from your glances, he eats praise from your hands.

He even believes your lies, when you lie well about him; for at bottom his heart sighs: "what am *I*?"

And if the truest virtue is the one that is not aware of itself, well; the vain man knows nothing of his modesty! –

But this is my third human prudence, that I do not allow my view of the *evil ones* to be spoiled by your fearfulness.

I am enchanted to see the wonders hatched by a hot sun: tigers and palm trees and rattle snakes.

Even among human beings there is a beautiful brood of the hot sun and much that is wonderworthy in those who are evil.

To be sure, just as your wisest did not strike me as quite so wise, so too I found the malice of human beings unequal to its reputation.

And often I shook my head and asked: Why do you keep rattling, you rattle snakes?

Indeed, even for evil there is still a future! And the hottest south has not yet been discovered for mankind.

How much is regarded today as the most egregious malice when in fact it is only twelve shoes wide and three months long! But some day bigger dragons will come into the world.

For in order for the overman to not lack his dragon, the over-dragon that is worthy of him, much hot sun must yet glow on humid jungle!

Your wild cats must first have turned to tigers and your poisonous toads to crocodiles; for the good hunter shall have a good hunt!

And truly, you good and just! In you there is much to laugh at and especially your fear of what up till now has been called "devil!"

So estranged from greatness are you in your souls that the overman would seem *terrible* to you in his kindness!

And you wise and knowing ones, you would flee from the sunburn of wisdom in which the overman joyfully bathes his nakedness!

You highest human beings whom I have ever laid eyes on – this is my doubt in you and my secret laughter: I suspect you would call my overman – devil!

Oh, I became weary of these highest and best; from their "height" I longed upward, outward, and away to the overman!

A dread overcame me when I saw these best human beings naked: then I sprouted wings to soar away into distant futures.

Into more distant futures, into more southern souths than ever a painter dreamed; there, where gods are ashamed of all clothing!

But I want to see *you* costumed, you neighbors and fellow human beings, and well groomed, and vain, and dignified, as "the good and the just" –

And costumed I myself want to sit among you – so that I might *not recognize* you and myself; for that is my final human prudence.

Thus spoke Zarathustra.

The Stillest Hour

What happened to me, my friends? You see me distraught, chased away, reluctantly obedient, prepared to go – alas, to go away from *you*!

Yes, once again Zarathustra must return to his solitude; but this time the bear returns to his cave unwillingly!

What happened to me? Who commanded this? – Alas, my angry mistress wills it so, she spoke to me – did I ever mention her name to you?

Yesterday toward evening *my stillest hour* spoke to me: that is the name of my terrible mistress.

And this is how it happened – for I must tell you everything, so your hearts do not harden against the one who must depart abruptly!

Do you know the terror of the one who is falling asleep? –

He is stricken with terror down to his toes because the ground is fading and the dream begins.

This I say to you as a parable. Yesterday, at the stillest hour, the ground faded from me, the dream began.

The hand advanced, the clock of my life drew a breath – never had I heard such stillness around me, so that my heart was terrified.

Then without voice it spoke to me: "*You know it, Zarathustra?*" –

And I cried out in terror on hearing this whispering, and the blood drained from my face, but I kept silent.

Then it spoke to me once more without voice: "You know it Zarathustra, but you do not speak it!" –

And at last I answered defiantly: "Indeed, I know it, but I do not want to speak it!"

Then it spoke to me again without voice: "You do not *want* to, Zarathustra? Is this even true? Do not hide in your defiance!" –

And I wept and trembled like a child and spoke: "Oh, I wanted to, yes, but how can I? Spare me this one thing! It is beyond my strength!"

Then it spoke to me again without voice: "What do you matter, Zarathustra? Speak your word and break!" –

And I answered: "Alas, is it *my* word? Who am I? I am waiting for one more worthy; I am not worthy even of breaking under it."

Then it spoke to me again without voice: "What do you matter? You are not yet humble enough for me. Humility has the toughest hide." –

And I answered: "What has the hide of my humility not borne already! I dwell at the foot of my height; how high are my peaks? No one yet has told me. But well do I know my valleys."

Then it spoke to me again without voice: "Oh Zarathustra, whoever has mountains to move must also move valleys and hollows." –

And I answered: "As of yet my words have moved no mountains, and what I spoke did not reach mankind. I went to human beings, to be sure, but I have not yet arrived among them."

Then it spoke to me again without voice: "What do you know *of that*! The dew lands on the grass when the night is most silent." –

And I answered: "They mocked me when I found and walked my own way; and in truth my feet trembled at that time.

And thus they spoke to me: 'You have forgotten the way, and now you are forgetting how to walk too!'"

Then it spoke to me again without voice: "What does their mockery matter! You are one who has forgotten how to obey; now you shall command!

Do you not know *who* is needed most by everyone? The one who commands great things.

To accomplish great things is difficult; but what is even more difficult is to command great things.

That is what is most unforgivable in you: you have the power, and you do not want to rule." –

And I answered: "I lack the lion's voice for all commanding."

Then it spoke to me again like a whispering: "The stillest words are those that bring the storm. Thoughts that come on the feet of doves steer the world.

Oh Zarathustra, you shall go as a shadow of that which must come; thus you will command and lead the way commanding." –

And I answered: "I am ashamed."

Then it spoke to me again without voice: "You must become a child again and without shame.

The pride of youth is still on you, you became young at a late time; but whoever would become a child must also overcome his youth." –

And I thought for a long time and trembled. At last however I said what I had said at first: "I do not want to."

Then laughter broke out around me. Alas, how this laughter tore my entrails and slit open my heart!

And it spoke to me one last time: "Oh Zarathustra, your fruits are ripe but you are not ripe for your fruits!

Thus you must return to your solitude, for you shall yet become mellow." –

And again there was laughing and it vanished; then it became still around me as if with twofold stillness. But I lay on the ground and the sweat poured from my limbs.

– Now you have heard everything, and why I must return to my solitude. I withheld nothing from you, my friends.

But hear this from me as well, *I* who am still the most tightlipped of human beings – and want to be so!

Oh my friends! There is still something I could tell you, there is still something I could give you! Why do I not give it? Am I stingy? –

But when Zarathustra had spoken these words he was overcome by the force of his pain and the nearness of parting from his friends, so that he wept out loud; and no one was able to comfort him. At night, however, he went away alone and left his friends.

Third Part

You look upward when you long for elevation. And I look down because I am elevated.

Who among you can laugh and be elevated at the same time?

Whoever climbs the highest mountain laughs at all tragic plays and tragic realities.

Zarathustra, "On Reading and Writing," (I, p. 28).

The Wanderer

It was around midnight that Zarathustra started his route over the ridge of the island, in order to arrive at the other coast by early morning; for there he intended to board a ship. At that location there was safe harborage where even foreign ships liked to anchor; these would take the occasional passenger who wanted to cross the sea from the blessed isles. Now as Zarathustra climbed up the mountain he thought as he traveled about his many lonely wanderings since the time of his youth, and about how many mountains and ridges and peaks he had already climbed.

I am a wanderer and a mountain climber, he said to his heart. I do not like the plains and it seems I cannot sit still for long.

And whatever may come to me now as destiny and experience – it will involve wandering and mountain climbing: ultimately one experiences only oneself.

The time has passed in which accidents could still befall me, and what *could* fall to me now that is not already my own?

It merely returns, it finally comes home to me – my own self and everything in it that has long been abroad and scattered among all things and accidents.

And I know one more thing: I am standing now before my last peak and before what has been saved for me for the longest time. Indeed, I must start my hardest path! Indeed, I have begun my loneliest hike!

But whoever is of my kind does not escape such an hour, the hour that speaks to him: "Only now do you go your way of greatness! Peak and abyss – they are now merged as one!

You go your way of greatness; now what was formerly your ultimate danger has become your ultimate refuge!

You go your way of greatness; now it must be your best courage that there is no longer a way behind you!

You go your way of greatness; here no one shall sneak along after you! Your foot itself erased the path behind you, and above it stands written: impossibility.

And if now all ladders should fail, then you must know how to climb on your own head – how else would you climb upward?

On your own head and over and beyond your own heart! Now what is mildest in you must become hardest.

Whoever has always spared himself much gets sick in the end from so much coddling. Praised be whatever makes hard! I do not praise the land where butter and honey flow!

It is necessary to *look away* from oneself in order to see *much*: this hardness is needed by every mountain climber.

But whoever is importunate with his eyes as a seeker of knowledge – how could he see more of things than their foregrounds?

But you, Zarathustra, you wanted to see the ground and background of all things, and so you must climb over yourself – up, upward, until you have even your stars *beneath* you!"

Yes, look down on myself and even on my stars: only that would I call my *peak*, that remains to me as my *ultimate* peak! –

Thus Zarathustra spoke to himself as he climbed, comforting his heart with hard sayings, for he was sore in his heart as never before. And as he came to the top of the mountain ridge, behold, there lay the other sea stretching before him, and he stood still and silent for a long time. But at this altitude the night was cold and clear and bright with stars.

I recognize my lot, he said at last, with sorrow. Well then! I am ready. Just now my ultimate solitude began.

Oh this black sad sea beneath me! Oh this pregnant nocturnal moroseness! Oh destiny and sea – now I must *descend* to you!

I stand before my highest mountains and before my longest hike: therefore I must descend deeper than I ever climbed before:

– descend deeper into suffering than I ever climbed before, down into its blackest flood! My destiny wills it so: Well then! I am ready.

Where did the highest mountains come from? Thus I once asked. Then I learned that they come from the sea.

This testimony is written into their stone and onto the walls of their peaks. From the deepest the highest must come into its height. –

Thus spoke Zarathustra at the pinnacle of the mountain, where it was cold. But as he came near to the sea and stood at last alone among the cliffs, then he had grown weary from his travels and felt even greater longing than before.

Everything is still sleeping, he said; even the sea sleeps. Drunk with sleep and strangely it looks at me.

But it breathes warmly, that I feel. And I also feel that it is dreaming. Dreaming it tosses on hard pillows.

Listen! Listen! How it moans with evil memories – or evil forebodings?

Yes, I am sad along with you, you dark monster, and for your sake annoyed even with myself.

Oh that my hand does not possess sufficient strength! Gladly indeed would I redeem you from evil dreams! –

And as Zarathustra spoke thus he laughed at himself with melancholy and bitterness. "What, Zarathustra!" he said. "Do you want to sing comfort even to the sea?

Oh you loving fool Zarathustra, you who are over-blessed with trust! But you have always been so; always you came trustingly to all that is terrible.

You wanted to caress every monster. A hint of warm breath, a bit of soft shag on the paw – and already you were prepared to love it and lure it.

Love is the danger of the loneliest one, love of everything *if only it lives*! Laughable indeed are my folly and my modesty in love!" –

Thus spoke Zarathustra and he laughed once again. But then he remembered the friends he left behind – and as if he had violated them with his thoughts, he became angry for his thoughts. And suddenly the laughing one began to weep – for wrath and longing Zarathustra wept bitterly.

On the Vision and the Riddle

1

When it was rumored among the sailors that Zarathustra was on the ship – for a man who came from the blessed isles went on board at the same time as him – then a great curiosity and anticipation arose. But Zarathustra kept silent for two days and was cold and deaf with sadness, such that he answered neither to glances nor questions. On the evening of the second day, however, he opened his ears again, even though he continued to be silent; for there was much that was peculiar and dangerous to be heard on this ship, which had come from far away and wanted to go still farther. But Zarathustra was a friend of all who make distant journeys and do not like to live without danger, and so, finally, his own tongue was freed while listening, and the ice of his heart broke: then he began to speak thus:

To you, bold searchers, researchers,[1] and whoever put to terrible seas with cunning sails –

to you, the riddle-drunk, the twilight-happy whose souls are lured by flutes to every maelstrom:

– because you do not want to probe along a thread with cowardly hands; and because where you can *guess*, there you hate to *deduce* –

to you alone I tell the riddle that I *saw* – the vision of the loneliest one. –

Darkly I walked recently through cadaver-colored twilight – darkly and hard, biting my lip. Not only one sun had set for me.

A path that climbed defiantly through boulders, a malicious, lonely path consoled neither by weed nor shrub – a mountain path crunched under the defiance of my foot.

Striding mutely over the mocking clatter of pebbles, crushing the rock that caused it to slip; thus my foot forced its way upward.

Upward – in defiance of the spirit that pulled it downward, the spirit of gravity, my devil and arch-enemy.

Upward – even though he sat atop me, half dwarf, half mole, lame, paralyzing, dripping lead into my ear, lead-drop thoughts into my brain.

"Oh Zarathustra," he murmured scornfully, syllable by syllable. "You stone of wisdom! You hurled yourself high, but every hurled stone must – fall!

Oh Zarathustra, you stone of wisdom, you sling stone, you star crusher! You hurled yourself so high – but every hurled stone – must fall!

Sentenced to yourself and to your own stoning; oh Zarathustra, far indeed you hurled the stone – but it will fall back down upon *you*!"

Then the dwarf became silent, and that lasted a long time. But his silence oppressed me, and being at two in such a way truly makes one lonelier than being at one!

I climbed, I climbed, I dreamed, I thought – but everything oppressed me. I resembled a sick person whose severe agonies make him

---

[1] *Euch, den kühnen Suchern, Versuchern . . .* When the prefix *ver-* is added to *suchen*, to seek or to search, the verb is modified to mean try, attempt, but also tempt, so that the noun *Versucher* means both one who attempts and one who tempts. The noun *der Versuch*, meanwhile, means both attempt and experiment. Nietzsche frequently alludes to his favorite deity, Dionysus, as the *Versucher-Gott*, i.e. as the tempter god, attempter god (experimenter). I render this wordplay as "searcher" and "researcher" to preserve the wordplay, but wherever this particular combination occurs in *TSZ* or elsewhere, one should suspect Nietzsche is exploring the relationship between searching, attempting (experimenting, researching) and tempting.

weary, and who is then jarred out of falling asleep by an even worse dream. –

But there is something in me that I call courage: this so far has slain my every discourage. This courage at last commanded me to stand still and to say: "Dwarf – you or I!" –

Courage after all is the best slayer – courage that *attacks*; for in every attack there is sounding brass.

But the human being is the most courageous animal, and so it overcame every animal. With sounding brass it even overcame every pain, but human pain is the deepest pain.

Courage also slays dizziness at the abyss; and where do human beings not stand at the abyss? Is seeing itself not – seeing the abyss?

Courage is the best slayer; courage slays even pity. But pity is the deepest abyss, and as deeply as human beings look into life, so deeply too they look into suffering.

But courage is the best slayer, courage that attacks; it slays even death, for it says: "Was *that* life? Well then! One More Time!"

In such a saying, however, there is much sounding brass. He who has ears to hear, let him hear!

2

"Stop, dwarf!" I said. "I – or you! But I am the stronger of us two – you do not know my abysmal thought! *That* – you could not bear!" –

Then something happened that made me lighter, for the dwarf jumped down from my shoulder, the inquisitive one, and he crouched upon a stone there before me. But right there where we stopped was a gateway.

"See this gateway, dwarf!" I continued. "It has two faces. Two paths come together here; no one has yet walked them to the end.

This long lane back: it lasts an eternity. And that long lane outward – that is another eternity.

They contradict each other, these paths; they blatantly offend each other – and here at this gateway is where they come together. The name of the gateway is inscribed at the top: 'Moment.'

But whoever were to walk one of them further – and ever further and ever on: do you believe, dwarf, that these paths contradict each other eternally?" –

"All that is straight lies," murmured the dwarf contemptuously. "All truth is crooked, time itself is a circle."

"You spirit of gravity!" I said, angrily. "Do not make it too easy on yourself! Or I shall leave you crouching here where you crouch, lamefoot – and I bore you *this high*!

See this moment!" I continued. "From this gateway Moment a long eternal lane stretches *backward*: behind us lies an eternity.

Must not whatever *can* already have passed this way before? Must not whatever *can* happen, already have happened, been done, passed by before?

And if everything has already been here before, what do you think of this moment, dwarf? Must this gateway too not already – have been here?

And are not all things firmly knotted together in such a way that this moment draws after it *all* things to come? Therefore – itself as well?

For, whatever *can* run, even in this long lane *outward* – *must* run it once more! –

And this slow spider that creeps in the moonlight, and this moonlight itself, and I and you in the gateway whispering together, whispering of eternal things – must not all of us have been here before?

– And return and run in that other lane, outward, before us, in this long, eerie lane – must we not return eternally? –"

Thus I spoke, softer and softer, for I was afraid of my own thought and secret thoughts. Then, suddenly, I heard a dog *howl* nearby.

Had I ever heard a dog howl like this? My thoughts raced back. Yes! When I was a child, in my most distant childhood:

– then I heard a dog howl like this. And I saw it too, bristling, its head up, trembling in the stillest midnight when even dogs believe in ghosts:

– so that I felt pity. For the full moon had passed over the house, silent as death, and it had just stopped, a round smolder – stopped on the flat roof just as if on a stranger's property –

that is the why the dog was so horror-stricken, because dogs believe in thieves and ghosts. And when I heard it howl like this again, I felt pity once more.

Where now was the dwarf? And the gateway? And the spider? And all the whispering? Was I dreaming? Was I waking? I stood all of a sudden among wild cliffs, alone, desolate, in the most desolate moonlight.

But there lay a human being! And there! The dog jumping, bristling, whining – now it saw me coming – then it howled again, it *screamed*: had I ever heard a dog scream like this for help?

And truly, I saw something the like of which I had never seen before. A young shepherd I saw; writhing, choking, twitching, his face distorted, with a thick black snake hanging from his mouth.

Had I ever seen so much nausea and pale dread in one face? Surely he must have fallen asleep? Then the snake crawled into his throat – where it bit down firmly.

My hand tore at the snake and tore – in vain! It could not tear the snake from his throat. Then it cried out of me: "Bite down! Bite down!

Bite off the head! Bite down!" – Thus it cried out of me, my dread, my hatred, my nausea, my pity, all my good and bad cried out of me with one shout. –

You bold ones around me! You searchers, researchers and whoever among you ever shipped out with cunning sails onto unexplored seas! You riddle-happy ones!

Now guess me this riddle that I saw back then, now interpret me this vision of the loneliest one!

For it was a vision and a foreseeing: *what* did I see then as a parable? And *who* is it that must some day come?

Who is the shepherd into whose throat the snake crawled this way? *Who* is the human being into whose throat everything that is heaviest, blackest will crawl?

– Meanwhile the shepherd bit down as my shout advised him; he bit with a good bite! Far away he spat the head of the snake – and he leaped to his feet. –

No longer shepherd, no longer human – a transformed, illuminated, *laughing* being!

Never yet on earth had I heard a human being laugh as *he* laughed!

Oh my brothers, I heard a laughter that was no human laughter – and now a thirst gnaws at me, a longing that will never be still.

My longing for this laughter gnaws at me; oh how can I bear to go on living! And how could I bear to die now! –

Thus spoke Zarathustra.

On Unwilling Bliss

With such riddles and bitterness in his heart Zarathustra traveled across the sea. But when he was four days removed from the blessed isles and from his friends, he had overcome all of his pain: triumphant and with firm footing he stood once again upon his destiny. And then Zarathustra spoke thus to his jubilating conscience:

I am alone again and want to be, alone with pure sky and open sea; and again it is afternoon around me.

In the afternoon I once found my friends for the first time, in the afternoon then a second time: at the hour when all light grows stiller.

For whatever happiness is still underway between sky and earth, it now seeks shelter for itself in a bright soul: *out of happiness* now all light has become stiller.

Oh afternoon of my life! Once *my* happiness too climbed to the valley to seek itself a shelter; there it found these open, hospitable souls.

Oh afternoon of my life! What have I not given up to have this one thing: this lively plantation of my thoughts and this morning light of my highest hope!

Companions the creator once sought and children *of his* hope, and truly, it turned out that he could not find them unless he first created them himself.

And so I am in the middle of my work, going to my children and returning from them; for the sake of his children Zarathustra must complete himself.

For at bottom one loves only one's own child and work; and where there is great love for oneself it is the hallmark of pregnancy – this is what I found.

My children are still greening in their first spring, standing close to one another and shaken by a common wind, the trees of my garden and best plot of soil.

And truly, where such trees stand next to one another, there *are* blessed isles!

But at some point I want to dig them up and set each one apart, so that it learns solitude and defiance and caution.

Gnarled and crooked and with pliant hardness it shall stand then beside the sea, a living lighthouse of invincible life.

There, where the storms plunge down into the sea and the mountain's trunk drinks water, there each one shall someday have his day and night watches, for *his own* testing and knowledge.

He shall be known and tested as to whether he is of my kind and kin –
whether he is the master of a long will, taciturn even when he speaks, and
yielding in such a way that he *takes* in giving –

– so that he might one day become my companion and a fellow creator
and fellow celebrator of Zarathustra: the kind who writes my will on my
tablets for the fuller completion of all things.

And for his sake and his kind I must complete *myself*; therefore I now
avoid my happiness and offer myself to all unhappiness – for *my* ultimate
testing and knowledge.

And truly, it was time that I left, and the wanderer's shadow and the
bitterest boredom and the stillest hour – all of them said to me: "it is high
time!"

The wind blew through my keyhole and said: "come!" The door sprang
open slyly and said: "go!"

But I lay chained to the love of my children; desire set this snare for
me, desire for love, that I might become the prey of my children and lose
myself to them.

Desire – to me that means: to have lost myself. *I have you, my children!*
In this having, everything shall be certain and nothing shall be desire.

But the sun lay brooding on my love, and Zarathustra cooked in his
own juice – then shadows and doubts flew over and past me.

I craved frost and winter: "Oh if only frost and winter made me snap
and crunch again!" I sighed – then icy fog rose up out of me.

My past broke open its graves; many a pain that had been buried
alive awakened – it had merely had a good night's sleep, hidden in burial
shrouds.

Thus everything cried out to me in signs: "it is time!" – But I – did not
hear. Until at last my abyss stirred and my thought bit me.

Oh, abysmal thought, you who are *my* thought! When will I find the
strength to hear you digging without trembling?

My heart pounds all the way up to my head when I hear you digging!
Even your silence wants to strangle me, you abysmally silent one!

Never yet have I dared to summon you *up*; it is enough that I carried
you around with me! As yet I have not been strong enough for the lion's
final overreaching and cheeky mischief.

Your gravity alone was always terrible enough for me; but one day I
shall yet find the strength and the lion's voice to summon you up!

When I have once overcome that challenge, then I want to overcome one still greater; and a *triumph* shall be the seal of my completion! –

Meanwhile I still drift on uncertain seas; accident flatters me with its smooth tongue, and though I look forward and backward, I still see no end.

As yet the hour of my final struggle has not come – or does it come just now? Indeed, with treacherous beauty the surrounding sea and life gaze at me!

Oh afternoon of my life! Oh happiness before evening! Oh harbor on the high sea! Oh peace in uncertainty! How I mistrust you all!

Indeed, I am mistrustful of your treacherous beauty! I resemble the lover who mistrusts the all too velvety smile.

As he pushes his most beloved before him, tender even in his hardness, the jealous one – so too I push this blissful hour before me.

Away with you, you blissful hour! Along with you an unwilling bliss came to me. Willing to take my deepest pain I stand here: you came at the wrong time!

Away with you, you blissful hour! Rather take shelter there – with my children! Hurry! And bless them before evening with *my* happiness!

The evening is coming now, the sun is sinking. Gone – my happiness! –

Thus spoke Zarathustra. And he waited for his unhappiness the whole night, but he waited in vain. The night remained bright and still, and happiness itself came closer and closer to him. Toward morning, however, Zarathustra laughed in his heart and said mockingly: "Happiness chases after me, and that is because I do not chase after women. But happiness is a woman."

Before Sunrise

Oh sky above me, you pure, you deep one! You abyss of light! Gazing at you I shudder with godlike desires.

To hurl myself into your height – that is *my* depth! To hide myself in your purity – that is *my* innocence.

The god is veiled by his beauty; thus you conceal your stars. You do not speak; *thus* you make your wisdom known to me.

Mutely you rose for me today over the roaring sea, your love and your modesty speak revelation to my roaring soul.

That you came to me beautiful, veiled in your beauty; that you speak to me mutely, revealed in your wisdom –

oh how could I not guess all that is modesty in your soul! *Before* the sun you came to me, the loneliest one.

We are friends from the beginning; we have grief and ghastliness and ground in common; even the sun we have in common.

We do not speak to one another because we know too much: we are silent to one another, we smile our knowledge to one another.

Are you not the light to my fire? Do you not have the sister soul to my insight?

Together we learned everything; together we learned to climb up to ourselves by climbing over ourselves, and to smile cloudlessly:

– smile down cloudlessly from bright eyes and from a distance of miles, when beneath us pressure and purpose and guilt steam like rain.

And if I wandered alone – for *whom* did my soul thirst in nights and on wrong paths? And if I climbed mountains, *whom* did I ever seek if not you on mountains?

And all my wandering and mountain climbing: they were only a necessity and a help to the helpless one – the only thing my will wants is *to fly*, to fly into you!

And whom did I hate more than drifting clouds and everything that stains you? And I hated even my own hatred because it stained you!

I grudge these drifting clouds, these creeping predator-cats; they take from you and me what we have in common – our awesome infinite saying of Yes and Amen.

We grudge these middle-men and mixers, these drifting clouds, these half-and-halfs who learned neither to bless, nor to curse whole heartedly.

I would rather sit in a barrel under a closed sky, would rather sit in an abyss without sky than see you, sky of light, stained by drifting clouds!

And often I wanted to tie them together with the jagged gold wires of lightning, and beat their kettle bellies like thunder –

– an angry kettle drummer because they rob me of your Yes! and Amen! – you sky above me, you pure, you bright one! You abyss of light! – Because they rob you of *my* Yes! and Amen!

For I would rather have din and thunder and stormy cursing than this deliberate, dubious cat calm; and even among humans the ones I hate most are the soft steppers and half-and-halfs and dubious, dawdling drift-clouds.

And "whoever cannot bless, let him *learn* to curse!" – this bright teaching fell to me from the bright sky, this star stands in my sky even in black nights.

I am a blesser and a Yes-sayer if only you are around me, you pure, you bright one, you abyss of light! Into all abysses then I carry my Yes-saying that blesses.

I have become a blesser and a Yes-sayer, and for this I wrestled long and was a wrestler, in order to free my hands one day for blessing.

But this is my blessing: to stand over each thing as its own sky, as its round roof, its azure bell and eternal security – and blessed is he who blesses so!

For all things are baptized at the well of eternity and beyond good and evil; good and evil themselves, however, are only shadows in between and damp glooms and drift-clouds.

Truly it is a blessing and no blasphemy when I teach: "Over all things stands the sky accident, the sky innocence, the sky chance, the sky mischief."

"By chance" – that is the oldest nobility in the world, I gave it back to all things, I redeemed them from their servitude under purpose.

This freedom and cheerfulness of the sky I placed like an azure bell over all things when I taught that over them and through them no "eternal will" – wills.

This mischief and this folly I placed in place of that will when I taught: "With all things one thing is impossible – rationality!"

A *bit* of reason to be sure, a seed of wisdom sprinkled from star to star – this sourdough is mixed into all things: for the sake of folly, wisdom is mixed into all things!

A bit of wisdom is indeed possible; but I found this blessed certainty in all things: that on the feet of accident they would rather – *dance*.

Oh sky above me, you pure, you exalted one! This your purity is to me now, that there is no eternal spider and spider web of reason:

– that you are my dance floor for divine accident, that you are my gods' table for divine dice throws and dice players! –

But you blush? Did I speak the unspeakable? Did I blaspheme when I wanted to bless you?

Or is it the shame of us two that made you blush? – Do you command me to go and be silent because now – the *day* is coming?

The world is deep – and deeper than the day has ever grasped. Not everything may be permitted to speak before day. But the day is coming, and so let us part now!

Oh sky above me, you bashful, you glowing one! Oh you my happiness before sunrise! The day is coming, and so let us part now! –

Thus spoke Zarathustra.

On Virtue that Makes Small

I

When Zarathustra was on dry land again he did not go directly to his mountains and his cave, but instead took many ways and asked many questions and found out about this and that, saying of himself jokingly: "Look at the river that flows back to its source in many windings!" For he wanted to learn what had transpired in the meantime *among human beings*; whether they had become bigger or smaller. And once he saw a row of new houses, and he was amazed then and he said:

"What do these houses mean? Truly, no great soul placed them here, as a parable of itself!

Probably some feeble-minded child took them out of its toy box? If only another child would put them back into its toy box!

And these parlors and chambers; can *men* go in and out here? To me they seem made for satin dolls, or for nibblers who probably let themselves be nibbled."

And Zarathustra stood still and reflected. At last he said sadly: "*Everything* has become smaller!

Everywhere I see lower gateways; whoever is like *me* can still pass through, but – he has to stoop!

Oh when will I return to my homeland where I no longer have to stoop – no longer have to stoop *before the small ones*!" – And Zarathustra sighed and gazed into the distance. –

On the same day, however, he delivered his speech on virtue that makes small.

2

I walk among these people and keep my eyes open; they do not forgive me that I am not envious of their virtues.

They bite at me because I say to them: for small people small virtues are necessary – and because I find it hard to grasp that small people are *necessary*!

I still resemble the rooster here in a strange barnyard, whom even the hens bite; and yet I am not bad to the hens because of that.

I am courteous toward them as toward all small annoyances; to be prickly toward what is small strikes me as wisdom for porcupines.

They all talk about me when they sit around the fire evenings – they talk about me, but no one thinks – about me!

This is the new stillness that I learned: their noise concerning me spreads a cloak over my thoughts.

They make noise among themselves: "What does this dark cloud want with us? Let's see to it that it does not bring us a plague!"

And recently a woman snatched her child to herself, who wanted to come to me: "Take the children away!" she shouted. "Such eyes singe children's souls."

They cough when I speak, they think that coughing is an objection to strong wind – they guess nothing of the roaring of my happiness!

"We still have no time for Zarathustra" – thus they object; but what does any time matter which "has no time" for Zarathustra?

And even if they were to praise me, how could I fall asleep on *their* praise? Their praise is a belt of thorns to me; it scratches me even when I take it off.

And this also I learned among them: the one who praises pretends that he is giving back, but in truth he wants to be given even more!

Ask my foot whether it likes their tune of praise and palaver! Indeed, to such a beat and tick-tock it wants neither to dance nor to stand still.

They want to palaver and praise me to their small virtue; they would like to persuade my foot to the tick-tock of their small happiness.

I walk among these people and keep my eyes open; they have become *smaller* and are becoming ever smaller: *but this is because of their teaching on happiness and virtue.*

For they are modest even in their virtue – because they want contentment. But only modest virtue goes along with contentment.

Even they, of course, learn to stride and to stride forward in their way – this is what I call their *hobbling*. This way they become an obstacle to anyone who is in a hurry.

And some of them look backward stiff-necked while walking forward; these I like to run into.

Foot and eye should not lie, nor rub each other's faces in their lies. But there is much lying among the small people.

A few of them will, but most of them are merely willed. A few of them are genuine, but most of them are bad actors.

There are unknowing actors among them and unwilling actors among them – the genuine are always rare, especially the genuine actors.

There is little here of the man, therefore their women masculinize themselves. For only he who is man enough will *redeem the woman* in woman.

And this hypocrisy I found to be the worst among them; that even those who command feign the virtues of those who serve.

"I serve, you serve, we serve" – this is how even the hypocrisy of the rulers prays here – and watch out if the first lord is *only* the first servant!

Oh, into their hypocrisies too the curiosity of my eyes flew astray, and well did I guess all their fly-happiness and their buzzing around sunny windowpanes.

So much kindness, so much weakness I see. So much justice and pity, so much weakness.

Round, righteous and kind they are to one another, like grains of sand are round, righteous and kind to one another.

To modestly embrace a small happiness – that they call "resignation" and already they are squinting around modestly for a new small happiness.

At bottom these simple ones want one simple thing: that no one harm them. And so they beat everyone to it by doing them a good deed.

But this is *cowardice*, even if it is called "virtue." –

And if they ever speak gruffly, these small people, *I* hear only their hoarseness – for every puff of wind makes them hoarse.

They are clever, and their virtues have clever fingers. But they lack fists; their fingers do not know how to form into fists.

To them virtue is whatever makes modest and tame; this is how they made the wolf into a dog and mankind himself into mankind's favorite pet.

"We place our chair in the *middle*" – that is what their grinning says to me – "and just as far away from dying fighters as from contented sows."

But this is – *mediocrity*: even if it is called moderation. –

3

I walk among these people and let many a word fall, but they know neither to take nor to keep.

They are amazed that I did not come to lambast lusting and malignancy, and truly, nor did I come to warn of pick-pockets!

They are amazed that I am not prepared to make their cleverness wittier and prettier, as if they did not have enough cleverlings already, whose voices scrape me like chalk on slate!

And when I shout: "A curse on all cowardly devils in you, who like to whine and fold their hands and worship," then they shout: "Zarathustra is godless."

And especially their teachers of resignation shout it – but they are precisely the ones into whose ears I like to shout: "Yes! I *am* Zarathustra, the godless one!"

These teachers of resignation! Wherever there is pettiness and sickness and scabs, they crawl to it like lice; and only my disgust prevents me from cracking them.

Well then! This is my sermon for *their* ears: I am Zarathustra, the godless, who says: "Who is more godless than I, so that I can enjoy his instruction?"

I am Zarathustra, the godless: where do I find my equal? And all those are my equal who give themselves their own will and put aside all resignation.

I am Zarathustra, the godless: I still cook every chance in *my* pot. And only when it has been well cooked in there do I welcome it as *my* food.

And truly, many a chance came to me imperiously, but my *will* spoke to it even more imperiously – and already it lay begging on its knees –

– begging me for protection and affection and addressing me with flattery: "Look, oh Zarathustra, it's only a friend coming to a friend!" –

But why do I speak where no one has *my* ears! And so I want to shout it out to the four winds:

You are becoming smaller and smaller, you small people! You are crumbling, you contented ones! You will yet perish –

– of your many small virtues, of your many small abstentions, of your many small resignations!

Too sparing, too yielding – that is your soil! But in order for a tree to grow *tall*, it needs to put down hard roots amid hard rock!

And even what you abstain from weaves at the web of all future humanity; even your nothing is a spider web and a spider that lives off the blood of the future.

And when you take, it's like stealing, you small-virtued ones; and even among rogues *honor* says: "One should only steal where one can not rob."

"It will give" – that too is a teaching of resignation. But I say to you contented people: *it will take* and it will take more and more from you!

Oh if only you would put aside all *half* willing and become as resolute in your sloth as in your deeds!

Oh if only you understood my words: "Go ahead and do whatever you will – but first be the kind of people who *can will*!

Go ahead and love your neighbors as you love yourselves – but first be the kind of people *who love themselves* –

love with the great love, love with the great contempt!" Thus speaks Zarathustra the godless. –

But why do I speak where no one has *my* ears! Here it is still one hour too early for me.

I am my own forerunner among these people, my own cock-crow through dark lanes.

But *their* hour is coming! And mine will come too! By the hour they become smaller, poorer, more sterile – poor weeds! Poor soil!

And *soon* they shall stand there before me like parched grass and steppe, and truly, weary of themselves – and yearning for *fire* more than for water!

Oh blessed hour of lightning! Oh secret before noon! – Wild fires I want to make of them some day and heralds with tongues of fire –

– some day they shall proclaim with tongues of fire: It is coming, it is near, *the great noon*!

Thus spoke Zarathustra.

On the Mount of Olives

The winter, a wicked guest, sits in my house; my hands are blue from his friendly handshake.

I honor him, this wicked guest, but I gladly let him sit alone. Gladly I run away from him, and if one runs *well*, then one can escape him!

With warm feet and warm thoughts I run to where the wind is calm – to the sunny spot of my mount of olives.

There I laugh at my fierce guest and still think well of him for catching the flies in my house and silencing much small noise.

For he does not tolerate it when a mosquito or two wants to sing; he also makes the lane so lonely that the moonlight is afraid in it at night.

A hard guest is he – but I honor him, and I do not pray to the pot-bellied fire idol like the weaklings.

Rather a bit of teeth chattering than worshiping idols – that is how my kind wants it! And I especially grudge all horny, steamy, musty fire idols.

Whomever I love, I love better in winter than in summer; better and more heartily I now mock my enemies since winter sits at home with me.

Heartily indeed, even when I *crawl* to bed – then even my hiding happiness laughs and makes mischief; even my lying dream laughs.

I, a crawler? Never in my life have I crawled before the mighty; and if I ever lied, then I lied out of love. That is why I am cheerful even in my winter bed.

A meager bed warms me more than a rich one, for I am jealous of my poverty, and in winter it is most faithful to me.

Each day I begin with a malice; I mock winter with a cold bath – that makes my fierce house guest growl.

I also like to tickle him with a little wax candle, so that finally he will release the sky from ashen grey twilight.

In the morning I am especially malicious, in the early hour when the pail clatters at the well and the horses whinny warmly through grey lanes:

Impatiently I wait for the bright sky to open at last, the snow-bearded winter sky, the old man and white-head –

– the winter sky, the silent one who often keeps even his sun silent!

Did I learn my long bright silence from him? Or did he learn it from me? Or did each of us invent it on his own?

The origin of all good things is thousandfold – all good mischievous things leap for joy into existence: so how are they supposed to do this – only once?

Long silence too is a good mischievous thing, and looking out of a round-eyed face like the winter sky –

– to be silent like the winter sky about one's sun and one's uncompromising solar will: indeed, this art and this winter mischief I learned *well*!

My favorite malice and art is that my silence learned not to betray itself through silence.

Rattling with diction and dice I outwit the solemn waiting ones; my will and purpose shall elude all these fierce watchers.

To prevent anyone from looking down into my ground and ultimate will, I invented my long bright silence.

Many a clever one I found, who veiled his face and muddied his water so that no one could see through him and down into him.

But precisely to him came the more clever mistrustful ones and nut crackers; precisely his most hidden fish they fished out of him!

But to me the bright, courageous, transparent ones are the most clever of those who keep silent; those whose ground is so *deep* that even the brightest water does not – betray it.

You snow-bearded silent winter sky, you round-eyed white-head above me! Oh you heavenly parable of my soul and its mischief!

And *must* I not conceal myself like someone who has swallowed gold – so that they do not slit open my soul?

Must I not wear stilts so that they *overlook* my long legs – all these plain jealous and pain zealous who surround me?

These smoky, room-temperature, used up, greened-out, grief ridden souls – how *could* their envy bear my happiness!

And so I show them only the ice and the winter on my peaks – and *not* that my mountain winds all the belts of the sun around itself!

They hear only my winter storms whistling, and *not* that I also glide over warm seas like longing, heavy, sultry south winds.

They still have mercy on my accidents and coincidences: but *my* words say: "Let accident come to me: it is innocent, like a little child!"

How *could* they bear my happiness if I did not cover my happiness with accidents and winter emergencies and polar bear caps and snow-sky sheets?

– If I myself didn't have mercy on their *pity*: the pity of these who are plain jealous and pain zealous!

– If I myself didn't sigh before them, teeth chattering, and patiently *allow* myself to be wrapped in their pity!

It is the wise mischief and benevolence of my soul that it *does not conceal* its winter and its ice storms; nor does it conceal its frostbites.

One person's loneliness is the escape of the sick; another's loneliness is the escape *from* the sick.

Let them *hear* me chatter and sigh from winter cold, all these wretched, leering rascals around me! With such sighing and chattering I still escape their heated rooms.

Let them sympathize and sympasigh[2] about my frostbite: "He will *freeze* yet from the ice of knowledge!" – so they lament.

Meanwhile I run with warm feet crisscross on my mount of olives; in the sunny spot of my mount of olives I sing and mock all pitying. –

Thus sang Zarathustra.

On Passing By

In this manner, hiking slowly through many peoples and towns, Zarathustra returned the long way to his mountains and his cave. And then, unexpectedly, he also arrived at the gate of the *big city*. Here, however, a foaming fool with outstretched hands leaped toward him and blocked his path. And this was the same fool whom the people called "Zarathustra's ape," because he had memorized some of the phrasing and tone of Zarathustra's speaking and also liked to borrow from the treasure of his wisdom. The fool spoke thus to Zarathustra:

"Oh Zarathustra, this is the big city: here you have nothing to gain and everything to lose.

Why do you want to wade through this mud? Have pity on your feet! Spit on the city gate instead and – turn around!

Here is hell for hermit's thoughts; here great thoughts are boiled alive and cooked till they are small.

Here all great feelings rot; here only tiny, rattlebone feelings are allowed to rattle!

Do you not already smell the slaughter houses and kitchens of the spirit? Does this town not steam with the reek of slaughtered spirit?

---

[2] "Mögen sie mich bemitleiden und bemitseufzen ob meiner Frostbeulen" – playful coinages such as *bemitseufzen*, of which there are several in TSZ, can often seem alienating and outrageous to readers of German, and clearly this was Nietzsche's intention. Though very difficult to translate, and frequently accompanied by internal rhyme, alliteration, and other lyrical devices, these vivacious puns and coinages nonetheless deserve an attempt on the translator's part.

Do you not see the souls hanging like limp dirty rags? – And they even make newspapers out of these rags!

Do you not hear how the spirit here turned into wordplay? It vomits dirty dish-word water! – And they even make newspapers out of this dirty dish-word water.

They hurry each other and know not where to. They heat each other up and know not why. They jingle with their tin, they jangle with their gold.

They are cold and they seek warmth in distilled liquors; they are overheated and seek coolness in frozen spirits; they are all sick and addicted to public opinion.

All lusting and malignancy are at home here; but here there are also virtuous types, there is much effective and affected virtue: –

Much effective virtue with scribble fingers and hard sit-and-wait flesh, blessed with little stars on their chests and padded fannyless daughters.

There is also much piety here and much devout spittle lick quaking and flatter cake baking before the God of Hosts.

'From on high' the star trickles down, and the merciful spittle; every starless chest meanwhile longs to get up high.

The moon has its farm, and the farm has its mooncalves; but the beggarly people and all effective beggarly virtue pray to everything that comes from the farm.

'I serve, you serve, we serve' – so begs all effective virtue to the prince, hoping that the deserved star will finally cling to the narrow chest!

But the moon still revolves around all that is earthly, and the prince too still revolves around what is most earthly – and that is the gold of the shopkeepers.

The God of Hosts is no God of gold bars; the prince proposes, but the shopkeeper – disposes!

By all that is bright and strong and good in you, oh Zarathustra, spit on this city of the shopkeepers and turn around!

Here all blood flows tainted and tepid and frothy decrepit through all veins; spit on the big city which is the big scum trap where all spumy crap spumes together!

Spit on this city of broken down souls and narrow chests, of prying eyes, of sticky fingers –

– on this city of the obtrusive, the insolent, the pencil- and roughnecks, the overheated and ambition eaten:

– where everything that is crumbly, corrupted, lusty, dusky, overly mushy and pussy festers together confederately: –

– spit on the big city and turn around!" –

At this point, however, Zarathustra interrupted the foaming fool and clapped his hand over the fool's mouth.

"Stop at last!" cried Zarathustra. "Your speech and your ways have nauseated me for a long time already!

Why have you lived so long near the swamp, that you yourself had to turn into a frog and a toad?

Doesn't tainted and frothy, decrepit swamp blood flow in your own veins now, since you have learned to croak and lambast this way?

Why didn't you go into the woods? Or plow the earth? Isn't the sea full of green islands?

I despise your despising; and if you warned me – why didn't you warn yourself?

Out of love alone shall my despising and my warning bird fly up: but not out of the swamp! –

They call you my ape, you foaming fool; but I call you my grunting swine – by grunting you will yet spoil my praise of folly.

What was it after all that made you start grunting? That no one *flattered* you enough – so you sat down to this garbage in order to have reason to grunt a lot –

– in order to have reason for a lot of *revenge*! Indeed, all your foaming is revenge, you vain fool; I guessed you well!

But your fool's words injure *me*, even where you are right! And if Zarathustra's words *were* right even a hundred times: you would always *do* wrong with my words!"

Thus spoke Zarathustra, and he looked at the big city, sighed, and kept silent for a long time. Finally he spoke thus:

"I am nauseated too by this big city and not only by this fool. Here as there nothing can be bettered, nothing can be worsened.

Woe to this big city! – And I wish I already saw the pillar of fire in which it will burn!

For such pillars of fire must precede the great noon. But this has its own time and its own destiny. –

Meanwhile, you fool, I give you this lesson in parting: where one can no longer love, there one should – *pass by*!" –

Thus spoke Zarathustra and he passed by the fool and the big city.

On Apostates

I

Alas, does everything lie wilted and grey that only recently stood green and colorful in this meadow? And how much honey of hope I carried from here to my beehives!

All these young hearts have already grown old – and not even old! Only weary, common, comfortable – as they put it: "We have become pious again."

Just recently I saw them set out by early morning on brave feet, but their feet of knowledge grew weary, and now they slander even their braveness of the morning!

Truly, many a one used to raise his legs like a dancer; the laughter in my wisdom beckoned to him – then he reconsidered. Just now I saw him crooked – and crawling to the cross.

Once they fluttered around light and freedom like gnats and young poets. A bit older, a bit colder, and already they monger rumors in the dark, thronging around the stove.

Did their hearts falter perhaps because solitude swallowed me like a whale? Did their ears listen perhaps longingly long *in vain* for me and my trumpet and herald calls?

Too bad! Those whose hearts have long courage and encourage mischief are always few; and in such the spirit too remains patient. But the rest are *cowardly*.

The rest: these are always the most by far, the day to day, the superfluous, the far-too-many – all of these are cowardly!

Whoever is of my kind also encounters my kind of experiences along the way, so that his first companions have to be corpses and jesters.

His second companions, however – they will call themselves his *believers*: a living swarm, much love, much folly, much beardless veneration.

Whoever is of my kind among human beings should not tie his heart to these believers; whoever knows capricious, cowardly humankind should not believe in these spring times and colorful meadows!

If they could do otherwise, then they would also *will* otherwise. Half-and-halfs spoil all that is whole. That leaves will wilt – what is to be lamented here!

Let them fly and fall, oh Zarathustra, and do not lament! Better yet blow among them with rustling wind –

– blow among these leaves, oh Zarathustra, so that everything *wilted* runs away from you even faster! –

2

"We have become pious again" – so these apostates confess, and some of them are still too cowardly to confess in this manner.

I look them in the eye – I tell them to their faces and to their blushing cheeks: You are the kind who *pray* again!

But it is a disgrace to pray! Not for everyone, but for you and me and whoever still has a conscience in his head. For *you* it is a disgrace to pray!

You know it well; your cowardly devil in you, who likes to fold his hands and lay his hands in his lap and wants to have it easier – this cowardly devil exhorts you: "There *is* a God!"

With that however you belong to the shade-loving variety who are never left in peace by light; now every day you must stick your head deeper into night and mist!

And truly, you chose the hour well, for just now the night birds are flying out. The hour has come for all shade-loving folk, the evening and commemoration hour when they do not "commemorate."

I hear and smell it: their hour came for the hunt and the procession, not for a wild hunt, to be sure, but for a tame, lame, snooping, up-buttering prayer muttering hunt –

– for a hunt for soulful mousy yes-men; all the heart's mousetraps have now been set again! And wherever I lift a curtain, a little night moth comes fluttering out.

Did it perhaps crouch there with another little night moth? For everywhere I smell little communities that have crept away; and where there are little rooms there are new Holy Joes in them and the reek of Holy Joes.

They sit long evenings together and say: "Let us become as little children again and say 'dear God'!" – their mouths and stomachs ruined by pious confectioners.

Or they watch long evenings the cunning lurking cross spider, which preaches cleverness to the spiders themselves and thus teaches: "There is good spinning among crosses!"

Or they sit the whole day with fishing rods at swamps and consider themselves *deep* for doing so; but whoever fishes where there are no fish – him I cannot even call superficial!

Or they learn piously, joyously to stroke the harp, from a writer of songs who would gladly harp his way into the hearts of little young women – having grown weary of the little old women and their praise.

Or they learn to shudder from a learned half-madman who waits in dark rooms for the spirits to come to him – and for the spirit to run away altogether!

Or they listen to an old wandering harebrained whistler, who learned the triste of tones from tristful winds; now he whistles after the wind and preaches triste in tristful tones.

And some of them have even become night watchmen; now they know how to blow into their horns and go around at night waking up old things that have long ago gone to sleep.

I heard five expressions of old things yesterday night at the garden wall – they came from such old, saddened, dried up night watchmen.

"For a father he doesn't care enough about his children: human fathers do this better!" –

"He is too old! He does not even care about his children at all anymore" – thus answered the other night watchman.

"Does he even have children? No one can prove it, if he himself doesn't prove it! I wish he would just go ahead and prove it properly for once."

"Prove it? As if *he* had ever proven anything! Proving is hard for him; he treasures instead that people have *faith* in him."

"Indeed! Indeed! Faith makes him blessed, faith in him. That's just the way of old people! That's how it is with us too!" –

– Thus the two old night watchmen and light chasers spoke to one another, and they tooted their horns sadly; so it was yesterday at the garden wall.

But my heart convulsed with laughter and wanted to break and did not know what next, and it sank into my diaphragm.

Indeed, this will be the death of me, that I choke from laughter when I see asses drunk and hear night watchmen doubting God's existence like this.

Has the time not *long* since past even for all such doubting? Who is allowed anymore to wake up such old, sleeping, shade-loving things!

It has been over for the old gods for a long time now – and truly, they had a good cheerful gods' end!

They did not "twilight" themselves to death – that is surely a lie! Instead, they just one day up and *laughed* themselves to death!

This happened when the most godless words were uttered by a god himself – the words: "There is one god. Thou shalt have no other god before me!" –

– an old grim-beard of a god, a jealous one forgot himself in this way:

And all the gods laughed then and rocked in their chairs and cried: "Is godliness not precisely that there are gods but no God?"

He who has ears to hear, let him hear. –

Thus spoke Zarathustra in the town that he loved and which is called The Motley Cow. From here he had only two more days to go to return to his cave and his animals, and his soul jubilated constantly at the nearness of his homecoming. –

The Homecoming

Oh solitude! Oh you my *home* solitude! I lived wild too long in wild foreign lands to not return to you with tears!

Now go ahead and threaten me with your finger, like mothers threaten; now smile at me, like mothers smile; now say to me: "And who was it that once stormed out on me like a storm wind? –

– who called out in leaving: 'too long have I sat with solitude, and I have forgotten how to keep silent!' *That* – you have learned now?

Oh Zarathustra, I know everything, and that you were *more forsaken* among the many, you solitary one, than ever with me!

Being forsaken is one thing, solitude is another: *that* – you have now learned! And that among human beings you will always be wild and foreign.

Wild and foreign even when they love you; for what they want above all is to be *spared*!

But here you are in your own home and house; here you can speak everything out and pour out all the reasons, nothing here is ashamed of obscure, obstinate feelings.

Here all things come caressingly to your rhetoric and they flatter you, for they want to ride on your back. Here you ride on every parable to every truth.

Here you may speak uprightly and forthrightly to all things, and truly, it rings like praise in their ears that someone talks straight with all things!

But being forsaken is another matter. For do you still recall, oh Zarathustra, when your bird called above you, when you stood in the woods, hesitating about which way to go, close to a corpse? –

When you spoke: 'May my animals guide me! I found it more dangerous among human beings than among animals' – *that* was forsaken!

And do you still recall, oh Zarathustra, when you sat on your island, a well of wine among empty buckets, giving and giving away, among the thirsty bestowing and flowing:

– until at last you alone sat thirsty among the drunk and lamented at night: 'is receiving not more blessed than giving? And stealing even more blessed than receiving?' – *That* was forsaken!

And do you still recall, oh Zarathustra, when your stillest hour came and drove you away from yourself, when with evil whispers it said: 'Speak and break!' –

– when it made you sorry for all your waiting and silence and discouraged your cautious courage: *that* was forsaken!" –

Oh solitude! You my home solitude! How blissfully and tenderly your voice speaks to me!

We do not implore one another, we do not deplore one another, we walk openly with one another through open doors.[3]

For at your house it is open and bright, and even the hours run here on lighter feet. In darkness, after all, time is heavier to bear than in the light.

Here all of being's words and word shrines burst open; here all being wants to become word, here all becoming wants to learn from me how to speak.

But down there – there all speaking is in vain! There forgetting and passing by are the best wisdom: *that* – I have now learned!

Whoever wanted to comprehend everything among human beings would have to apprehend everything. But for that my hands are too clean.

I cannot stand even to inhale their breath; too bad that I have lived so long among their noise and bad breath!

---

[3] "Wir gehen offen miteinander." Kaufmann misread *offen*, openly, as *oft* or *öfters*: "we often walk together."

Oh blissful silence around me! Oh clean fragrances around me ! Oh how this silence takes a deep clean breath! Oh how it listens, this blissful silence!

But down there – everyone talks there, everyone is ignored there. One could ring in his wisdom with bells, and the shopkeepers in the market place would jingle it out with pennies.

Everyone talks among them, no one knows any more how to understand. Everything falls in the water, nothing falls anymore into deep wells.

Everyone talks among them, nothing works out anymore and comes to an end. Everyone cackles, but who wants to sit still in the nest anymore and hatch eggs?

Everyone talks among them, everything gets talked to death. And whatever was still too hard yesterday for time itself and for its tooth, today it hangs scraped up and chewed up from the snouts of today's people.

Everyone talks among them, everything is betrayed. And what was once called secret and secrecy of deep souls, today it belongs to the street trumpeters and other butterflies.

Oh human nature, you strange thing! You noise in dark lanes! Now you lie behind me again – my greatest danger lies behind me!

In sparing and pitying my greatest danger always lay; and all human nature wants to be spared and pitied.

With concealed truths, with a fool's hand and a fooled, infatuated heart, rich in pity's petty lies – this is how I lived among human beings.

Disguised I sat among them, ready to misjudge *myself* in order to stand *them*, and gladly urging myself: "You fool, you do not know human beings!"

One forgets about human beings when one lives among human beings; there is too much foreground in all human beings – what use are far-sighted, far-seeking eyes *there*!

And when they misjudged me, I, fool, spared them more than myself, since I am accustomed to hardness, and often I even took revenge on myself for being so sparing.

Covered in bites by poisonous flies and hollowed out, like a stone, by many drops of malice, I sat among them and still I told myself: "Everything small is innocent of its smallness!"

Especially those who call themselves "the good," I found to be the most poisonous flies; they sting in all innocence, they lie in all innocence – how *could* they be just toward me!

Whoever lives among the good is taught by pity to lie. Pity fouls the air for all free souls. The stupidity of the good, after all, is unfathomable.

To conceal myself and my wealth – *that* is what I learned down there, for I found each of them poor in spirit. And it was the lie of my pitying that I knew with each one,

– that I saw and smelled with each one, what was *enough* spirit for him and what was already *too much*!

Their stiff wise men – I call them wise, not stiff – that is how I learned to swallow words. Their gravediggers – I called them researchers and testers – that is how I learned to switch words.

The gravediggers dig themselves diseases. Under ancient ruins rest noxious fumes. One should not stir up the morass. One should live on mountains.

With blissful nostrils I once again breathe mountain freedom! My nose is finally redeemed of the odor of all human nature!

Tickled by sharp breezes as if by sparkling wines, my soul *sneezes* – sneezes and jubilates to itself: *Gesundheit*!

Thus spoke Zarathustra.

On the Three Evils

1

In a dream, in the last dream of morning I stood today on a foothill – beyond the world, holding a scale, and I *weighed* the world.

But the dawn came too early, and glowed me awake, this jealous one! She is always jealous of my morning dream embers.

Measurable for the one who has time, weighable for a good weigher, flyable for strong wings, guessable for divine nut crackers: thus my dream found the world.

My dream, a daring sailor, half ship, half whirlwind, silent as butterflies, impatient as falcons: how did it have the patience and while today for world-weighing?

Did my wisdom perhaps encourage it, my laughing, waking day wisdom, which mocks all "infinite worlds"? For it says: "Where there is force, *number* will become the master: it has more force."

How certainly my dream looked upon this finite world, not inquisitively, not curiously, not incuriously, not fearfully, not beseechingly:

– as if a plump apple offered itself to my hand, a ripe golden apple, with cool soft velvety peel – thus the world offered itself to me:

– as if a tree waved to me, a broad-limbed, strong-willed tree, bent as a support and even as a footrest for the weary traveler: thus stood the world on my foothill:

– as if delicate hands carried a shrine toward me – a shrine open for the delight of bashful, venerating eyes: thus the world offered itself to me today:

– not riddle enough to chase away human love, not solution enough to lull human wisdom to sleep – a humanly good thing the world was for me today, of which so much evil is spoken!

How do I thank my morning dream for allowing me to weigh the world early this morning? As a humanly good thing it came to me, this dream and consoler of the heart!

And in order to do by day what it does, and to imitate it and learn its best, I now want to place the three most evil things on the scale and weigh them humanly well.

He that taught to bless here also taught to curse: what are the three best-cursed things in the world? These I want to place on the scale.

Sex, lust to rule, selfishness: these three have been cursed best and slandered and lied about most so far – these three I want to weigh humanly well.

Well then! Here is my foothill and there is the sea; *it* rolls up to me, shaggy, flattering, the faithful old hundred-headed behemoth hound that I love.

Well then! Here I want to hold the scale over rolling seas, and I also choose a witness to look on – you, you hermit tree, you strongly fragrant, broadly vaulted tree that I love!

On what bridge does the now get to the someday? By what compulsion does the high compel itself to the low? And what commands even the highest – to grow higher?

Now the scale stands balanced and still: three weighty questions I threw into it, three weighty answers are borne by the other pan.

2

Sex: the thorn and stake of all hair-shirted body despisers, and cursed as "world" among all hinterworldly, because it mocks and fools all teachers of muddle and mistakes.

Sex: the slow fire on which the rabble are burned, the ready rut and rolling boil oven of all wormy wood, all stinking rags.

Sex: innocent and free for free hearts, the garden happiness of earth, all the future's exuberant gratitude for the now.

Sex: a sweetish poison only for the wilted, but for the lion-willed a great fortifying of the heart, and the respectfully reserved wine of wines.

Sex: the great parable-happiness for higher happiness and highest hope. For to many marriage is promised and more than marriage –

– To many who are stranger to one another than man and woman – and who has ever completely grasped *how strange* man and woman are to one another!

Sex – but I want fences around my thoughts and around my words too, so that the pigs and the partiers do not break into my garden! –

Lust to rule: the searing scourge of the hardest of the hard hearted, the creepy torture that is reserved for the very cruelest person, the dark flame of living funeral pyres.

Lust to rule: the grim gadfly imposed on the vainest peoples, the mocker of all insecure virtue, the rider on every horse and every pride.

Lust to rule: the earthquake that breaks and breaks open everything rotten and hollow, the rolling, growling, punishing smasher of whitewashed tombs, the flashing question mark next to premature answers.

Lust to rule: before whose gaze human beings crawl and cower and drudge and become lower than snake and swine – until at last the great contempt cries out of them –

Lust to rule: the terrible teacher of the great contempt who preaches "away with you!" to the faces of cities and empires – until they themselves cry out "away with *me!*"

Lust to rule: which also ascends luringly to the pure and the solitary and into self-sufficient heights, glowing like a love that luringly paints purple bliss on earth's skies.

Lust to rule: but who would call it *lust* when the high longs downward for power! Indeed, there is nothing sick and addicted in such longing and descending!

That the solitary height not isolate and suffice itself eternally; that the mountain come to the valley and the winds of the height to the lowlands –

Oh who would find the right christening and glistening name for such longing! "Bestowing virtue" – thus Zarathustra once named the unnameable.

And it was then that it happened – indeed happened for the first time! – that his words pronounced *selfishness* blessed, the sound, healthy selfishness that wells from a powerful soul –

– from a powerful soul to which the high body belongs, the beautiful, triumphant, invigorating body, around which every manner of thing becomes mirror:

– the supple persuading body, the dancer whose parable and epitome is the self-joyous soul. Such self-joy of body and soul calls itself: "Virtue."

With its words of good and bad such self-joy shields itself as if with sacred groves; with the names of its happiness it banishes from itself everything contemptible.

From itself it banishes all that is cowardly, saying: "Bad – *that is cowardly!*" It considers contemptible those who always worry, sigh, complain, and whoever picks up even the smallest advantages.

It also despises all woe-wallowing wisdom, for indeed, there is also wisdom that blossoms in darkness, a night shadow wisdom that always sighs: "All is vain!"

It holds shy mistrust in low esteem, and everyone who wants oaths instead of gazes and hands; and all wisdom that is all too mistrustful – because this is the way of cowardly souls.

Even lower it esteems those quick to please, the dog-like who lie on their backs right away, the humble; and there is wisdom too that is humble and dog-like and pious and quick to please.

Utterly disgusting and despicable to it are those who never defend themselves, who swallow poisonous spittle and evil stares; the all too patient, all-enduring, all-complacent: for they are the servile kind.

Whether a person is servile before gods and gods' kicks, or before human beings and stupid human opinions: *all* servile kind it spits on, this blissful selfishness!

Bad: that is what it calls everything that is struck down, stingy and servile; fettered blinking eyes, oppressed hearts, and those false, yielding types who kiss with broad cowardly lips.

And pseudo-wisdom: that is what it calls everything that servants and old men and weary people witticize; and especially the whole nasty nitwitted, twitwitted foolishness of priests!

The pseudo-wise, however, all the priests, the world weary and whoever's souls are of the woman's and servant's kind – oh how their game has always played tricks on selfishness!

And precisely *that* was supposed to be virtue and be called virtue, that they played evil tricks on selfishness! And "selfless" – that is how they wished themselves, with good reason, all these world-weary cowards and cross spiders!

But for all of them now the day is coming, the transformation, the judgement sword, *the great noon*: then much shall be revealed!

And whoever pronounces the ego hale and holy and selfishness blessed, indeed, he tells what he knows, this foreteller: "*Look, it is coming, it is near, the great noon!*"

Thus spoke Zarathustra.

On the Spirit of Gravity

1

My mouth – is of the people: I speak too crudely and sincerely for Angora rabbits. And my words sound even stranger to all cephalopods and pen pushers.

My hand – is a fool's hand: watch out, all tables and walls, and whatever else has space for foolish trim and foolish whim!

My foot – is a cloven foot; with it I clip-clop and trot over sticks and stones, crissing and crossing the countryside, and devilish fun is my fast run.

My stomach – it must be the stomach of an eagle? Because what it loves best is flesh of lamb. Certain at least, it is the stomach of a bird.

Nourished by innocent things and by a little, ready and impatient to fly, to fly away – that is just my way: why should there not be something of the bird's way in this!

And especially since I am the enemy of the spirit of gravity, that is the bird's way; and truly, deadly enemy, arch-enemy, ancient enemy! Oh where has my enmity not already flown and flown astray!

Of that I could even sing a song – and I *want* to sing it; even though I am alone in my empty house and have to sing it to my own ears.

There are other singers, to be sure, for whom only for a full house softens the vocal chords, makes the hands eloquent, the eyes expressive, the heart alert – I am not like those.

2

Whoever one day teaches humans to fly, will have shifted all boundary stones; for him all boundary stones themselves will fly into the air, he will christen the earth anew – as "the light one."

The ostrich runs faster than the fastest horse, but it also sticks its head heavily into the heavy earth; so too the human being who cannot yet fly.

Heavy do earth and life seem to him; and the spirit of gravity *wants* it so! But whoever wants to become light and a bird must love himself – thus *I* teach.

Not, to be sure, with the love of the sick and addicted, because among them even self-love stinks!

One has to learn to love oneself – thus I teach – with a hale and healthy love, so that one can stand oneself and not have to roam around.

Such roaming around christens itself "love of the neighbor": these words so far have produced the best lying and hypocrisy, and especially from those whom all the world found heavy.

And truly, this is not a command for today and tomorrow, this *learning* to love oneself. Instead, of all arts this is the most subtle, cunning, ultimate and most patient.

For one's own, you see, all one's own is well hidden; and of all buried treasures, one's own is the latest to be dug up – this is the spirit of gravity's doing.

Almost from the cradle, grave words and values are imparted to us; "good" and "evil" this dowry calls itself. For its sake we are forgiven for being alive.

And for this reason one lets the little children come to one, in order to restrain them early on from loving themselves: this is the spirit of gravity's doing.

And we – we faithfully lug what is imparted to us on hard shoulders and over rough mountains! And if we sweat, then we are told: "Yes, life is a heavy burden!"

But only the human being is a heavy burden to himself! This is because he lugs too much that is foreign to him. Like a camel he kneels down and allows himself to be well burdened.

Especially the strong human being who is eager to bear and inherently reverent: too many *foreign* words and values he loads upon himself – now life seems a desert to him!

And true enough, much that is one's own is also a heavy burden! And much of what people are on the inside is like an oyster, namely disgusting and slimy and hard to grasp –

– so that a noble shell with noble ornamentation must intercede for it. But one must also learn this art: *to have* a shell and seemly sight and clever blindness!

Once more what is deceiving about people is that many a shell is meager and sad and too much a shell. Much hidden goodness and strength is never guessed; the most exquisite delicacies find no tasters!

Women know this, the most exquisite ones: a bit fatter, a bit thinner – oh how much destiny lies in so little!

The human being is hard to discover and hardest still for himself; often the spirit lies about the soul. This is the spirit of gravity's doing.

But he will have discovered himself who speaks: "This is *my* good and evil." With this he has silenced the mole and dwarf who says: "Good for all, evil for all."

Indeed, nor do I like those for whom each thing is good and this world seems the very best. Such types I call the all-complacent.

All-complacency that knows how to taste everything – that is not the best taste! I honor the obstinate, choosy tongues and stomachs, which have learned to say "I" and "Yes" and "No."

But chewing and digesting everything – that is truly the swine's style! To always say hee-yaw – only the ass learned that, and whoever is of its spirit! –

Deep yellow and hot red: this is what *my* taste wants – it mixes blood into all colors. But whoever whitewashes his house betrays to me a whitewashed soul.

One is in love with mummies, the other with ghosts; and both alike hostile to all flesh and blood – oh how they both offend my taste! For I love blood.

And I do not want to dwell and dawdle where everyone spits and spews: that is just *my* taste – I would rather live among thieves and perjurers. No one carries gold in their mouth.

But even more repugnant to me are all lick spittles; and the most revolting animal of a human being that I found I christened "parasite": it did not want to love and yet wanted to live off love.

Damned I call all those who have only one choice: to become evil beasts or evil beast tamers: I would not build my hut among them.

Damned I also call those who must always *wait* – they offend my taste: all the publicans and grocers and kings and other shop- and country-keepers.

Indeed, I too learned to wait, and thoroughly – but only to wait for *myself*. And above all I learned to stand and walk and run and leap and climb and dance.

But this is my teaching; whoever wants to fly someday must first learn to stand and walk and run and climb and dance – one cannot fly one's way to flight!

On rope ladders I learned to climb to many a window, with agile legs I climbed up high masts: to sit atop tall masts of knowledge struck me as no small bliss –

– to flicker like small flames atop tall masts; a small light, to be sure, and yet a great comfort for stranded sailors and shipwreck survivors!

By many a trail and manner I came to my truth; not on one ladder did I climb to my height, where my eye roams out into my distance.

And I never liked asking the way – that always offended my taste! I preferred to question and try the ways myself.

All my coming and going was a trying and questioning – and truly, one must also *learn* to answer such questioning! That, however – is my taste:

– not good, not bad, but *my* taste, of which I am no longer shameful nor secretive.

"This – it turns out – is *my* way – where is yours?" – That is how I answered those who asked me "the way." *The* way after all – it does not exist!

Thus spoke Zarathustra.

On Old and New Tablets

I

Here I sit and wait, old broken tablets around me and also new tablets only partially written upon. When will my hour come?

– the hour of my going down, going under: for I want to return to mankind once more.

This is what I wait for now; signs must come to me first that it is *my* hour – namely the laughing lion with a swarm of doves.

Meanwhile I talk to myself as one who has time. No one tells me anything new, and so I tell myself to myself.

2

When I came to mankind, I found them sitting on an old conceit: they all conceited to have known for a long time what is good and evil for humanity.

To them all talk of virtue seemed an old worn out thing; and whoever wanted to sleep well even spoke about "good" and "evil" before going to bed.

I disturbed this sleepiness when I taught: what is good and evil *no one knows yet* – except for the creator!

He, however, is the one who creates a goal for mankind and gives the earth its meaning and its future: This one first *creates* the possibility *that* something can be good and evil.

I told them to overthrow their old professorial chairs wherever that old conceit had sat; I told them to laugh at their great masters of virtue and their saints and poets and world redeemers.

I told them to laugh at their gloomy wise men and at any who ever perched in warning, like black scarecrows, in the tree of life.

I sat down alongside their great road of graves and even among carrion and vultures – and I laughed at all their yesteryear and its rotting, decaying glory.

Indeed, like preachers of repentance and fools I screamed bloody murder about all their great and small – that their best is so very small! that their most evil is so very small! – I had to laugh.

Thus my wild longing cried and laughed out of me, born in the mountains, a wild wisdom surely! – my great, winging, roaring longing.

And often it swept me off my feet and up and away, in the midst of my laughter, where I flew quivering, an arrow, through sun-drunken delight:

– off into distant futures not yet glimpsed in dreams, into hotter souths than any artist ever dreamed of; there, where dancing gods are ashamed of all clothing:

– so that I must speak in parables and limp and stutter like the poets; and truly, I am ashamed that I must still be a poet! –

Where all becoming seemed to me the dance of gods and the mischief of gods, and the world seemed unloosed and frolicsome and as though it were fleeing back to itself:

– as an eternal fleeing from and seeking each other again of many gods, as the blissful contradicting, again-hearing, again-nearing each other of many gods:

Where all time seemed to me a blissful mockery of moments, where necessity was freedom itself, which played blissfully with the sting of freedom:

Where I once again found my old devil and arch-enemy, the spirit of gravity, and everything he created: compulsion, statute, necessity and consequence and purpose and will and good and evil:

For must there not exist something *over* which one dances, dances away? Must not, for the sake of the light and the lightest – moles and heavy dwarves exist? –

3

It was there too that I picked up the word "overman" along the way, and that the human is something that must be overcome,

– that human being is a bridge and not an end; counting itself blessed for its noon and evening as the way to new dawns:

– the Zarathustra-words about the great noon, and whatever else I suspended above mankind like purple second sunsets.

Truly, I allowed them to see new stars together with new nights; and over clouds and day and night I even spread laughter like a colorful tent.

I taught them all *my* creating and striving: to carry together into one what is fragment in mankind and riddle and horrid accident –

– as poet, riddle guesser and redeemer of chance I taught them to work on the future, and to creatively redeem everything that *was*.

To redeem what is past in mankind and to recreate all "It was" until the will speaks: "But I wanted it so! I shall want it so –"

This I told them was redemption, this alone I taught them to call redemption. –

Now I wait for *my* redemption – so that I can go to them for the last time.

And I want to go to mankind one more time: *among* them I want to go under, dying I want to give them my richest gift!

I learned this from the sun when it goes down, the super-rich one: it pours gold into the sea from its inexhaustible wealth –

– such that even the poorest fisherman rows with *golden* oars! Because I saw this once and did not tire of my tears as I gazed on. –

Zarathustra too wants to go under like the sun; now he sits and waits, old broken tablets around him and also new tablets – partially written upon.

4

Look here, here is a new tablet, but where are my brothers to help me carry it to the valley and into hearts of flesh?

This is what my great love of the farthest demands: *do not spare your neighbor*! Human being is something that must be overcome.

There are manifold ways and means of overcoming: *you* see to it! But only a jester thinks: "human being can also be *leaped over*."

Overcome yourself even in your neighbor; and you should not let anyone give you a right that you can rob for yourself!

What you do no one can do to you in turn. Observe, there is no retribution.

Whoever cannot command himself should obey. And though many a person *can* command himself, much is still missing before he also obeys himself!

5

This is how souls of the noble kind would have it: they want nothing *for free*, and life least of all.

Whoever is of the rabble wants to live for free; we others, however, to whom life gave itself – we always reflect on *what* we can best give *in exchange*!

And truly, it is a noble phrase that says: "what life promises *us*, *we* want to keep – for life!"

One should not want to enjoy where one gives nothing to enjoy. And, one should not *want* to enjoy!

Enjoyment and innocence, you see, are the most bashful things: both do not want to be sought. One should *have* them – but one should sooner *seek* guilt and suffering! –

6

Oh my brothers, whoever is a firstborn is always sacrificed. But now we are the firstborns.

We all bleed on secret sacrificial altars; we all burn and broil in honor of old idols.

Our best is still young; that tempts old gums. Our flesh is tender, our hide is mere lambskin – how could we not tempt old idol priests!

Even in ourselves he still lives, the old idol priest, who roasts up our best for his banquet. Oh my brothers, how could firstborn not be sacrifices!

But our kind wants it so; and I love those who do not want to preserve themselves. Those who are going under I love with my whole love: because they are going over. –

7

To be true – this few *can* do! And whoever can, does not yet want to! But least of all the good can do it.

Oh these good! – *Good people never speak the truth*; for the spirit, being good in this manner is a disease.

They give way, these good, they give themselves up, their heart repeats words, their ground obeys; but whoever obeys, *he does not hear himself*!

Everything that the good call evil must come together, in order to give birth to one truth; oh my brothers, are you also evil enough for *this* truth?

Audacious daring, long mistrust, the cruel no, surfeit, the cutting into what is alive – how rarely *this* comes together! But from such semen – truth is begotten!

Side by side with bad conscience all *science* has grown so far. Break, break me these old tablets, you seekers of knowledge!

8

If timbers span the water, if footbridges and railings leap over the river, then surely the one who says "Everything is in flux" has no credibility.

Instead, even the dummies contradict him. "What?" say the dummies, "everything is supposed to be in flux? But the timbers and the railings are *over* the river!

Over the river everything is firm, all the values of things, the bridges, concepts, all 'good' and 'evil' – all of this is *firm!*" –

But when the hard winter comes, the beast tamer of rivers, then even the wittiest learn to mistrust, and, sure enough, then not only the dummies say: "Should everything not – *stand still?*"

"Basically everything stands still" – that is a real winter doctrine, a good thing for sterile times, a good comfort for hibernators and stove huggers.

"Basically everything stands still" – but *against this* preaches the thaw wind!

The thaw wind, a bull that is no plowing bull – a raging bull, a destroyer that breaks ice with its wrathful horns! But ice – *breaks footbridges!*

Yes my brothers, is everything not *now in flux?* Have all railings and footbridges not fallen into the water? Who could still *hang on* to "good" and "evil"?

"Woe to us! Hail to us! The thaw wind is blowing!" – Preach me this, oh my brothers, in all the streets!

9

There is an old delusion called good and evil. So far the wheel of this delusion has revolved around soothsayers and astrologers.

Once people *believed* in soothsayers and astrologers, and *therefore* they believed "Everything is fate: you should, because you must!"

Then later people mistrusted all soothsayers and astrologers, and *therefore* they believed "Everything is freedom: you can, because you want to!"

Yes, my brothers, so far we have merely deluded ourselves, but not known about the stars and the future, and *therefore* we have merely deluded ourselves, but not known about good and evil!

10

"Thou shalt not rob! Thou shalt not kill!" – such words were once held holy; before them one bent the knee, bowed the head and removed one's shoes.

But I ask you: where in the world have there ever been better robbers and killers than such holy words?

Is there not in all life itself – robbing and killing? And for such words to have been called holy, was *truth* itself not – killed?

Or was it a sermon of death that pronounced holy what contradicted and contravened all life? – Yes my brothers, break, break me the old tablets!

11

This is my pity for everything past, that I see it is abandoned –

– abandoned to the favor, the spirit, the madness of each generation that comes along, and interprets everything that was as the bridge to itself!

A great despot could come along, a shrewd monster, who with his favor and disfavor could force and forge the whole past, until it became a bridge to him, and omen and herald and harbinger.

But this is the other danger and my other pity: whoever is of the rabble, their remembrance goes no further back than their grandfather – and with their grandfather time ends.

Thus all the past is abandoned; because it could happen one day that the rabble would become ruler and in its shallow water all time would drown.

Therefore, my brothers, we need a *new nobility*, which is the adversary of all rabble and all despotic rule and which writes anew the word "noble" on new tablets.

Many noble ones are needed, to be sure, and many kinds of noble ones *for nobility to exist*! Or, as I once spoke in parables: "Precisely that is godliness, that there are gods but no God!"

12

Oh my brothers, I consecrate and conduct you to a new nobility: you shall be my begetters and growers and sowers of the future –

– to be sure, not to a nobility that you could buy like the shopkeepers and with shopkeepers' gold, for everything that has a price has little value.

Not where you come from shall constitute your honor from now on, but instead where you are going! Your will and your foot, which wants to go over and beyond yourself – let that constitute your new honor!

Certainly not that you served a prince – what do princes matter anymore! Or that you became a bulwark for what stands, to make it to stand more firmly!

Not that your kinfolk became courtiers at court, and learned to stand long hours like a colorful flamingo in shallow ponds.

– For *being able* to stand is a merit among courtiers; and all courtiers believe that part of blessedness after death is – *being allowed* to sit!

Nor that a spirit they called holy led your forefathers to promised lands, which *I* do not praise; because where the worst of all trees grew, the cross – there is nothing to praise about that land!

And truly, wherever this "holy ghost" led its knights, in such crusades goats and geese and pious crisscrossing contradictors ran *in front*!

Oh my brothers, your nobility should not look back, but *out there*! You should be exiles from all father- and forefatherlands!

You should love your *children's land*; let this love be your new nobility – the undiscovered land in the furthest sea! For that land I command your sails to seek and seek!

You should *make it up* in your children that you are the children of your fathers; *thus* you should redeem all that is past! This new tablet I place above you!

13

"Why live? All is vain! Life – that is threshing straw; life – that is burning oneself and yet not getting warm."

Such archaic babble still passes for "wisdom"; but it is honored more highly *because* it smells old and musty. Even mustiness ennobles.

Children might speak like this: they *fear* fire because it burned them! There is much childishness in the old books of wisdom.

And whoever is always "threshing straw," why should he be allowed to revile threshing? One really should muzzle such oxen!

Such people sit down at the table and bring nothing along, not even a good appetite – and now they revile saying "All is vain!"

But eating and drinking well, my brothers, is really no vain art! Break, break me the tablets of the never-glad!

14

"To the clean all is clean" – that is what folks say. But I say to you: "to swine all becomes swine!"

This is why the rapturous and the head-hangers, whose hearts also hang down, preach: "The world itself is a filthy monster."

Because they are all unclean in spirit, especially those who have neither rest nor respite, unless they see the world *from the hinter side* – these hinterworldlings!

To their faces I say, even if it does not sound kind: the world resembles a human being in that it has a behind – *that much* is true!

There is much filth in the world: *that much* is true! But the world itself is not therefore a filthy monster!

There is wisdom in the fact that much in the world smells foul: nausea itself creates wings and water-divining powers!

Even in the best there is something that nauseates; and the best is still something that must be overcome!

Yes my brothers, there is much wisdom in the fact that there is much filth in the world! –

15

Such sayings I heard the pious hinterworldlings speak to their conscience, and truly, without malice and falseness – even though there is nothing more false in the world, nor more malicious.

"Just let the world be the world! Do not lift so much as a finger against it!"

"If someone wants to strangle and stab and slice and dice the people, let him; do not lift so much as a finger against it! That way they will yet learn to renounce the world."

"And your own reason – this you yourself should smother and strangle, because it is a reason of this world – that way you yourself will learn to renounce the world." –

– Break, break me these old tablets of the pious, my brothers! Gainsay me the sayings of the world slanderers!

16

"Whoever learns much, he forgets all vehement desire" – today this is whispered throughout all dark lanes.

"Wisdom makes weary, nothing is worth it; thou shalt not desire!" – this new tablet I found hanging even in the open markets.

Break, my brothers, break me this *new* tablet too! The world-weary hung it there and the preachers of death, and the jailers as well; just look, it too is a sermon for slavery!

The reason they have such ruined stomachs is because they learned badly and not what was best, and everything too early and everything too fast; and they *ate* badly –

– you see, their spirit is a ruined stomach: *it* recommends death! Because truly, my brothers, the spirit *is* a stomach!

Life is a well of joy; but for those out of whom the ruined stomach speaks, the father of gloom, all wells are poisoned.

Knowing: that is *joy* to the lion-willed! But whoever has grown weary is himself merely being "willed," and all waves toss him around.

And so it always is with weak willed persons; they lose themselves along the way. And finally their own weariness asks: "Why did we ever embark on ways! It's all the same!"

To their ears it is music when they hear preached: "Nothing is worth it! You shall not will!" But this is a sermon for slavery.

Yes my brothers, as a fresh roaring wind Zarathustra comes to all who are weary of their way; many noses he will yet make sneeze!

My free breath also blows through walls, and down into prisons and imprisoned spirits!

Willing liberates because willing is creating: thus I teach. And you should learn *only* for creating!

And even this learning you shall first *learn* from me, namely learning-well! – He who has ears to hear, let him hear!

17

There sits the skiff – over there perhaps is the entryway to the great nothing. But who wants to board this "perhaps"?

None of you wants to board the death skiff! Then why do you want to be *world-weary*!

World-weary! And you have not even become earth-alienated yet! I found you still lusting for the earth, still in love with your own earthly weariness!

Not for nothing does your lip hang – a little earthly wish still sits on it! And in your eye – doesn't a little cloud of unforgotten earthly joy float there?

There are many good inventions on earth, some useful, others pleasant, for whose sake the earth is lovable.

And some of what is there has been invented so well that it is like a woman's breasts: useful and pleasant at the same time.

But you world-weary! You earth-lazy! You should be flogged with switches! With floggings you should be made to step lively again.

After all, if you are not misfits and moribund wretches of whom the earth is weary, then you are sly sloths or nibbling, creeping pleasure cats. And if you do not want to *run* again with gusto, then you should – pass away!

One should not try to be a physician for the incurable: thus Zarathustra teaches – and so you should pass away!

But it takes more *courage* to make an end than to make a new verse: that all physicians and poets know.

18

Oh my brothers, there are tablets created by weariness, and tablets created by rotten laziness; even though they talk the same, still they want to be heard differently.

See this languishing specimen here! He is merely one span away from his goal, but out of weariness he has laid himself defiantly here in the dust – this valiant man!

Out of weariness he yawns at the road and the earth and the goal and himself; not one more step will he take – this valiant one!

Now the sun burns on him and the dogs lick at his sweat; but he lies there in his defiance and would rather die of thirst –

– die of thirst one span away from his goal! Truly, you will yet have to drag him to his heaven by the hair – this hero!

Better still, just let him lie where he has laid himself so that sleep can come to him, the comforter, with its cooling rushing rain:

Let him lie until he awakens on his own – until he renounces all weariness on his own and whatever weariness taught through him!

Only, my brothers, chase the dogs away from him, the lazy creepers and the whole raving rout –

– the whole raving rout of "the educated" that *feasts* on the sweat of every hero!

19

I draw circles around me and sacred borders; ever fewer climb with me on ever higher mountains – I build a range of mountains out of ever more sacred mountains.

But wherever you may climb with me, my brothers, see to it that a *parasite* does not climb with you!

Parasite: that is a worm, a crawling writhing worm that wants to glut itself on your infected nicks and niches.

And *its* art consists in guessing where climbing souls are weary; in your grief and dismay, in your tender modesty it builds its disgusting nest.

Where the strong is weak, the noble one all too mild – in that place it builds its disgusting nest; the parasite lives where the great person has little nicks and niches.

What is the highest species of all being and what is the least? The parasite is the least of species, but whoever is of the highest species nourishes the most parasites.

After all, the soul that has the longest ladder and reaches down farthest – how could it not have the most parasites clinging to it?

The most encompassing soul, which can run and stray and roam farthest within itself; the most necessary soul, which out of joy plunges itself into chance –

– the soul that loves being, but submerges into becoming; the having soul that *wants* to rise to willing and desiring –

– the soul that flees itself and catches up to itself in the widest circle; the wisest soul which folly persuades most sweetly –

– the one that loves itself most, in which all things have their current and recurrent and ebb and flow – indeed, how could *the highest soul* not have the worst parasites?

20

Oh my brothers, am I perhaps cruel? But I say: if something is falling, one should also give it a push!

Everything of today – it is falling, it is failing: who would want to stop it! But I – I *want* to push it too!

Do you know the kind of lust that rolls stones down into steep depths? – These people of today; just look at how they roll into my depths!

I am a prelude of better players, my brothers! An exemplary play! *Act* according to my example!

And whomever you cannot teach to fly, him you should teach – *to fall faster*!

21

I love the valiant, but it is not enough to be a fierce combatant – one must also know *whom* to combat!

And often there is more valiance in someone controlling himself and passing by, *so that* he saves himself for the worthier enemy!

You should have only those enemies whom you hate, but not enemies to despise; you must be proud of your enemy: this I taught you already once before.

For the worthier enemy, my friends, you should save yourselves, and therefore you must pass by much –

– especially pass by much rabble that thunders in your ears about folk and peoples.

Keep your eye clear of their pros and cons! There is much justice, much injustice here; whoever watches becomes angry.

Look around, beat them down – it's all the same here; therefore go away into the woods and lay your swords to sleep!

Go *your* ways! And let folk and peoples go theirs! – dark ways, to be sure, on which not a single hope flashes anymore!

Let the shopkeeper rule where all that is left to glitter – is shopkeepers' gold! The time of kings is no more; what calls itself a people today deserves no kings.

Just look at how these peoples themselves do the same as the shop-keepers; they pluck themselves the tiniest advantage from any dustpan!

They lie in wait for one another, they look in hate at one another – this they call "good neighbors." Oh happy distant time when a people said to themselves: "I want to be *ruler* over peoples!"

For the best should rule, my brothers, and the best also *want to* rule! And wherever the teaching says differently, there – the best are *missing*.

22

If *they* had bread for free, oh no! What would *they* clamor for! Their sustainment – that is their real entertainment, and they should have it hard!

They are beasts of prey: in their "working" – preying is there too; in their "earning" – outwitting is there too! Therefore they should have it hard!

They should become better beasts of prey, more subtle, more clever, *more human-like*: the human being, after all, is the best beast of prey.

Human beings have already successfully preyed upon the virtues of all animals; this is because human beings have had the hardest time of all animals.

Only the birds are above him. And if human beings were to learn even to fly, watch out! *How high* – would his lust to prey fly!

23

This is how I want man and woman: fit for war the one, fit for bearing children the other, but both fit to dance in head and limb.

And let each day be a loss to us on which we did not dance once! And let each truth be false to us which was not greeted by one laugh!

24

In taking your wedding vows – see to it that you are not making your *bedding vows*. Vowing too quickly *results* in – breaking vows! And better vow breaking than vow bending and vow pretending! A woman once said to me: "Sure, I broke my wedding vows, but first my wedding vows broke – me!"

The worst of the vengeful I always found to be the mismatched couples: they take it out on the whole world that they are no longer singles.

This is why I want honest people to speak honestly to one another: "We love each other; let us *see to it* that we keep loving each other! Or did we promise by mistake?"

– "Give us a trial period and a small marriage, so that we can see whether we are fit for a big marriage! It is a big thing to always be in twos!"

Thus I counsel all honest people; and what then would my love for the overman be, and for everything else that is to come, if I counseled and conveyed otherwise!

Not merely to reproduce, but instead to *sur*produce – to that goal, my brothers, may the garden of marriage help you!

25

Whoever has become wise about ancient origins will surely, in the end, seek new wells of the future and new origins.

Yes my brothers, it will not be overly long and *new peoples* will originate and new wells will roar down into new depths.

An earthquake, after all – it buries many wells, it causes much dying of thirst: it also brings to light inner powers and secrets.

An earthquake reveals new wells. In an earthquake of ancient peoples new wells break out.

And whoever cries out there: "Look, here is a fountain for many who thirst, a heart for many who long, a will for many tools" – around him gathers a *people*, that is: many who try.

Who can command, who must obey – *here it is tried*! Indeed, with what long searching and guessing and lack of success and learning and trying again!

Human society: it is an experiment, this I teach – a long search: but it searches for the commander! –

– an experiment, oh my brothers! And *not* a "contract!" Break, break me such words of the soft hearted and half-and-halfs!

26

My brothers! In whom does the greatest danger lie for all of future humanity? Is it not in the good and the just?

– is it not in those who speak and feel in their hearts: "We already know what is good and just, and we have it too; woe to any who still search here!"

And whatever harm the evil may do, the harm of the good is the most harmful harm!

And whatever harm the world slanderers may do, the harm of the good is the most harmful harm!

My brothers, there was a man who once looked into the hearts of the good and the just, and he spoke: "They are pharisees." But he was not understood.

The good and the just themselves were not permitted to understand him: their spirit is imprisoned in their good conscience. The stupidity of the good is unfathomably clever.

But this is the truth: the good *must* be pharisees – they have no choice!

The good *must* crucify the one who invents his own virtue! This *is* the truth!

The second one, however, who discovered their land, the land, hearts and soil of the good and just: he was the one who asked: "Whom do they hate the most?"

The *creator* they hate the most; he who breaks tablets and old values, the breaker – him they call the lawbreaker.

Because the good, you see – they *can* not create: they are always the beginning of the end –

– they crucify the one who writes new values on new tablets, they sacrifice the future to *themselves* – they crucify all future humanity!

The good – they were always the beginning of the end. –

27

Oh my brothers, have you even understood these words? And what I once said about the "last human being?" –

In whom does the greatest danger lie for all of future humanity? Is it not in the good and the just?

Break, break me the good and the just! – Oh my brothers, have you even understood these words?

28

You flee from me? You are frightened? You tremble before these words?

My brothers, when I told you to break the good and the tablets of the good, then for the first time I launched mankind onto their high seas.

And only now the great fright comes to them, the great looking-around oneself, the great sickness, the great nausea, the great seasickness.

False coasts and false securities were taught you by the good; in the lies of the good you were born and bielded. Everything has been duplicitous and twisted from the ground up by the good.

But whoever discovered the land "human being" also discovered the land "human future." Now you will be seafarers, brave and patient!

Walk upright for once, my brothers, learn to walk upright! The sea is stormy: Many want to right themselves again on you.

The sea is stormy: Everything is in the sea. Well then! Well now! You old salts!

What fatherland! *There* our helm wants to steer, where our *children's land* is! Out there, stormier than the sea, storms our great longing! –

29

"Why so hard!" – the kitchen coal once said to the diamond. "Are we not close relatives?"

Why so soft? Oh my brothers, this *I* ask you: for are you not – my brothers?

Why so soft, so retiring and yielding? Why is there so much denying and denial in your hearts? And so little destiny in your gazes?

And if you do not want to be destinies and inexorable, how could you triumph with me?

And if your hardness does not want to flash and undo and cut through, how could you one day create with me?

The creators are hard after all. And it must seem like bliss to you to press your hand upon millennia as if upon wax –

– bliss to write upon the will of millennia as if upon bronze – harder than bronze, more noble than bronze. Only the most noble is perfectly hard.

This new tablet, my brothers, I place above you: *become hard*! –

30

Oh you my will! You turning point of all need, you point of *my* necessity! Preserve me from all small victories!

You ordaining of my soul, that I call destiny! You in-me, over-me! Preserve and save me for a great destiny!

And your ultimate greatness, my will, save that for your ultimate – that you be inexorable *in* your victory! Indeed, who was not defeated in his victory!

Indeed, whose eye did not darken in this drunken twilight! Indeed, whose foot did not stagger and forget how to stand in victory!

– That I may one day be ready and ripe in the great noon; ready and ripe like glowing bronze, clouds pregnant with lightning and swelling udders of milk –

– ready for myself and for my most hidden will; a bow burning for its arrow, an arrow burning for its star –

– a star ready and ripe in its noon, glowing, skewered, blissful with annihilating arrows of the sun –

– a sun itself and an inexorable will of the sun, ready for annihilating in victory!

Oh will, turning point of all need, you *my* point of necessity! Save me for a great victory! –

Thus spoke Zarathustra.

The Convalescent

I

One morning not long after his return to his cave, Zarathustra sprang from his bed like a madman, screamed with a terrifying voice and behaved as though someone else were lying on his bed, who did not want to get up. And Zarathustra's voice reverberated so much that his animals rushed to him frightened, and from every cave and hiding place neighboring on Zarathustra's cave, all the animals scurried away – flying, fluttering, crawling, leaping in whatever manner of foot or feather they were given. But Zarathustra said these words:

Up, abysmal thought, out of my depths! I am your rooster and dawn, you sleepy worm: up! Up! My voice will yet crow you awake!

Unsnap the straps of your ears: listen! Because I want to hear you! Up! Up! Here there is thunder enough to make even graves learn to listen!

And wipe the sleep and all that befogs and blinds you from your eyes! Hear me with your eyes too: my voice is a remedy even for those born blind.

And once you are awake, you shall remain awake eternally. It is not *my* manner to wake great-grandmothers from their sleep only to tell them – go back to sleep!

You stir, you stretch, you gasp? Up! Up! No gasping – you will speak to me! Zarathustra summons you, the godless one!

I, Zarathustra, the advocate of life, the advocate of suffering, the advocate of the circle – you I summon, my most abysmal thought!

Hail to me! You are coming – I hear you! My abyss *speaks*, I have unfolded my ultimate depth to the light!

Hail to me! Here now! Give me your hand – ha! Let go! Haha! – Nausea, nausea, nausea – oh no!

2

Scarcely had he spoken these words, however, when Zarathustra collapsed like a dead man and long remained as if dead. But when he came to he was pale and he trembled, still lying down, and for a long time he wanted neither to eat nor drink. This behavior lasted seven days; meanwhile, his animals did not leave his side day and night, unless the eagle flew out to fetch food. And whatever prey it fetched together it laid on Zarathustra's bed until eventually Zarathustra lay among yellow and red berries, grapes, red apples, aromatic herbs and pine cones. At his feet, however, two lambs were spread out, which the eagle with difficulty had taken as prey from their shepherds.

Finally, after seven days, Zarathustra sat up on his bed, picked up one of the red apples, smelled it, and found its aroma lovely. Then his animals believed the time had come to speak with him.

"Oh Zarathustra," they said. "Now you have been lying like this for seven days, with heavy eyes: do you not want at last to get on your feet?

Step out of your cave: the world awaits you like a garden. The wind is playing with heady fragrances that make their way to you; and all brooks want to run after you.

All things long for you, while you have stayed alone for seven days – step out of your cave! All things want to be your physician!

Did perhaps some new knowledge come to you, something sour, heavy? You lay there like leavened dough, your soul rose up and swelled over all its rims. –"

– "Oh my animals," answered Zarathustra. "Just keep babbling and let me listen! It invigorates me so when you babble: where there is babbling the world indeed lies before me like a garden.

How lovely it is that there are words and sounds; aren't words and sounds rainbows and illusory bridges between things eternally separated?

To each soul belongs another world; for each soul every other soul is a hinterworld.

Illusion tells its loveliest lies about the things that are most similar, because the tiniest gap is hardest to bridge.

For me – how would there be something outside me? There is no outside! But we forget this with all sounds; how lovely it is that we forget!

Have names and sounds not been bestowed on things so that human beings can invigorate themselves on things? It is a beautiful folly, speaking: with it humans dance over all things.

How lovely is all talking and all lying of sounds! With sounds our love dances on colorful rainbows." –

– "Oh Zarathustra," said the animals then. "To those who think as we do, all things themselves approach dancing; they come and reach out their hands and laugh and retreat – and come back.

Everything goes, everything comes back; the wheel of being rolls eternally. Everything dies, everything blossoms again, the year of being runs eternally.

Everything breaks, everything is joined anew; the same house of being builds itself eternally. Everything parts, everything greets itself again; the ring of being remains loyal to itself eternally.

In every Instant being begins; around every Here rolls the ball There. The middle is everywhere. Crooked is the path of eternity." –

– "Oh you foolish rascals and barrel organs!" answered Zarathustra, smiling again. "How well you know what had to come true in seven days –

– and how that monster crawled into my throat and choked me! But I bit off its head and spat it away from me.

And you – you have already made a hurdy-gurdy song of it? Now I lie here, weary still from this biting and spitting out, sick still from my own redemption.

And you looked on at all of this? Oh my animals, are you also cruel? Did you want to watch my great pain the way people do? For human beings are the cruelest animal.

Tragic plays, bullfights and crucifixions have always made them feel best on earth; and when they invented hell for themselves, see here – it was their heaven on earth.

When a great human being cries out – in a flash the little ones come running, and their tongues hang out with lasciviousness. But they call it their 'pity.'

The little human being, especially the poet – how eagerly he puts his accusations against life into words! Hear him, but do not fail to hear the lust that is in all his accusing!

Such accusers of life are overcome by life in a blink of an eye. 'You love me?' says the flirt. 'Wait just a while longer, I don't have time for you yet.'

The human being is the cruelest animal against itself; and with all those who call themselves 'sinner' and 'cross bearer' and 'penitent,' do not fail to hear the lust in such complaining and accusing!

And I myself – do I want therefore to be the accuser of mankind? Oh my animals, this alone have I learned so far, that for mankind their most evil is necessary for their best –

– that whatever is most evil is their best *power* and the hardest stone for the highest creator; and that mankind must become better *and* more evil –

The cross on which I suffered was not that I know human beings are evil – instead, I cried as no one yet has cried:

'A shame that their most evil is so very small! A shame that their best is so very small!'

My great surfeit of human beings – *that* choked me and crawled into my throat; and what the soothsayer said: 'All is the same, nothing is worth it, knowledge chokes.'

A long twilight limped ahead of me, a tired to death and drunk to death sadness that spoke with a yawning mouth:

'Eternally he returns, the human of whom you are weary, the small human being' – thus my sadness yawned and dragged its foot and could not fall asleep.

For me the human earth transformed into a cave, its chest caved in; everything living became human mold and bones and crumbling past.

My sighing sat upon all human graves and could no longer stand up; my sighing and questioning croaked and choked and gnashed and lashed day and night:

– 'alas, human beings recur eternally! The small human beings recur eternally!' –

Naked I once saw them both, the greatest human and the smallest human: all too similar to one another – all too human still even the greatest one!

All too small the greatest one! That was my surfeit of humans! And eternal recurrence of even the smallest! – That was my surfeit of all existence!

Oh nausea! Nausea! Nausea!" – Thus spoke Zarathustra and sighed and shuddered, because he remembered his sickness. But his animals did not allow him to continue.

"Speak no more, you convalescent!" – answered his animals. "Rather go outside where the world awaits you like a garden.

Go outside to the roses and bees and swarms of doves! Especially to the song birds, so that you can learn *to sing* from them!

Singing after all is for convalescents, let the healthy person talk. And even if the healthy person also wants songs, he wants different songs than the convalescent."

– "Oh you foolish rascals and barrel organs, shut up!" – answered Zarathustra, and he smiled at his animals. "How well you know which comfort I invented for myself in seven days!

That I must sing once again – *this* comfort I invented for myself and *this* convalescence; but do you want to make that into a hurdy-gurdy song right away too?"

– "Speak no more," answered his animals again. "Instead, you convalescent, fashion yourself a lyre first, a new lyre!

Behold oh Zarathustra! For your new songs new lyres are needed.

Sing and foam over, Zarathustra; heal your soul with new songs so that you can bear your great destiny, which was never before a human's destiny!

For your animals know well, oh Zarathustra, who you are and must become; behold, *you are the teacher of the eternal recurrence* – that now is *your* destiny!

That you must teach this teaching as the first – how could this great destiny not also be your greatest danger and sickness!

Behold, we know what you teach: that all things recur eternally and we ourselves along with them, and that we have already been here times eternal and all things along with us.

You teach that there is a great year of becoming, a monster of a great year; like an hourglass it must turn itself over anew, again and again, so that it runs down and runs out anew –

– so that all these years are the same as each other, in what is greatest and also in what is smallest – so that we ourselves in every great year are the same, in what is greatest and also in what is smallest.

And if you wanted to die now, oh Zarathustra: behold, we know too how you would speak to yourself then: – but your animals beg you not to die yet!

You would speak and without trembling, rather taking a deep breath, blissfully; for a great weight and oppressiveness would be taken from you, you most patient one!

'Now I die and disappear,' you would say, 'and in an instant I will be a nothing. Souls are as mortal as bodies.

But the knot of causes in which I am entangled recurs – it will create me again! I myself belong to the causes of the eternal recurrence.

I will return, with this sun, with this earth, with this eagle, with this snake – *not* to a new life or a better life or a similar life:

– I will return to this same and selfsame life, in what is greatest as well as in what is smallest, to once again teach the eternal recurrence of all things –

– to once again speak the word about the great earth of noon and human beings, to once again proclaim the overman to mankind.

I spoke my word, I break under my word: thus my eternal fate wills it – as proclaimer I perish!

The hour has now come for the one who goes under to bless himself. Thus – *ends* Zarathustra's going under!'" –

When the animals had spoken these words they fell silent and waited for Zarathustra to say something to them: but Zarathustra did not hear that they were silent. Instead he lay still, with eyes closed, like someone sleeping – even though he was not sleeping. Indeed, at this moment he was conversing with his soul. The snake and the eagle, however, finding him silent in this manner, honored the great stillness around him and cautiously slipped away.

On Great Longing

Oh my soul, I taught you to say "today" and "once" and "formerly," and to dance your round over all here and then and there.

Oh my soul, I redeemed you from all nooks, I swept dust, spiders and twilight off of you.

Oh my soul, I washed the petty bashfulness and the nook-virtue from you and persuaded you to stand naked before the eyes of the sun.

With the storm called "spirit" I blew over your choppy sea; I blew all clouds away, I even choked the choker who is called "sin."

Oh my soul, I gave you the right to say no like the storm and to say yes as the open sky says yes: still as light you now stand and even if you pass through storms of denial.

Oh my soul, I gave you back your freedom over what is created and uncreated: and who knows as you know the lust of future things?

Oh my soul, I taught you contempt that does not come like a gnawing worm, the great, loving contempt that loves most where it has the most contempt.

Oh my soul, I taught you to persuade such that you persuade even the grounds; like the sun that persuades even the sea into its heights.

Oh my soul, I took from you all obeying, knee-bending and sir-saying; I myself gave you the name "turning point of need" and "destiny."

Oh my soul, I gave you new names and colorful playthings, I called you "destiny" and "compass of compasses" and "umbilical cord of time" and "azure bell."

Oh my soul, to your soil I gave all wisdom to drink, all new wines and also all old strong wines of wisdom from time immemorial.

Oh my soul, I poured every sun upon you and every night and every silence and every longing – then you grew up for me like a grapevine.

Oh my soul, super-rich and heavy you stand there now, a grapevine with swelling udders and crowded, brownish gold grapes –

– crowded and crushed by your happiness, waiting out of superabundance and even bashful because of your waiting.

Oh my soul, nowhere now is there a soul that could be more loving and more compassing and encompassing! Where would future and past be closer together than in you?

Oh my soul, I gave you everything and all my hands have become empty on you – and now! Now you say to me smiling and full of melancholy: "Who of us is supposed to be thankful?

– does the giver not have to give thanks that the receiver received? Is bestowing not a bare necessity? Is receiving not – mercy?"

Oh my soul, I understand the smiling of your melancholy: your super-richness itself reaches out with longing hands!

Your fullness gazes out over roaring seas and searches and waits; the longing of over-fullness gazes smilingly from your sky-like eyes!

And truly, oh my soul! Who could see your smile and not melt into tears! The angels themselves melt into tears at the super-goodness of your smile.

It is your goodness and super-goodness that do not want to lament and weep; and yet, oh my soul, your smile longs for tears and your trembling mouth for sobs.

"Is not all weeping a lamentation? And is not all lamentation an accusation?" This is how you speak to yourself, and this is why, oh my soul, you would rather smile than pour out your suffering –

– pour out your suffering in gushing tears over your fullness and over all the aching of the grapevine for the vintner and his knife!

But if you do not want to weep and weep out your purple melancholy, then you must *sing*, oh my soul! – Look, I too smile for telling you this in advance:

– sing with a roaring song until all seas become silent, to listen for your longing –

– until the skiff floats over silent longing seas, the golden wonder around whose gold all good and bad and wonderful things hop –

– even many great and small animals and everything that has light, wondrous feet, and can run on paths of violet blue –

– over to the golden wonder, the voluntary skiff and to its master: but he is the vintner who waits with his diamond knife –

– your great redeemer, oh my soul, the nameless one – for whom only future songs will find a name! And truly, your breath is fragrant already with future songs! –

– already you glow and dream, already you drink thirstily at all deep, resounding wells of comfort, already your melancholy rests in the bliss of future songs! –

Oh my soul, now I have given you everything and even my ultimate, and all my hands have become empty on you: – *that I commanded you to sing*, indeed, that was my ultimate!

That I commanded you to sing – speak now, speak: *who* of us now must be thankful? – Better yet: sing to me, sing oh my soul! And let me give thanks! –

Thus spoke Zarathustra.

The Other Dance Song

1

Into your eyes I looked recently, oh life: I saw gold gleaming in your night eyes – my heart skipped a beat at this thrill:

– I saw a golden boat gleaming on nocturnal waters, a sinking, drinking, winking golden rocking boat!

You cast a glance at my foot, at my dance-drunken foot; a laughing, asking, melting rocking glance:

Two times only your little hands shook their maracas – and already my dance-drunk foot began to rock. –

I kicked up my heels, my toes fairly strained to hear you disclose: after all, a dancer has ears in his toes!

I leaped over to you; you dodged my advance, retreating deftly; and only the licking, fleeing, trailing tongues of your hair were left me!

I leaped away from your hair's lurid snaking; and there you stood, half facing me, your eyes afire with aching.

Your crooked gazes teach me – crooked running; on crooked paths my foot learns – crooked cunning!

I fear you up close, and I love you away; your leaving spells me, your seeking compels me – I suffer, but suffer gladly for you any day!

You whose coldness ignites, whose hate is alluring; whose fleeing invites, whose scorn is – stirring:

– who would not hate you, you great binder, and winder, temptress, attemptress, and finder! Who would not love you, you innocent, ardent one, wind-bride and child-eyed sinner!

Where are you pulling me now, you standout and upstart? And now you flee me again, sweet wildcat, thankless heart!

I dance after you, and follow your trail using any clue. Where are you? Give me your hand! Even a finger will do!

Here are caves and thickets, we could get lost in there! – Stop! Stand still! Do you not see owls and bats in the air?

You owls! You bats! This leaves you in stitches? Where are we? Such howling and yelping you learned from the bitches.

You gnash at me sweetly with little white teeth; your curly little mane, evil eyes peeking out from beneath!

This is a dance moving every which way; I am the hunter – are you my hound or my prey?

Next to me now! And quick, you evil little jumper! Up now! And over! – Oh no! I slipped and now I'm on my rump here!

Oh see me lying, miss mischief, have mercy on me! There are paths to sweet places – where I would rather be!

– Paths of love through silent blooming plants! Or down there along the lake, where goldfish swim and dance!

Are you weary now? Over there are sheep and sunset-swoons; is it not sweet to sleep when shepherds play their tunes?

Are you so bitter weary! I will carry you there, just relax and let your arms sink! And if you thirst – I have something, but nothing you would drink! –

– Oh this cursed clever, supple snake and slippery witch! Gone without a trace? But left behind, and left by hand, I feel two red spots on my face!

I am truly tired of always playing your sheepish shepherd pal! You witch, if I have so far sung for you, now *you* for me will – yell!

To the beat of my whip you will dance so and yell so! But did I forget the whip? – Oh no! –

2

Then life answered me like this and covered her dainty little ears:

"Oh Zarathustra! Please do not crack your whip so fearfully! Surely you know: noise murders thoughts – and just now the most tender thoughts are coming to me.

We are both a couple of real do-no-goods and do-no-evils. Beyond good and evil we found our island and our green meadow – we two alone! Therefore we at least have to like each other!

And just because we do not love each other from the heart – must we grudge one another for not loving each other from the heart?

That I like you, and often too much, this you know; and the reason is that I am jealous of your wisdom. Ah, this crazy old fool of a wisdom!

If your wisdom ever ran away from you, oh! Then my love would also quickly run away from you too." –

Then life looked pensively behind her and around her and said softly: "Oh Zarathustra, you are not faithful enough for me!

You do not love me nearly as much as you say; I know you are thinking of leaving me soon.

There is an old heavy, heavy growling bell: it growls at night all the way up to your cave –

– when you hear this bell toll the hour at midnight, then you think between one and twelve about –

– you think, oh Zarathustra, I know it, about how you will soon leave me!" –

"Yes," I answered, hesitating. "But you also know –" And I said something in her ear, right in it between her tangled yellow, foolish shaggy locks.

"You *know* that, oh Zarathustra? No one knows that." –

And we looked at each other and gazed at the green meadow, over which the cool evening had just spread, and we wept together. – But at that moment I loved life more than I ever loved all my wisdom. –

Thus spoke Zarathustra.

3

One!

Oh mankind, pray!

Two!

What does deep midnight have to say?

Three!

"From sleep, from sleep –

Four!

From deepest dream I made my way –

Five!

The world is deep,

Six!

And deeper than the grasp of day.

Seven!

Deep is its pain –,

Eight!

Joy – deeper still than misery:

Nine!

Pain says: refrain!

Ten!

Yet all joy wants eternity –,

Eleven!

– wants deep, wants deep eternity!"

Twelve!

The Seven Seals (Or: the Yes and Amen Song)

1

If I am a soothsayer and full of that soothsaying spirit that hikes on a high pass between two seas –

hikes between the past and the future as a heavy cloud – the enemy of oppressive lowlands and everything that is weary and can neither die nor live:

ready in its dark bosom for lightning and for the redeeming ray of light, pregnant with lightning bolts that say Yes! and laugh Yes! to soothsaying bolts of lightning –

– but blessed is the one who is pregnant like this! And truly, whoever will one day kindle the light of the future must hang long on the mountain like a heavy storm! –

oh how then could I not lust for eternity and for the nuptial ring of rings – the ring of recurrence!

Never yet have I found the woman from whom I wanted children, unless it were this woman whom I love: for I love you, oh eternity!

For I love you, oh eternity!

2

If my wrath ever broke open graves, moved boundary stones and rolled old broken tablets down into steep depths:

If my scorn ever blew apart moldy words, and I came upon the cross spiders like a broom, and as a sweeping wind to old musty burial chambers:

If I ever sat jubilating where old gods lie buried, blessing the world, loving the world next to the monuments of ancient world maligners –

– because I love even churches and God's graves once the sky's pure eye gazes through their broken roofs; gladly do I sit like grass and red poppies on broken churches –

Oh how then could I not lust for eternity and for the nuptial ring of rings – the ring of recurrence!

Never yet have I found the woman from whom I wanted children, unless it were this woman whom I love: for I love you, oh eternity!

For I love you, oh eternity!

3

If ever a breath came to me of creative breath and of that heavenly necessity that forces even accidents to dance astral rounds:

If ever I laughed with the laugh of creative lightning that follows rumbling but obediently the long thunder of the deed:

If ever I rolled dice with gods at the gods' table of the earth, so that the earth quaked and ruptured and snorted up rivers of fire –

– because the earth is a gods' table, and it trembles with creative new words and gods' throws –

Oh how then could I not lust for eternity and for the nuptial ring of rings – the ring of recurrence!

Never yet have I found the woman from whom I wanted children, unless it were this woman whom I love: for I love you, oh eternity!

For I love you, oh eternity!

4

If ever I drank my fill from that foaming mug of mixed spices, in which all good things are mixed:

If my hand ever poured the farthest to the closest and fire to spirit and joy to sorrow and the most wicked to the kindest:

If I myself am a grain of that redeeming salt that makes all things in the mixing mug mix well –

– because there is a salt that binds good with evil; and even what is most evil is worthy as a spice and for the final foaming over –

Oh how then could I not lust for eternity and for the nuptial ring of rings – the ring of recurrence!

Never yet have I found the woman from whom I wanted children, unless it were this woman whom I love: for I love you, oh eternity!

For I love you, oh eternity!

5

If I favor the sea and everything that is of the sea, and even favor it most when it angrily contradicts me:

If ever that joy of searching is in me that drives sails toward the undiscovered, if a seafarer's joy is in my joy:

If ever my jubilating cried: "The coast disappeared – now the last chain has fallen from me –

– infinity roars around me, way out there space and time glitter, well then, what of it old heart!" –

Oh how then could I not lust for eternity and for the nuptial ring of rings – the ring of recurrence!

Never yet have I found the woman from whom I wanted children, unless it were this woman whom I love: for I love you, oh eternity!

For I love you, oh eternity!

6

If my virtue is a dancer's virtue and I often leaped with both feet into golden emerald delight:

If my malice is a laughing malice, at home beneath rosy slopes and lily hedges:

– for in laughter everything evil is together, but pronounced holy and absolved by its own bliss:

And if that is my alpha and omega, that all heaviness becomes light, all body dancer, all spirit bird – and truly, that is my alpha and omega! –

Oh how then could I not lust for eternity and for the nuptial ring of rings – the ring of recurrence!

Never yet have I found the woman from whom I wanted children, unless it were this woman whom I love: for I love you, oh eternity!

For I love you, oh eternity!

7

If ever I spread silent skies above me and flew into my own sky with my own wings:

If I playfully swam in deep expanses of light, and my freedom's bird-wisdom came –

– but bird-wisdom speaks like this: "See, there is no up, no down! Throw yourself around, out, back you light one! Sing! Speak no more!

– are not all words made for the heavy? Do not all words lie to the light? Sing! Speak no more!" –

Oh how then could I not lust for eternity and for the nuptial ring of rings – the ring of recurrence!

Never yet have I found the woman from whom I wanted children, unless it were this woman whom I love: for I love you, oh eternity!

For I love you, oh eternity!

Fourth and Final Part

Oh, where in the world has greater folly occurred than among the pitying? And what in the world causes more suffering than the folly of the pitying?

Woe to all lovers who do not yet have an elevation that is above their pitying!

Thus the devil once spoke to me: "Even God has his hell: it is his love for mankind."

And recently I heard him say these words: "God is dead; God died of pity for mankind."

Zarathustra, "On the Pitying" (II, p. 69).

The Honey Sacrifice

– And again moons and years passed over Zarathustra's soul and he took no notice of it; but his hair had turned white. One day as he sat on a stone before his cave and gazed outward – there where one looks out upon the sea and beyond twisting abysses – his animals walked around him pensively until finally they stood before him.

"Oh Zarathustra," they said. "Are you perhaps on the lookout for your happiness?" – "What does happiness matter!" he answered. "I haven't strived for happiness for a long time, I strive for my work." – "Oh Zarathustra," said the animals again. "You say that as one who has had overly much of the good. Do you not lie in a sky-blue lake of happiness?" – "You foolish rascals," answered Zarathustra, smiling. "How well you chose your metaphor! But you also know that my happiness is heavy and not like a fluid wave of water; it presses me and will not leave me alone and it acts like melted tar." –

Then the animals again walked around him pensively and once more they stood before him. "Oh Zarathustra," they said, "is *that* why you yourself are becoming ever yellower and darker, even though your hair looks white and flaxen? Don't you see, you are bogged down in your misfortune!" – "What are you saying, my animals?" said Zarathustra, and he laughed. "Truly, I smeared when I used the word tar. What's happening to me is common to all fruits that ripen. It's the *honey* in my veins that makes my blood thicker and also makes my soul calmer." – "It will be as you say, oh Zarathustra," answered the animals, and they pressed up against him. "But do you not want to climb a high mountain today? The air is pure and today one sees more of the world than ever before." – "Yes, my animals," he answered. "Your advice is superb and after my own heart: I do want to climb a high mountain today! But see to it that there is honey at hand for me there; yellow, white, good, icy fresh golden honey from the comb. Because know this: I want to offer the honey sacrifice up there." –

But when Zarathustra was up on the summit he sent home the animals which had accompanied him, and he found that he was alone now – then he laughed with his whole heart, looked around and spoke thus:

That I spoke of sacrifices and honey sacrifices was merely a sleight of speech and, truly, a useful folly! Up here I may speak more freely than before hermits' caves and hermits' pets.

What sacrifice! I squander what was bestowed me, I the squanderer with a thousand hands: How could I call that – sacrificing!

And when I desired honey I merely desired bait and sweet ooze and mucus, for which even growling bears and odd, surly, evil birds lick with their tongues:

– the best bait, as it is needed by hunters and fishermen. Because if the world is like a dark jungle and a pleasure garden for all wild hunters, to me it seems even more, and preferably, an abysmal rich sea,

– a sea full of colorful fishes and crabs, for whose sake even gods would crave to become fishermen and net casters: so rich is the world in odd things great and small!

Especially the human world, the human sea – toward *it* I now cast my golden fishing rod and say: open up, you human abyss!

Open up and toss me your fishes and glittering crabs! With my best bait today I bait the oddest human fishes!

– my very happiness I cast far and wide, between sunrise, noon and sunset, to see if many human fishes learn to jiggle and wiggle on my happiness.

Until, biting on my sharp hidden hooks, they have to emerge into *my* height, the motliest gorge gudgeons to the most spiteful of all fishers of human fish.

That's what I am, after all, at bottom and from the start; reeling, reeling in, raising up, raising, a raiser, a cultivator and taskmaster who not for nothing once told himself: "Become who you are!"

So now human beings may come *up* to me; you see, I am still waiting for the sign that it is time for my descent; I myself will not go under yet, as I must, and among human beings.

That's why I'm waiting here, cunning and mocking on high mountains, not impatient, not patient, but instead one who has forgotten even forbearance – because he no longer "bears."

My destiny leaves me time for this: surely it has forgotten me? Or does it sit behind a big rock in the shade, catching flies?

And really, I like my eternal destiny for not rushing and pressing me and for leaving me time for jests and spite, so that today I climbed this high mountain to catch fish.

Did a human being ever catch fish on high mountains? And even if what I want and do up here is folly, this is still better than becoming pompous and green and gold down there from waiting –

– a swaggering wrath snorter from waiting, a holy, howling mountain storm, an impatient one who cries down into the valleys: "Hear me, or I shall whip you with the lash of God!"

Not that I would grudge such angry men for it; they are good enough for me to laugh at! They have to be impatient anyway, these big noisy drums, who either get to speak today or never!

But I and my destiny – we do not speak to today, nor do we speak to never: we have patience enough and time and overtime for speaking. Because it must come someday and may not pass by.

What must come someday and may not pass by? Our great *Hazar*, that is our great distant human empire, the Zarathustra empire of a thousand years –

How distant might such a "distance" be? What do I care! But it is no less firm to me on that account – with both feet I stand firmly on this ground,

– on an eternal ground, on hard primeval rock, on this highest, hardest primeval mountain chain, to which all winds come as if to a weathershed, asking Where? and from Where? and Where to?

Laugh, laugh here my bright hearty spite! Throw down your glittering, mocking laughter from high mountains! Bait me the most beautiful human fish with your glittering!

And whatever in all the seas belongs to *me*, my actual me in all things – fish *that* out for me, bring *that* up to me – that's what I am waiting for, I the most spiteful of all fishermen.

Out, out my fishing rod! Into and down, bait of my happiness! Drip your sweetest dew, my heart's honey! Bite, my fishing rod, into the belly of all black gloom!

Out there, out there my eye! Oh how many seas surround me, what dawning human futures! And above me – what rosy red stillness! What cloudless silence!

The Cry of Distress

The next day Zarathustra again sat on the stone before his cave, while the animals roamed about in the world to bring home new nourishment – and new honey too, because Zarathustra had spent and squandered the old honey to the last drop. But as he sat there like this, with a stick in his hand and tracing the outline of his shadow on the ground, reflecting and, truly, not about himself and his shadow – then all at once he was frightened and startled, because next to his own shadow he saw another shadow. And as he quickly looked around and stood up, there was the soothsayer standing next to him, the same one whom he had wined and dined at his table, the proclaimer of the great weariness who taught: "All is the same, nothing is worth it, the world is without meaning, knowledge chokes." But his face had transformed in the meantime; and when Zarathustra looked him in the eyes, his heart was frightened again – so many grave proclamations and ashen gray lightning bolts animated this face.

The soothsayer, who read what was going on in Zarathustra's soul, wiped his hand over his face as if he wanted to wipe it away; Zarathustra did the same. And when both had silently composed and strengthened themselves in this manner, they shook hands as a sign that they wanted to recognize one another.

"Welcome," said Zarathustra, "you soothsayer of the great weariness; not for nothing were you once a guest at my table. Eat and drink with me today too, and forgive that a contented old man joins you at the table!" "A contented old man?" answered the soothsayer, shaking his head. "Whoever you are or want to be, oh Zarathustra, you've been that long enough up here – in a short time your skiff will no longer be on the rocks!" – "Am I on the rocks then?" asked Zarathustra, laughing. – "The waves around your mountain," answered the soothsayer, "rise and rise; the waves of great distress and gloom: soon they will lift your skiff as well and carry you away." – Zarathustra was silent on hearing this and surprised. – "Do you not hear anything yet?" continued the soothsayer. "Is there not a rushing and roaring up from the depths?" – Zarathustra kept silent and listened; then he heard a long, long cry that the abysses threw back and forth to each other, as if none wanted to keep it – so evil did it sound.

"You wicked proclaimer," spoke Zarathustra at last. "That's a cry of distress and the cry of a human being, even if it comes out of a black sea. But what is human distress to me! My final sin, the one saved up for me – do you know what it's called?"

– "*Pity!*" answered the soothsayer from his overflowing heart, and he raised both hands high – "oh Zarathustra, I come to seduce you to your last sin!" –

And scarcely had these words been spoken when the cry rang out again, and longer and more anxious than before, also much closer now. "Do you hear? Do you hear, oh Zarathustra?" cried the soothsayer. "The cry is meant for you, it calls you: come, come, come, it is time, it is high time!" –

Zarathustra was silent after this, confused and shaken; finally he asked, like one who hesitates inwardly: "And who is it there that calls me?"

"But you know it already," answered the soothsayer vehemently. "Why do you conceal yourself? It is *the higher man* who calls for you!"

"The higher man?" cried Zarathustra, seized by horror. "What does *he* want? What does *he* want? The higher man! What does he want here?" – And his skin was bathed in sweat.

But the soothsayer did not respond to Zarathustra's fear, and instead he listened and listened toward the depths. But after it was quiet there for a long time, he turned his glance back and saw Zarathustra standing and trembling.

"Oh Zarathustra," he began with a sad voice. "You do not stand there like one whose happiness makes him giddy: you will have to dance to keep from falling down!

But even if you were to dance before me and leap all your side-leaps, no one should be allowed to tell me: 'Look, here dances the last gay human being!'

Anyone who came to this height looking for *him* would come in vain; caves he would find, to be sure, and hinter-caves, hiding places for hiders, but no shafts of happiness and treasure chambers and new golden veins of happiness.

Happiness – how could anyone find happiness among those who are buried away and hermits? Must I seek the last happiness far away on blessed isles between forgotten seas?

But all is the same, nothing is worth it, searching does not help, and there are no blessed isles anymore!" –

Thus sighed the soothsayer; but at his last sigh Zarathustra became bright and certain once more, like someone who comes from a deep chasm into the light. "No! No! No! Three times no!" he cried in a strong voice, stroking his beard. "*That* I know better! There are still blessed isles! Be silent *about that*, you sighing sadsack!

Stop splashing *about that*, you rain cloud of the morning! Do I not already stand here soaked by your gloom and drenched like a dog?

Now I'll shake myself and run away from you, so that I can dry off again; that shouldn't surprise you! Do I seem discourteous to you? But this is *my* court.

But as far as your higher man is concerned: let's go! I'll search for him right now in those woods – *from there* his cry came. Perhaps he is beset by some evil beast.

He is in *my* territory, and in here he shall not come to harm! And truly, there are many evil beasts in my territory." –

With these words Zarathustra turned to leave. Then the soothsayer spoke: "Oh Zarathustra, you are a rogue!

I already know that you want to get rid of me! You would rather run into the woods and pursue evil beasts!

But what will it help you? By evening you will have me again anyway, I will be sitting in your own cave, patient and heavy like a block – and I will be waiting for you!"

"So be it!" called Zarathustra over his shoulder as he departed. "And whatever is mine in my cave, it belongs to you too, my guest!

But if you should find honey in there, good! Then just lick it up, you old growling bear, and sweeten your soul! Because by evening we will both want to be in a good mood,

– in a good mood and glad that this day came to an end! And you yourself will dance to my songs as my dancing bear.

You don't believe it? You shake your head? Well then! We'll see, old bear! But I too am – a soothsayer."

Thus spoke Zarathustra.

Conversation with the Kings

I

Zarathustra had been underway in his mountains and woods for not even one hour when all at once he saw a strange procession. On precisely the path he wanted to take down, two kings came walking, adorned with crowns and purple sashes and as colorful as flamingoes; before them they drove a burdened ass. "What do these kings want in my kingdom?" spoke Zarathustra to his astonished heart, and he hid himself quickly behind a bush. But when the kings caught up to him he said, half out loud like a person talking to himself: "Strange! Strange! What rhyme or reason can this have? I see two kings – and only one ass!"

Then the two kings stopped, smiled, looked toward the place from which the voice had come and then turned to face one another. "Such things are also thought among us," said the king to the right, "but one does not speak it."

But the king to the left shrugged his shoulders and answered: "It's probably a goatherd. Or a hermit who has lived too long among cliffs and trees. After all, no society at all also ruins good manners."

"Good manners?" retorted the other king indignantly and bitterly. "Then what are we trying to run away from? Is it not 'good manners'? Is it not our 'good society?'

Better, truly, to live among hermits and goatherds than live with our gilded, fake, make-up wearing rabble – even if it calls itself 'good society,'

– even if it calls itself 'nobility.' But there everything is fake and foul, starting with the blood, thanks to old diseases and even worse healers.

Best and dearest to me today is still a healthy peasant, coarse, cunning, stubborn, enduring: that is the most noble type today.

The peasant today is the best; and peasant-type should be ruler! But it is the kingdom of the rabble – I will not be deceived anymore. Rabble now, that means: mishmash.

Rabble mishmash: in it everything is jumbled together, saint and scoundrel and Junker and Jew and every beast from the ark of Noah.

Good manners! Everything among us is fake and foul. No one knows how to revere anymore – *that* precisely is what we are running away from. They are mawkish, obtrusive dogs, they are gilders of palm leaves.

This nausea chokes me, that we kings ourselves became fake, decked out and dressed up in old yellowed grandfathers' pomp, medals for the most moronic and the slyest and whoever the hell haggles today for power!

We *are not* the first – and yet we must *signify* that we are: it is this deception that we have finally had enough of, that nauseates us.

We got away from the riffraff, all these screamers and scribble-blowflies, all the shopkeeper stench, all the twitching ambition, all the bad breath – phooey to living among the riffraff,

– phooey to signifying the first among the riffraff! Oh nausea! Nausea! Nausea! What do we kings matter anymore!" –

"Your old illness befalls you again," said now the king on the left. "Nausea befalls you, my poor brother. But you know too that someone is listening to us."

At once Zarathustra, whose ears and eyes had opened wide at this conversation, rose from his hiding place, approached the kings and began:

"The one who listens to you, who listens gladly to you, you kings, is called Zarathustra.

I am Zarathustra, who once spoke: 'What do kings matter anymore!' Forgive me, I was so pleased when you said to one another: 'What do we kings matter!'

But here is *my* realm and my rule: what might you be seeking now in my realm? Or perhaps you have *found* along the way what *I* am seeking, namely the higher man."

When the kings heard this they beat their breasts and exclaimed with one voice: "We have been found out!

With the sword of your words you strike through our hearts' thickest darkness. You discover our distress, for behold! We are on our way to find the higher man –

– the man who is higher than we, even though we are kings. To him we lead this ass. The highest man, you see, should be the highest ruler on earth.

There is no harder misfortune in all human destiny than when the powerful of the earth are not also the first human beings. Then everything becomes fake and crooked and monstrous.

And should they even be last and more beast than human; then the rabble rises and rises in price, until finally even rabble virtue speaks: 'Behold, I alone am virtue!'" –

"What did I just hear?" answered Zarathustra. "What wisdom among kings! I am delighted, and truly, I'm already in the mood to make a rhyme of it: –

– even if it turns out to be a rhyme that is not suitable for everyone's ears. Long ago I gave up being considerate of long ears. Well then! Well now!

(But here it happened that the ass too got in a word; and clearly and malevolently he said hee-yaw.)

Once – I think in anno domini one –

The Sybil said, drunk, though wine she'd had none:

'Oh no, how badly things go!

Decline! Decline! The world has sunk so low!
Rome sank to whore and to a whorehouse too,
Rome's Caesar to beast, God himself – turned Jew!'"

2

The kings were enchanted by these rhymes of Zarathustra, but the king to the right spoke: "Oh Zarathustra, how well we did in going forth to see you!

For your enemies showed us your image in their mirror: there you were with your devil's grimace and laughing scornfully, such that we were afraid of you.

But what good did it do? Again and again you pricked our ears and hearts with your sayings, then we said at last: what does it matter how he looks!

We have to *hear* him, the one who teaches 'you shall love peace as a means to new wars, and the short peace more than the long one!'[1]

No one has ever spoken such warlike words: 'What is good? Being brave is good. The good war hallows any cause.'

---

[1] The frequent quotes of Zarathustra throughout Part IV are not verbatim but close enough to indicate that Zarathustra's words have caught on and are being interpreted with varying degrees of success. Parts I and II appeared in 1883, Part III was written later in 1883 and early 1884, and published in 1884 – it was intended as the final part of TSZ. Part IV was originally planned as a separate work under the title "Noon and Eternity," but Nietzsche found no publisher for it, and decided instead to make it the fourth part of TSZ and to publish it at his own expense. Part IV appeared in only 40 copies in 1885, and was distributed to friends only. In 1886 the first edition of TSZ Parts I–III appeared; the complete work in four parts did not appear until 1892. When Nietzsche boasts in *Ecce Homo* (*Kritische Studienausgabe* VI:341) that he needed no more than ten days to finish each part of TSZ, the information is misleading if we do not also consider his method of composition. The ten-day periods do not refer to the idea and its execution in the various parables, speeches, frame narratives, characters etc, i.e. each part did not take ten days from start to finish. This can be illustrated by the fact that the final aphorism of *The Gay Science*, as well as notes from the period, already deal with Zarathustra. Instead, Nietzsche constantly worked out various drafts related to the basic Zarathustra idea, often even during his long walks, and these he copied into larger notebooks at home. When he sat down to compose one of the parts of TSZ, it then took him approximately ten days to structure his already existing material into its finished literary form (see *Kritische Studienausgabe* XIV: 280-2). When Nietzsche speaks in *Ecce Homo* of his phenomenal inspiration, and how ideas simply flooded over and through him ("I never had a choice," *Kritische Studienausgabe* VI:339), this should not be taken to mean that he experienced four ten-day periods of Zarathustra inspiration. Nietzsche, Jung, Kaufmann all appear to have contributed to this myth. Part IV differs structurally from the earlier parts but also in tone; it represents a very sober "revisiting" of the original work, a retreat from the teaching and preaching, includes several "dithyrambs" later revised and added to the *Dionysus Dithyrambs*, and displays a narrow scope of interaction with only "higher men." Notably it takes place entirely on Zarathustra's mountain.

Oh Zarathustra, our fathers' blood stirred in our bodies at the sound of such words; it was like the speech of springtime to old casks of wine.

When swords ran every which way like red-stained snakes, our fathers warmed to life; the sun of all peace seemed limp and lackluster to them, but the long peace caused them shame.

How they sighed, our fathers, when they saw gleaming bright, dried up swords on the wall! Like them, they thirsted for war. For a sword wants to drink blood and sparkles with desire." –

– As the kings talked in this manner and gabbed enthusiastically about the happiness of their fathers, Zarathustra was overcome by no small desire to mock their enthusiasm; after all, these were visibly very peaceful kings he saw standing before him, the kind with old and refined faces. But he restrained himself. "Well then!" he said. "The path leads there, Zarathustra's cave lies there, and this day shall also have a long evening! But now a cry of distress hurries me away from you.

It will honor my cave if kings want to sit and wait in it, but, to be sure, you will have to wait long!

Alright! What's the harm? Where does one learn to wait better today than at court? And the whole virtue of kings that is left to them – is it not today called: *being able* to wait?"

Thus spoke Zarathustra.

The Leech

And Zarathustra walked on pensively, farther and deeper through woods and past swampy valleys; but as happens to anyone who reflects on grave matters, he unintentionally stepped on someone. And behold, all at once he was sprayed in the face with one scream of pain and two curses and twenty wicked invectives, such that in his fright he raised his staff and also started beating the man he had just stepped on. Immediately thereupon he gained his composure, and his heart laughed at the folly that he had just committed.

"Forgive me," he said to the man he had stepped on, who stood up grimly and then sat down. "Forgive and partake, above all, in a parable first.

Of how a wanderer who is dreaming of distant things unintentionally stumbles over a sleeping dog on a lonely lane, a dog lying in the sun:

– how both startle then, and attack each other like deathly enemies, these two who are scared to death: so it went with us too.

And yet! And yet – how little was missing and they would have caressed each other, this dog and this lonely man! Are they not after all both – lonely!"

– "Whoever you may be," said the stepped on man, still grimly, "you step on my dignity with your parable too, and not only with your foot!

See here, am I some kind of dog?" – and then the sitting man got up and pulled his bare arm out of the swamp. Because at first he had lain stretched out on the ground, hidden and unrecognizable like those who lie in wait for swamp quarry.

"But what in blazes are you doing!" cried Zarathustra, shocked. For he saw that much blood was flowing over the man's bare arm. "You wretch, did some wicked beast bite you?"

The bleeding man laughed, but still angrily. "What concern is it of yours!" he said, and made to leave. "Here I am at home and in my territory. Anyone who wants may question me, but I will hardly answer a stumbling fool."

"You are mistaken," said Zarathustra, with pity, and he held on to him. "You are mistaken: here you are not in your home, but in my realm, and in here no one comes to harm.

Meanwhile call me whatever you want – I am who I must be. I call myself Zarathustra.

Well then! Up there is the path to Zarathustra's cave; it isn't far – wouldn't you like to care for your wounds at my place?

Things have gone badly for you in this life, you wretch; first you were bitten by the beasts, and then – you were stepped on by a human being!" –

But when the stepped on man heard the name of Zarathustra, he transformed. "What is happening to me!" he cried out. "*Who* concerns me anymore in this life other than this one person, namely Zarathustra, and that one animal that lives off blood, the leech?

For the leech's sake I lay here at this swamp like a fisher, and already my outstretched arm had been bitten ten times, then an even more beautiful leech bites on my blood, Zarathustra himself!

Oh happiness! Oh miracle! Praised be the day that lured me to this swamp! Praised be the best, liveliest cupping glass living today, praised be the great conscience-leech Zarathustra!" –

Thus spoke the stepped on man; and Zarathustra was pleased at his words and their fine, respectful manner. "Who are you?" he said, and offered him his hand. "Between us there is much to clear up and to cheer up; but already it seems to me the day is growing pure and bright."

"I am *the conscientious of spirit*," answered the man, "and in matters of the spirit one can hardly be more rigorous, vigorous and venomous than I, except the one from whom I learned it, Zarathustra himself.

Rather know nothing, than know much half way! Rather be a fool in one's own right than a wise man according to strangers. I – go to the ground of things:

– what does it matter whether it is big or small? Whether it is called swamp or sky? A hand's breadth of ground is enough for me, if only it is real ground and bottom!

– a hand's breadth of ground: on that one can stand. In proper science and conscience there is nothing great and nothing small."

"So perhaps you are the expert on the leech?" asked Zarathustra. "And you pursue the leech down to its ultimate grounds, you conscientious one?"

"Oh Zarathustra," answered the stepped on man. "That would be a monstrous undertaking, how could I presume to such a thing!

What I am master and expert of, however, is the leech's *brain* – that is *my* world!

And it is a world too! But forgive me that my pride speaks up here, for in this matter I have no equal. That is why I said 'here I am at home.'

How long already have I pursued this one thing, the brain of the leech, so that the slippery truth no longer slips away from me here? Here is *my* realm!

– this is why I threw away everything else, this is why all else is the same to me; and right next to my knowledge my black ignorance lurks.

My conscience of spirit wants of me that I know one thing and do not know everything else; I am nauseated by all halfness of spirit, all hazy, soaring, rapturous people.

Where my honesty ceases I am blind and also want to be blind. But where I want to know, I also want to be honest, namely venomous, rigorous, vigorous, cruel and inexorable.

That *you* once said, oh Zarathustra: 'Spirit is the life that itself cuts into life,' that induced and seduced me to your teaching. And truly, with my own blood I increased my own knowledge!"

– "And it shows too," interrupted Zarathustra; for blood was still flowing from the bare arm of the conscientious one. No fewer than ten leeches, after all, had bored themselves into it.

"Oh you weird fellow, how much is revealed to me by your appearance, namely you yourself! And maybe I should not pour all of it into your rigorous ears!

Well then! Let's part here! But I would like to find you again. Up there leads the path to my cave; tonight you shall be my dear guest there!

I would also like to make it up to your body that Zarathustra stepped on you with his feet; I'll be thinking about that. But now a cry of distress hurries me away from you."

Thus spoke Zarathustra.

The Magician

I

But as Zarathustra made his way around a boulder he saw someone not far below him on the same path, flailing his limbs like a raving madman, who finally flopped belly-first to the ground. "Stop!" said Zarathustra to his heart. "That one there must be the higher man, that awful cry of distress came from him – I'll go see if I can help." But when he ran to the spot where the person lay on the ground, he found a trembling old man with a fixed gaze; and as hard as Zarathustra tried to prop him up and stand him on his feet again, it was in vain. Nor did the unfortunate man seem to notice that someone was with him; instead he kept looking around with pitiful gestures, like someone who had been abandoned and left stranded by the whole world. At last, however, after much trembling and twitching and writhing he began to wail thus:

> Who will warm me, who loves me still?
> Give me hot hands!
> Give me braziers for my heart!
> Laid out, shuddering,
> Like something half-dead whose feet one warms –
> Racked, oh! by unknown fevers,
> Shivering from pointy icy arrows of frost,
> Hunted by you, thought!
> Unnameable! Disguised! Horrendous one!

You hunter behind clouds!
Struck down by your lightning,
You scornful eye that looks at me from darkness:
– I lie here,
Doubled up, writhing, tortured
By all eternal torments,
Struck
By you, cruelest hunter,
You unknown – god!

Strike deeper,
Strike one more time!
Skewer, smash this heart!
Why this torment
With blunt-toothed arrows?
Why do you look again,
Not weary of human agony,
With gloating gods' eyes flashing lightning?
You do not want to kill,
Only torment, torment?
Why torment *me*,
You gloating unknown god? –

Aha! You sneak close?
At such midnight
What do you want? Speak!
You press me, squeeze me –
Ha! too close already!
Away! Away!
You hear me breathing,
you listen to my heart,
You jealous one –
But of what are you jealous?
Away! Away! Why the ladder?
Do *you* want *in*,
Into my heart,
To climb in, to climb into
My most secret thoughts?
Shameless one! Unknown – thief!
What would you gain by stealing,
What would you gain by eavesdropping,
What would you gain by torturing,

You torturer!
You executioner god!
Or should I, like a dog,
Roll over before you?
Devotedly, ecstatically beside myself
Wag love – to you?

In vain! Stab deeper,
Cruelest thorn! No,
Not dog, only your prey am I,
Cruelest hunter!
Your proudest captive,
You robber behind clouds!
Speak at last,
What do you want, waylayer, *from me?*
You disguised in lightning! Unknown one! Speak,
What do you *want*, unknown god? –
What? Ransom?
Why do you want ransom?
Demand much – thus my pride counsels!
And speak briefly – thus my other pride counsels!
Aha!

Me – you want? Me?
Me – entirely?
Aha!

And you torment me, fool that you are,
Torment my pride?
Give me *love* – who will warm me still?
Who loves me still? – give me hot hands,
Give me braziers for my heart,
Give me, the loneliest one,
Whom ice, alas, sevenfold ice
Teaches to yearn,
To yearn even for enemies,
Give, yes give,
Cruelest enemy,
Give me – *yourself!* –

Gone!
He himself fled,
My last, my only companion,

My great enemy,
My unknown,

My executioner god! –
– No! Come back,
With all your torments!
To the last of all lonely ones
Oh come back!
All my rivers of tears flow
Their course to you!
And my last heart flames –
For you they flicker!
Oh come back,
My unknown god! My pain! My last –
       happiness!

2

– But at this point Zarathustra could no longer restrain himself, grabbed his staff and began beating the wailing man with all his strength. "Shut up!" he cried to him, with grim laughter. "Shut up, you actor! You counterfeiter! You liar from top to bottom! I recognize you well!

I'll give you warm legs, you wicked magician, I'm very good at heating up people like you!"

– "Desist," said the old man and he leaped to his feet. "Beat me no more, oh Zarathustra! I only did this as a game!

Such things belong to my art; you yourself I wanted to put to the test, when I gave you this test. And verily, you saw through me well!

But you yourself – you also tested me with no small sample of yourself: you are *hard*, you wise Zarathustra! You hit hard with your 'truths,' your cudgel forces *this* truth out of me!"

– "Do not flatter," answered Zarathustra, still upset and frowning darkly, "you actor from top to bottom! You're fake – why do you talk – of truth!

You peacock of peacocks, you sea of vanity, *what* are you playing before me, you wicked magician, in *whom* am I supposed to believe when you wail in this form?"

"*The penitent of the spirit*," said the old man. "*Him* I played: you yourself once coined this phrase –

– the poet and magician who ultimately turns his spirit against himself, the transformed one who freezes to death from his own evil science and conscience.

And just admit it: it took you a long time, oh Zarathustra, before you saw through my art and lie! *You believed* in my distress when you cradled my head with both hands –

– I heard you wail 'they loved him too little, loved him too little!' That I was able to deceive you to such an extent, that causes my malice to jubilate secretly."

"You may have deceived finer heads than me," said Zarathustra harshly. "I am not on my guard for deceivers, I *have* to be without caution – my fate wants it so.

But you – *have* to deceive: that much I know about you! You always have to be e-quivocal, tri-, quad- and quinquivocal! Even what you just now confessed was not nearly true nor false enough for me!

You wicked counterfeiter, how could you do otherwise! You would even put make-up on your disease when you show yourself naked to your physician.

Just like you put make-up on your lie before me when you said 'I *only* did this as a game!' There was *earnest* in it, you *are* something of a penitent of the spirit!

I guessed you well: you became everyone's enchanter, but against yourself you have no lie and no guile left over – you are disenchanted of yourself!

You harvested nausea as your single truth. Not a word of yours is genuine anymore, except your mouth: namely the nausea that clings to your mouth." –

– "Who *are* you!" yelled the old magician at this point, with defiance in his voice. "Who is permitted to speak with *me* thus, the greatest person living today?" – and an emerald bolt of lightning shot from his eye toward Zarathustra. But then he transformed immediately and said sadly:

"Oh Zarathustra, I am weary of and nauseated by my arts, I am not *great*, why do I pretend! But, you know it well – I sought greatness!

I wanted to represent a great human being and I persuaded many; but this lie was beyond my powers. On it I break down.

Oh Zarathustra, everything about me is a lie; but that I am breaking down – this breaking down is *genuine*!" –

"It does you honor," spoke Zarathustra somberly and glancing down to the side, "it does you honor that you sought greatness, but it also betrays you. You are not great.

You wicked old magician, *that* is your best and most honest, and what I honor in you, namely that you wearied of yourself and said so: 'I am not great.'

In that I honor you as a penitent of the spirit; and even if it was only for a whiff and a wink, for this one moment you were – genuine.

But tell me, what do you seek here in *my* woods and cliffs? And when you laid yourself in *my* path, what did you want to test in me? –

– why did you research *me*?" –

Thus spoke Zarathustra, and his eyes flashed. The old magician was silent for a while, then he said: "Did I research you? I merely – search.

Oh Zarathustra, I seek someone who is genuine, proper, simple, unequivocal, a human being of all honesty, a vessel of wisdom, a saint of knowledge, a great human being!

Do you not know it, oh Zarathustra? *I seek Zarathustra.*"

– And here a long silence ensued between the two; but Zarathustra became deeply immersed in himself, such that he closed his eyes. But then, turning back to his interlocutor, he seized the hand of the magician and spoke, full of kindness and craftiness:

"Well then! Up there leads the path, there lies the cave of Zarathustra. In it you may seek whomever you wish to find.

And ask my animals for advice, my eagle and my snake: they shall help you seek. But my cave is big.

For my part – I've never seen a great human being. The eyes of the finest are too coarse today for what is great. It is the kingdom of the rabble.

Many a one I found already, who stretched and puffed himself up, and the people cried: 'See here, a great human being!' But what good are all bellows! In the end only wind comes out.

In the end a frog will burst if it puffs itself up too long: then only wind comes out. To stab a swollen person in the belly – that's what I call great fun. Hear me, you little boys!

Today belongs to the rabble; who *knows* anymore what is great, what is small! Who could successfully search for greatness! Only a fool – fools would succeed.

You seek great human beings, you queer fool? Who *taught* you that? Is the time for that today? Oh you wicked searcher – why do you research me?" –

Thus spoke Zarathustra, comforted in his heart, and off he went again on his way, laughing.

Retired

Not long after he had freed himself from the magician, however, Zarathustra again saw someone sitting beside the path that he walked, namely a tall man in black with a gaunt, pale face: *this man* dismayed him tremendously. "Oh no," he spoke to his heart, "there sits depression in disguise, and its looks remind me of priests: what do *they* want in my kingdom?

What! Scarcely did I escape that magician, now another practitioner of black arts has to cross my path –

– some kind of sorcerer with laying-on of hands, a dark miracle worker of God's grace, an anointed world slanderer, may the devil take him!

But the devil is never in place where he would be in the right place; he always comes too late, this damned dwarf and clubfoot!" –

Thus cursed Zarathustra impatiently in his heart and he considered how he might avert his gaze and slip by the man in black; but behold, it happened differently. For in the same moment the sitting man had already caught sight of him, and not unlike a person who has run into unexpected luck, he leaped to his feet and approached Zarathustra.

"Whoever you may be, you wanderer," he said, "help a lost, seeking old man who could easily come to harm here!

This world here is foreign to me and far off, I even heard wild beasts howling; and the one who could have offered me protection, he himself no longer exists.

I sought the last pious human being, a saint and a hermit who alone in his woods had not yet heard what the whole world today knows."

"*What* does the whole world know today?" asked Zarathustra. "This perhaps, that the old God no longer lives, the one in whom the whole world once believed?"

"You said it," answered the old man gloomily. "And I served this old God until his final hour.

But now I am retired, without a master, and yet I am not free, nor merry for a single hour unless in my memories.

And so I climbed into these mountains to finally have a festival for myself, as is proper for an old pope and church father: for know this, I am the last pope! – a festival of pious memories and divine worship.

But now he himself is dead, this most pious human being, this saint in the woods who constantly praised his god with singing and growling.

I did not find him when I found his hut – but two wolves were in it, howling at his death – for all animals loved him. Then I ran away.

Did I arrive in vain in these woods and mountains? Then my heart resolved to seek another, the most pious of all those who do not believe in God – to seek Zarathustra!"

Thus spoke the oldster and he looked with a sharp eye at the man who stood before him; but Zarathustra grasped the old pope's hand and regarded it admiringly for a long time.

"See here, you reverend one," he said then, "what a beautiful and long hand! This is the hand of one who has always dispensed blessings. Now, however, it holds on to the one you seek, to me, Zarathustra.

I am he, godless Zarathustra, who speaks: who is more godless than I, that I may enjoy his instruction?" –

Thus spoke Zarathustra and with his gaze he penetrated the thoughts and secret thoughts of the old pope. At last the latter began:

"The one who loved and possessed him most has now also lost him most – :

– behold, perhaps I myself am now the more godless of us two? But who could take pleasure in that!" –

"You served him up until the end," said Zarathustra, pensively, after a deep silence. "Do you know *how* he died? Is it true, as they say, that pity choked him to death,

– that he saw how *the human being* hung on the cross, and couldn't bear that his love for mankind became his hell and ultimately his death?" –

But the old pope did not answer, and instead he looked to the side awkwardly and with a pained and dark expression.

"Let him go," said Zarathustra after a long thoughtful pause, while still looking the old man straight in the eye.

"Let him go, he's gone. And even though it honors you that you speak only good of this dead one, still you know as well as I *who* he was; and that he walked queer ways."

"For our three eyes only," said the old pope cheerfully (because he was blind in one eye), "in matters of God I am more enlightened than Zarathustra himself – and am permitted to be.

My love served him long years, my will followed his will in all things. But a good servant knows everything, and also some things that his master conceals from himself.

He was a concealed god, full of secretiveness. Indeed, even in getting himself a son he used nothing other than sneaky means. At the doorway of his faith stands adultery.

Whoever praises him as a god of love does not think highly enough of love itself. Did this god not also want to be judge? But the loving one loves beyond reward and retribution.

When he was young, this god from the East, then he was harsh and vengeful and he built himself a hell for the amusement of his favorites.

But at last he became old and soft and mellow and pitying, more like a grandfather than a father, but most like a wobbly old grandmother.

There he sat, wilted, in his nook by the stove, grousing about his weak legs, weary of the world, weary of willing, and one day he choked to death on his all too great pity." –

"You old pope," said Zarathustra here, interrupting. "Did you see *that* with your own eyes? It certainly could have happened that way; that way, *and* another way too. When gods die, they always die many kinds of death.

But well then! This way or that, this way and that – he's gone! He was offensive to the taste of my ears and eyes, I do not wish to speak anything worse of him.

I love everything that gazes brightly and speaks honestly. But he – you know it well, you old priest, there was something of your kind in him, something priest-like – he was equivocal.

He was also unclear. How he raged at us, this wrath snorter, because we understood him poorly! But why did he not speak more purely!

And if the fault was in our ears, why did he give us ears that heard him poorly? If mud was in our ears, well then – who put it there?

He failed at too much, this potter who never completed his training! But that he avenged himself on his clay formations and his creations because they turned out badly for him – that was a sin against *good taste*.

In piousness too there is good taste; *it* said at last: "Away with *such* a god! Rather no god, rather meet destiny on one's own, rather be a fool, rather be a god oneself!""

– "What do I hear!" spoke the old pope at this point with pricked up ears. "Oh Zarathustra, you are more pious than you believe, with such disbelief! Some kind of god in you converted you to your godlessness.

Is it not your very piousness that no longer allows you to believe in a god? And your overly great honesty will yet lead you away beyond good and evil!

Take a good look: what is left for you? You have eyes and hands and mouth that have been preordained for blessing since eternity. One does not bless with hands alone.

In your proximity, even though you claim to be the most godless man, I detect a secret, sacred and sweet aroma of long blessings: it makes me happy and it makes me hurt.

Let me be your guest, oh Zarathustra, for one single night! Nowhere on earth do I feel happier now than with you!" –

"Amen! It shall be so!" spoke Zarathustra with great astonishment. "Up there leads the path, there lies the cave of Zarathustra.

Gladly, to be sure, I would guide you there myself, you reverend one, because I love all pious people. But now a cry of distress hurries me away from you.

In my realm no one shall come to harm; my cave is a safe harbor. And I would like nothing better than to place every sad person back on firm land and firm legs.

But who could take *your* melancholy off your shoulders? For that I'm too weak. We may have to wait a long time, truly, before someone awakens your god again.

For this old god does not live anymore: he is thoroughly dead." –

Thus spoke Zarathustra.

The Ugliest Human Being

– And again Zarathustra's feet ran through mountains and woods, and his eyes searched and searched, but nowhere to be seen was the one whom they wanted to see, the great sufferer of distress and crier of distress. But along the whole way he jubilated in his heart and was thankful. "What good things," he said, "this day has bestowed on me, as compensation for having begun so badly! What strange interlocutors I found!

Now I want to chew on their words for a long time, as on good kernels; my teeth will grind and grate them down until they flow like milk into my soul!" –

But when the path disappeared again around a boulder, all at once the landscape changed and Zarathustra stepped into a realm of death. Here black and red cliffs jutted upward: no grass, no tree, no birdsong. For it was a valley that all animals avoided, even the predators; except for a species of hideous, thick, green snakes that would come here to die when they grew old. And for this reason the shepherds called this valley: Snake Death.

Now Zarathustra sank into a black reminiscence, for it seemed to him that he had already stood in this valley once before. And much graveness spread itself over his mind, such that he walked slowly and ever more slowly until finally he stood still. But then, when he opened his eyes he saw something sitting beside the path, shaped like a human but scarcely like a human, something unspeakable. And all of a sudden Zarathustra was overcome with great shame for having looked upon such a thing with his own eyes; blushing all the way up to his white hair, he averted his gaze and picked up his foot, intending to leave this wicked spot. But then a noise animated the dead wasteland; it welled up from the ground gurgling and rattling, like water gurgles and rattles at night through clogged water pipes, until finally it turned into a human voice and human speech – that sounded like this.

"Zarathustra! Zarathustra! Guess my riddle! Speak, speak! What is *revenge against the witness?*

I lure you back, there is slippery ice here! See to it, see to it that your pride does not break its legs here!

You consider yourself wise, you proud Zarathustra! Then go ahead and guess the riddle, you hard nut cracker – the riddle that I am! So tell me: who am *I?*"

– But when Zarathustra had heard these words – what do you think took place in his soul? *He was overwhelmed with pity;* and he collapsed at once like an oak tree that has long withstood many wood cutters – heavily, suddenly, to the terror of even those who wanted to fell it. But right away he picked himself up from the ground and his face had become hard.

"I recognize you alright," he spoke with a voice of bronze: " *You are the murderer of God!* Let me go.

You *could not bear* the one who saw *you* – who saw you always and through and through, you ugliest human being! You took revenge on this witness!"

Thus spoke Zarathustra and wanted to leave; but the unspeakable one latched on to a corner of his garment and began again to gurgle and to search for words. "Stay!" he said at last –

– "Stay! Do not pass by! I guessed what kind of axe knocked you to the ground: Hail to you, oh Zarathustra, that you stand again!

You guessed, I know it well, how he who killed him feels – the murderer of God. Stay! Sit down here with me, it will not be in vain.

To whom did I want to go, if not to you? Stay, sit down! But do not look at me! Honor thus – my ugliness!

They persecute me; now *you* are my last refuge. *Not* with their hatred, *not* with their bailiffs – oh such persecution I would mock and be proud and glad!

Has not everything successful hitherto been done by the well-persecuted? And whoever persecutes well easily learns to *succeed* – after all he is already – after somebody! But it's their *pity* –

– their pity is what I flee and why I flee to you. Oh Zarathustra, protect me, you my last refuge, you the only one to guess me:

– you guessed how he who killed *him* feels. Stay! And if you want to go, you impatient one: do not go the way that I came. *That* way is bad.

Are you angry with me that I've already spoken broken words for too long? That I even counsel you? But know this, it's me, the ugliest human being,

– who also has the biggest, heaviest feet. Where *I* walked, the way is bad. I trample all ways to death and to ruin.

But that you passed me by, silently; that you blushed, I saw it well: that's how I recognized you as Zarathustra.

Any other would have tossed me his alms, his pity, with looks and speech. But for that – I am not beggar enough, you guessed that –

–for that I am too *rich*, rich in what is great, what is terrible, what is ugliest, what is most unspeakable! Your shame, oh Zarathustra, *honored* me!

With difficulty I managed to escape the throng of the pitying – to find the only one today who teaches 'pitying is obtrusive' – you, oh Zarathustra!

– Be it a god's, be it the pity of mankind: pitying is offensive to shame. And not wanting to help can be more noble than the virtue that leaps to help.

But today *that* is what passes for virtue itself among all small people, pity – they have no respect for great misfortune, for great ugliness, for great failure.

I look away over all these people like a dog looks away over the backs of teeming flocks of sheep. They are small, good-wooled and good-willed gray people.

Like a heron looks away contemptuously over shallow ponds, its head tossed back; thus I look away over teeming gray little waves and wills and souls.

They have been deemed to be right for too long, these small people; and *so* in the end they were given might too – now they teach: 'the only good is what small people call good.'

And 'truth' today is what the preacher spoke, the one who himself came from among them, that odd holy man and advocate of small people who testified of himself: 'I – am the truth.'

This immodest person has for a long time now caused small people to get big heads – he who taught no small error when he taught 'I – am the truth.'

Was an immodest person ever answered more courteously? – But you, oh Zarathustra, passed him by and said: 'No! No! Three times no!'

You warned against his error, you were the first to warn against pity – not all, not none, but yourself and your kind.

You are ashamed of the shame of the great sufferer; and indeed, when you say 'from pitying a great cloud is coming, beware, you human beings!'

– when you teach 'all creators are hard, all great love is above pitying': oh Zarathustra, how well schooled you seem to me in predicting the weather!

But you yourself – warn yourself too against *your* pitying! Because many are on their way to you, many who are suffering, doubting, despairing, drowning, freezing –

I warn you against me too. You guessed my best and worst riddle, me myself and what I did. I know the axe that fells you.

But he – *had* to die: he saw with eyes that saw *everything* – he saw the depths and grounds of human beings, all their hidden disgrace and ugliness.

His pitying knew no shame: he crawled into my filthiest nook. This most curious, super-obtrusive, super-pitying one had to die.

He always saw *me*: I wanted revenge on such a witness – or to no longer live myself.

The god who saw everything, *even human beings*: this god had to die! Human beings cannot *bear* that such a witness lives."

Thus spoke the ugliest human being. But Zarathustra rose and set about to leave, because he was chilled down to his entrails.

"You unspeakable one," he said, "you warned me against your way. Out of gratitude I now commend mine to you. Look, up there lies Zarathustra's cave.

My cave is big and deep and has many nooks; there the most hidden person will find a hiding place. And close by are a hundred burrows and tunnels for crawling, flapping and leaping wildlife.

You outcast, who cast himself out, you no longer want to dwell among human beings and human pity? Well then, do as I do! Thus you'll also learn from me; only the doer learns.

And speak first and foremost with my animals! The proudest animal and the wisest animal – they are surely the right counselors for both of us!" –

Thus spoke Zarathustra and continued on his way, pensive and even more slowly than before; because he had much to ask himself and knew no easy way to answer.

"How poor indeed is a human being!" he thought in his heart, "how ugly, how gasping, how full of concealed shame!

They tell me that human beings love themselves; oh, how great this self-love must be! How much contempt it has against it!

Even this man here loved himself, as he despised himself – to me he seems a great lover and a great despiser.

I've never found anyone who despised himself more deeply; *that* too is elevation. Oh no, was *he* perhaps the higher man whose cry I heard?

I love the great despisers. Human being, however, is something that must be overcome." –

The Voluntary Beggar

When Zarathustra had left the ugliest human being, he was freezing and he felt lonely; after all, so much that was cold and lonely went through his mind, to the point where even his limbs grew colder because of it. But as he climbed further and further, up, down, now past green meadows, but then also across wild stony deposits where previously an impatient brook might have laid itself to bed, then all at once his mood became warmer and more cordial.

"What happened to me?" he asked himself, "something warm and lively refreshes me, something that must be close to me.

Already I am less alone; unknown companions and brothers roam around me, their warm breath touches on my soul."

But when he peered about himself and searched for the comforters of his solitude, oddly enough, it was cows huddled together on a knoll; their nearness and smell had warmed his heart. Now these cows seemed engrossed in listening to someone speaking, and they paid no attention to the one who approached them. But when Zarathustra was quite near them he heard clearly how a human voice spoke from the midst of the cows; and evidently they had all turned their heads toward the speaker.

Then Zarathustra leaped up eagerly and pushed the animals apart, fearing that someone might have come to harm here, which could scarcely be remedied by the pity of cows. But in this he had deceived himself; for indeed, there sat someone on the ground and appeared to be persuading the animals to not be afraid of him, a peaceful man and mountain preacher from whose eyes goodness itself preached. "What are you seeking here?" cried Zarathustra, astonished.

"What am I seeking here?" he answered: "The same thing you seek, you trouble maker! Namely happiness on earth.

But for that I want to learn from these cows. And you should know, I've already persuaded them half the morning, and just now they wanted to tell me for sure. Why do you have to disturb them?

Unless we are converted and become as cows, we will by no means enter the kingdom of heaven. For there is one thing that we ought to learn from them: chewing the cud.

And truly, what profit is it to a man if he gains the whole world, and did not learn this one thing, chewing the cud: what would it help? He would not be rid of his misery

– his great misery: which today is called *nausea*. Who today does not have heart, mouth and eyes full of nausea? You too! You too! But just look at these cows here!" –

Thus spoke the mountain preacher and then he turned his own gaze on Zarathustra – for till now his gaze hung lovingly on the cows – then, however, it transformed. "Who is this with whom I speak?" he cried, startled, and jumped up from the ground.

"This is the man without nausea, this is Zarathustra himself, the one who overcame great nausea, this is the eye, this is the mouth, this is the heart of Zarathustra himself."

And while he spoke thus he kissed the hands of the one to whom he spoke, and tears streamed from his eyes, and he behaved quite like someone to whom a precious gift and treasure falls unexpectedly from heaven. The cows, meanwhile, watched all of this and were amazed.

"Do not speak of me, you odd, you lovely man!" said Zarathustra and he restrained his tenderness. "Tell me first about yourself! Are you not the voluntary beggar who once threw away great wealth –

– who once was ashamed of his wealth and of the wealthy, and fled to the poorest people, to give them his fullness and his heart? But they did not accept him."

"But they did not accept me," said the voluntary beggar, "you know it already. So in the end I went to the animals and to these cows."

"Then you learned," Zarathustra interrupted the speaker, "how it is harder to grant right than to take right, and that bestowing well is an *art* and the ultimate, craftiest master-art of kindness."

"Especially nowadays," answered the voluntary beggar. "Nowadays, namely, where everything lowly has become rebellious and skittish and haughty in its own way: namely in a rabble way.

For the hour has come, you know it well, for the great, terrible, long, slow rabble and slave rebellion: it grows and grows!

Now the lowly are outraged by all benevolence and little charities; and the super-rich should be on their guard!

Whoever dribbles these days like portly bottles with all too narrow necks – people like to break the necks of such bottles today.

Lascivious greed, galling envy, aggrieved vengefulness, rabble pride: all of that leaped into my face. It is no longer true that the poor are blessed. But the kingdom of heaven is among the cows."

"And why is it not among the wealthy?" asked Zarathustra, temptingly, as he warded off the cows that trustingly snorted at the peaceful man.

"Why do you tempt me?" he answered. "You yourself know it even better than I. What drove me to the poorest, oh Zarathustra? Was it not my nausea for our wealthiest people?

– for the convicts of wealth who cull their advantage out of every dustpan, with cold eyes, horny thoughts; for this mob that stinks to high heaven,

– for this gilded, fake rabble, whose fathers were pick-pockets or vultures or rag pickers, with women who were willing, lascivious, forgetful – all of them after all are not far from being whores –

rabble above, rabble below! What do 'poor' and 'rich' mean anymore today! I forgot this difference – then I fled, farther, ever farther, until I got to these cows."

Thus spoke the peaceful man and he himself snorted and sweated at these words, such that the cows once again were amazed. But Zarathustra continued to look him in the face, smiling as he spoke so harshly, and he silently shook his head.

"You do violence to yourself, you mountain preacher, when you use such harsh words. Not for such harshness were your mouth or your eyes made.

Nor, it seems to me, your stomach itself: *it* resists all such raging and hating and foaming over. Your stomach wants gentler things: you are no butcher.

Rather, you seem to me a vegetarian and a root man. Perhaps you crunch grains. But certainly you are ill disposed toward pleasures of the flesh and you love honey."

"You guessed me well," responded the voluntary beggar, with relief in his heart. "I love honey, I also crunch grains, because I sought what tastes lovely and makes for clean breath:

– also what takes a long time, a day's and mouth's work for gentle idlers and bums.

The ones who have excelled the most, to be sure, are these cows: they invented chewing the cud for themselves and lying in the sun. They also refrain from all weighty thoughts, which bloat the heart."

– "Well then!" said Zarathustra. "You should also see *my* animals, my eagle and my snake – their equal exists nowhere today on earth.

Look, there the path leads to my cave; be its guest tonight. And speak with my animals about the happiness of animals –

– until I myself come home. Because now a cry of distress hurries me away from you. You'll also find new honey at my place, icy-fresh golden honey from the comb – eat it!

But now quickly take leave of your cows, you odd, you lovely man! Even if it is difficult for you. For they are your warmest friends and teachers!" –

"– With the exception of one person, whom I love even more," answered the voluntary beggar. "You yourself are good and even better than a cow, oh Zarathustra!"

"Away, away with you! You nasty flatterer!" cried Zarathustra with malice, "why do you spoil me with such praise and flatter-honey?

Away, away from me!" he cried once more and brandished his staff at the affectionate beggar, who ran away swiftly.

The Shadow

But scarcely had the voluntary beggar run away and Zarathustra was again alone with himself, than he heard a new voice behind him, crying "Stop! Zarathustra! Stop already! It's me, oh Zarathustra, me, your shadow!" But Zarathustra did not wait, because he was suddenly overcome with annoyance at the excessive hustle and bustle in his mountains. "Where's my solitude gone?" he said.

"This is really becoming too much for me; this mountain is teeming, my kingdom is no longer of *this* world, I need new mountains.

My shadow is calling me? What does my shadow matter! Let him run after me – I'll run away from him."

Thus Zarathustra spoke to his heart and ran away. But the one who was behind him continued to follow, so that soon three runners were after each other, namely the voluntary beggar in front, then Zarathustra and third and furthest behind, his shadow. Not long had they run in this manner when Zarathustra came to his senses about his folly and with one great effort shook off all that cloyed and annoyed him.

"What!" he said, "haven't the most ridiculous things always happened among us old hermits and holy men?

Truly, my folly grew tall in the mountains! Now I hear six old fools' legs rattling along after each other!

But can Zarathustra afford to be afraid of a shadow? And it seems to me, when all's said and done, that he has longer legs than I."

Thus spoke Zarathustra, laughing with his eyes and his entrails, then he stopped, turned around abruptly – and behold, he almost hurled his successor and shadow to the ground – so closely did the latter follow on his heels, and so weak was he too. When he took a close look at him, he shrank back as if before a sudden ghost: so thin, blackish, hollow and outdated did this successor look.

"Who are you?" asked Zarathustra, intensely, "what are you doing here? And why do you call yourself my shadow? I don't like you."

"Forgive me," answered the shadow, "that it is I; and if you do not like me, well then, oh Zarathustra, for that I praise you and your good taste!

I am a wanderer, who has already walked much at your heels; always on my way, but without goal, without home too, such that very little is lacking, truly, and I would be the Eternal Jew – except that I am not eternal and neither am I Jew.

What? Must I always be on my way? Whirled by every wind, unsteady, driven out? Oh earth, you have become too round for me!

I've already sat on every surface, like weary dust I have slept on mirrors and window panes: Everything takes from me, nothing gives, and I grow thin – I almost resemble a shadow.

But after you, oh Zarathustra, I've flown and followed longest, and even when I concealed myself from you, I was still your best shadow: wherever you sat, I sat too.

With you I have haunted the remotest, coldest worlds, like a ghost that runs voluntarily over winter rooftops and snow.

With you I strived to enter everything forbidden, worst, remotest; and if anything of mine is a virtue, then it is that I have feared no ban.

With you I smashed anything my heart ever honored, I overthrew all boundary stones and images, I pursued the most dangerous wishes – indeed, I have passed over every crime once.

With you I unlearned my faith in words and values and great names. When the devil sheds his skin, does his name not fall off too? For it too is skin. Perhaps the devil himself is – skin.

'Nothing is true, all is permitted': thus I persuaded myself. I plunged into the coldest waters, with head and heart. Oh how often I paid for it by standing there naked as a red crab!

Oh where has all my goodness and all my shame and all my faith in the good gone! Oh where has that mendacious innocence that I once possessed gone, the innocence of the good and their noble lies!

Too often, to be sure, I followed on the heels of truth: and it kicked me in the head. Sometimes I believed I was lying and behold – that's where I first hit – the truth.

Too much became clear to me, now it doesn't matter to me anymore. Nothing that I love lives anymore – how am I supposed to still love myself?

'Live as I please or don't live at all' – that's how I want it, and that's how the saintliest person wants it too. But alas, how could *I* still have – pleasure?

Do *I* – still have a goal? A harbor toward which *my* sail turns?

A good wind? Indeed, only the one who knows *where* he's sailing knows also which wind is good and which is his favorable wind.

What did I have left? A heart weary and insolent; a restless will; fluttering wings; a broken backbone.

Ever a visitor, searching for *my* home, oh Zarathustra, you well know, this visiting was *my* visitation, and it devours me.

'Where is – *my* home?' I asked, and I search and searched for it, but I have not found it. Oh eternal everywhere, oh eternal nowhere, oh eternal – in vain!"

Thus spoke the shadow, and Zarathustra's face lengthened at these words. "You are my shadow!" he said at last, with sadness.

"Your danger is no small one, you free spirit and wanderer! You've had a bad day: see to it that you do not have an even worse evening!

To such restless ones as you even a jail ends up looking like bliss. Have you ever seen how captured criminals sleep? They sleep peacefully, they enjoy their new security.

Beware that you are not captured in the end by a narrow belief, a harsh, severe delusion! Because now you are seduced and tempted by anything that is narrow and solid.

You have lost your goal: indeed, how will you get rid of and get over this loss? Along with it – you have also lost your way!

You poor roamer and raver, you weary butterfly! Do you want to have a rest and a home this evening? Then go up to my cave!

There leads the path to my cave. And now I have to run away from you quickly again. Already it's as though I'm covered in shadow.

I want to run alone, so that things clear up around me again. For that I'll yet have to be long on my legs and like it. But this evening at my place – there will be dancing!" –

Thus spoke Zarathustra.

At Noon

– And Zarathustra ran and ran and found no one anymore, and he was alone and found himself again and again, and he enjoyed and sipped his solitude and thought about good things – for hours. At the hour of noon, however, as the sun stood directly over Zarathustra's head, he passed by an old crooked and knotty tree, embraced by the luxurious love of a grapevine and hidden away from itself; from it hung abundant yellow grapes, trailing toward the wanderer. Then he got a craving to quench a slight thirst and to pluck himself a grape; but when he had already stretched out his arm to do so, then he got an even stronger craving to do something else, namely to lie down beside the tree, at the hour of perfect noon, and to sleep.

This Zarathustra did; and as soon as he lay on the ground, in the quiet and secrecy of the colorful grass, he quickly forgot about his slight thirst and fell asleep. For, as Zarathustra's proverb says, one thing is more needful than the other. Only his eyes remained open – because they did not tire of seeing and praising the tree and the grapevine's love. As he was falling asleep, however, Zarathustra spoke thus to his heart:

Still! Still! Didn't the world become perfect just now? What's happening to me?

Like a delicate wind, unseen, dancing on a paneled sea, light, feather light – thus sleep dances on me.

He does not close my eyes, he leaves my soul awake. Light is he, truly, feather light!

He persuades me, I don't know how. He pats me on the inside with flattering hand, he conquers me. Yes, he conquers me until my soul stretches out –

– how she grows long and weary, my strange soul! Did a seventh day's evening come to her precisely at noon? Did she wander blissfully too long already between good and ripe things?

She stretches herself out, long – longer! She lies still, my strange soul. She's already tasted too much that is good, this golden melancholy oppresses her, she grimaces.

– Like a ship that sailed into its stillest bay – now it leans against the earth, weary of the long journeys and the uncertain seas. Is the earth not more faithful?

How such a ship moors and nestles itself to the land – now it's enough for a spider to spin a web to it from the land. It needs no stronger lines now.

Like such a weary ship in the stillest bay, thus I too rest now close to the earth, faithfully, trusting, waiting, bound to it with the lightest threads.

Oh happiness, oh happiness! Do you want to sing, oh my soul? You lie in the grass. But this is the secret solemn hour when no shepherd plays his flute.

Stand back! Hot noon sleeps on the meadows. Do not sing! Still! The world is perfect.

Do not sing, you winged bug in the grass, oh my soul! Do not even whisper! Look here – still! Old noon is sleeping, he's moving his mouth: didn't he just drink a drop of happiness –

– an old brown drop of golden happiness, golden wine? It flits over him, his happiness is laughing. Thus laughs – a god. Still! –

– "Happily, how little suffices for happiness!" Thus I spoke once, and deemed myself clever. But it was a blasphemy: *this* I learned now. Clever fools speak better.

Precisely the least, the softest, the lightest, a lizard's rustling, a breath, a wink, a blink of an eye – *a little* is the stuff of the *best* happiness. Still!

– What happened to me: listen! Didn't time just fly away? Am I not falling? Did I not fall – listen! – into the well of eternity?

– What's happening to me? Still! Something is stinging me – oh no – in the heart? In the heart? Oh break, break, heart, after such happiness, after such a sting!

– What? Did the world not become perfect just now? Round and ripe? Oh the golden round ring – where is it flying to now? I'll run after it! Rush!

Still – (and here Zarathustra stretched and felt that he was sleeping).

"Get up!" he said to himself, "you sleeper! You noon sleeper! Well then, well now, you old legs! It's time and overtime, many a good piece of road is still waiting for you –

Now you've slept yourself out, for how long? Half an eternity! Well then, well now, my old heart! How long after such a sleep will it take you to wake yourself out?

(But then he fell asleep anew, and his soul spoke against him and resisted and laid itself down again) – "Let me be! Still! Didn't the world become perfect just now? Oh the golden round ball!" –

"Get up," spoke Zarathustra, "you little thief, you loafing thief! What? Still stretching, yawning, sighing, falling down into deep wells?

Who are you? Oh my soul!" (and here he started, because a sunbeam fell down from the sky onto his face)

"Oh sky above me," he said, sighing, and sat upright. "You're looking at me? You're listening to my strange soul?

When will you drink this drop of dew that has fallen upon all earthly things – when will you drink this strange soul – when, well of eternity! You cheerful, dreadful noon abyss! When will you drink my soul back into yourself?"

Thus spoke Zarathustra and he rose from his sleeping place at the tree as if from a strange drunkenness; and behold, the sun was still standing straight over his head. But from this one might justifiably infer that Zarathustra had not slept long.

The Welcome

It was not until late afternoon that Zarathustra returned home to his cave after much searching and roaming around in vain. But as he stood facing the cave, not more than twenty paces away from it, something happened that he least expected now: once again he heard the great *cry of distress*. And, amazingly, this time it came from his own cave! But it was a protracted, manifold, peculiar cry, and Zarathustra clearly differentiated that it was composed of many voices; even if, heard from a distance, it sounded like the cry of a single mouth.

Then Zarathustra bounded toward his cave, and behold, what an eyeful awaited him after this earful! Indeed, there sitting all together were the ones he had passed by during the day: the king on the right and king on the left, the old magician, the pope, the voluntary beggar, the shadow, the conscientious of spirit, the sad soothsayer and the ass; the ugliest human being, however, had donned a crown and draped two purple sashes around himself – for like all ugly people he loved to disguise himself and act beautiful. But in the midst of this gloomy company stood Zarathustra's eagle, bristling and restless because he was pressed to answer too much for which his pride had no answer; meanwhile the wise snake hung around his neck.

All of this Zarathustra observed with great amazement; then he examined each one of his guests with affable curiosity, read their souls and was amazed once more. In the meantime the assembled had risen from their seats and they waited respectfully for Zarathustra to speak. But Zarathustra spoke thus:

"You despairing ones! You strange ones! So it was *your* cry of distress I heard? And now I also know where to find the one whom I have sought in vain today: *the higher man* – :

– in my own cave he's sitting, the higher man! But why am I amazed? Did I myself not lure him to me with honey sacrifices and the cunning calls of my happiness?

Yet it seems to me you are not fit company for each other; sitting here together you strain each other's nerves, you criers of distress. First someone has to come,

– someone to make you laugh again, a good gay buffoon, a dancer and a wind and wildcat, some old fool – what do you think?

Forgive me please, you despairing ones, for speaking to you with such small words, unworthy, truly, of such guests! But you cannot guess *what* makes my heart so mischievous –

You yourselves are responsible, and how you look, forgive me! After all, everyone who looks at a despairing person becomes mischievous. To give encouragement to someone who despairs – for that everyone thinks they're strong enough.

You yourselves gave me this strength – a good gift, my elevated guests! A righteous gift for your host! Well then, don't be angry now when I offer you something of my own.

This here is my kingdom and my dominion; but whatever is mine shall be yours for this evening and this night. My animals shall serve you; my cave shall be your resting place!

In my home and house no one shall despair; in my territory I protect everyone from his wild animals. And that is the first thing I offer you: security!

But the second thing is: my little finger. And once you've got hold of *it*, just go ahead and take the whole hand! And my heart too! Welcome to this place, welcome, my guests! "

Thus spoke Zarathustra and he laughed with love and malice. After this welcome his guests bowed repeatedly and maintained a respectful silence; then the king on the right responded in their name.

"By the manner, oh Zarathustra, that you offered us your hand and your greeting, we recognize you as Zarathustra. You humbled yourself before us; you almost offended our sense of respect –

– but who is able to humble himself like you with such pride? *That* in itself uplifts us, it refreshes our eyes and hearts.

To behold this alone we would have gladly climbed higher mountains than this one here. We came hungry for something to behold, we wanted to see what brightens gloomy eyes.

And behold, already we have ceased all our crying of distress. Already our minds and hearts stand open and are delighted. Little is missing and our spirits will become spirited.

Nothing more delightful grows on earth, oh Zarathustra, than a tall, strong will: that is the earth's most beautiful plant. An entire landscape is invigorated by one such tree.

Whoever grows tall like you, oh Zarathustra, I compare to the stone-pine: long, silent, hard, solitary, of the most resilient wood, magnificent –

– but in the end reaching out with strong green branches for *its* dominion, asking strong questions before the winds and weather and whatever else is at home in the heights,

– answering even more strongly, a commander, a victor: oh who would not climb high mountains to look upon such plants?

Even the gloomy, the failures are invigorated by your tree, oh Zarathustra, even the hearts of the unsteady are made sure and are healed at the sight of you.

And truly, many eyes today are trained on your mountain and tree; a great longing has opened up, and many have learned to ask: who is Zarathustra?

And those into whose ears you ever dripped your song and your honey: all the hidden ones, the solitary and the dualitary, said at once to their hearts:

'Does Zarathustra still live? It's not worth it anymore to live, all is the same, all is in vain: or – we must live with Zarathustra!'

'Why does he not come, he who announced himself for so long?' thus many ask. 'Did solitude swallow him up? Or should we perhaps go to him?'

Now it happens that solitude itself is becoming brittle and is breaking apart, like a grave that breaks open and can no longer contain its dead. Everywhere one sees the resurrected.

Now the waves rise and rise around your mountain, oh Zarathustra. And as high as your height may be, many must go up to you; your skiff shall not be on the rocks much longer.

And that we who despair have now come to your cave and no longer despair: this is merely a token and an omen that better ones are on their way to you –

– for what is on its way to you is nothing less than the last remnant of God among human beings, that is: all human beings of great longing, of great nausea, of great surfeit,

– all who do not want to live unless they once again learn to *hope* – unless they learn from you, oh Zarathustra, the *great* hope!"

Thus spoke the king on the right and he grasped Zarathustra's hand in order to kiss it; but Zarathustra rebuffed his veneration and stepped back startled, silent, and as if he were fleeing suddenly into remote distances. But after a brief while he was once again among his guests, looking at them with bright, piercing eyes, and he said:

"My guests, you higher men, I want to speak in German and intelligibly with you. Not for *you* did I wait here in these mountains.

('In German and intelligibly? May God have mercy!' said the king on the left, as an aside. 'One notices that he does not know our dear Germans, this wise man from the East!

But he really means "in German and in-eptly" – well then! Nowadays that is not the worst of tastes!')

"You may indeed be higher men, collectively," Zarathustra continued. "But for me – you are not high and strong enough.

For me, that is: for the inexorable that remains silent in me but will not always remain silent. And if you belong to me, then surely not as my right arm.

For whoever stands on sick and frail legs himself, as you do, wants above all to be *spared*, whether he knows it or conceals it from himself.

But I do not spare my arms and legs, *I do not spare my warriors*: how could you be fit for *my* war?

With you I would only ruin every victory. And many of you would already fall over just to hear the loud pounding of my drums.

Nor are you beautiful enough for me and wellborn. I need clean, smooth mirrors for my teachings; on your surfaces even my own image is distorted.

Your shoulders are weighed down by many a burden, many a memory; in your corners many a wicked dwarf crouches. There is hidden rabble in you as well.

And even if you are higher and of a higher kind: much in you is crooked and deformed. There's no smith in the world who could hammer you right and straight for me.

You are mere bridges – may higher people stride across on you! You represent steps – so do not be angered by the one who steps over you into *his* height!

From your seed perhaps a genuine son and perfect heir will grow someday for me; but that is far off. You yourselves are not the ones to whom my inheritance and my name belong.

Not for you do I wait here in these mountains, not with you shall I go down for the last time. You came to me only as an omen that higher ones are on their way to me –

– *not* the people of great longing, of great nausea, of great surfeit and that which you called the remnant of God.

– No! No! Three times no! I wait for *others* here in these mountains and will not lift a foot from here without them,

– for higher, stronger, more victorious, more cheerful ones, those who are built right-angled in body and soul: *laughing lions* must come!

Oh my guests, you strange ones – have you not yet heard anything of my children? And that they are on their way to me?

Speak to me of my gardens, of my blessed isles, of my beautiful new species[2] – why don't you speak to me of that?

This host's gift I beg of your love, that you speak of my children. It is for this that I am rich, for this that I became poor: what did I not give,

---

[2] Kaufmann in his translation deleted the word "species" (*Art*), writing instead: "Speak to me of my gardens, of my blessed isles, of my new beauty." Nietzsche referred to the overman as a new species, even while he insisted that the current human being cannot be "leaped over" in the pursuit of the overman.

– what would I not give just to have this one thing: *these* children, *this* living plantation, *these* life-trees of my will and my highest hope!"

Thus spoke Zarathustra and suddenly he stopped in his speech, because his longing overcame him, and his eyes and his mouth were closed by the turmoil in his heart. And all his guests were silent as well, and they stood still and dismayed; except that the old soothsayer made signs and gestures with his hands.

The Last Supper

At this point, however, the soothsayer interrupted the welcome of Zarathustra and his guests; he pushed forward like someone who has no time to lose, grabbed Zarathustra's hand and shouted: "But Zarathustra!

One thing is more needful than the other, so you yourself say: well then, one thing is more needful to *me* now than everything else.

A word at the right time: did you not invite me to *supper*? And here are many who traveled a long way. Surely you do not intend to feed us with speeches?

Also, you have all given too much thought already to freezing, drowning, suffocating and other bodily emergencies: but no one has thought about *my* emergency, namely starving –"

(Thus spoke the soothsayer; but when Zarathustra's animals heard these words, they ran away terrified, seeing that whatever they had brought home by day would not suffice to stuff even this one soothsayer.)

"Including dying of thirst," continued the soothsayer. "And even though I hear water splashing here, like the speeches of wisdom, namely abundantly and tirelessly, I want – *wine*!

Not everyone is a born water drinker, like Zarathustra. Nor is water fit for the weary and the wilted: *we* deserve wine – only *it* provides sudden convalescence and instant health!"

At this opportunity, since the soothsayer demanded wine, it happened that the king on the left, the silent one, also spoke up at last. "*We* have taken care of the wine," he said, "I together with my brother, the king on the right: we have wine enough – an entire ass-load. So nothing is lacking but bread."

"Bread?" countered Zarathustra, and he laughed. "Bread is the one thing hermits do not have. But man does not live by bread alone, but also on the meat of good lambs, of which I have two:

230

– *These* we'll quickly slaughter and spice with sage; that's how I love it. And we do not lack for roots and fruits, good enough even for sweet-tooths and big eaters; nor for nuts and other riddles to crack.

And so we'll make a good meal in short order. But whoever wants to share in the eating must also lend a hand, even the kings. In Zarathustra's home, even a king may be a cook."

This suggestion appealed to the hearts of everyone, except that the voluntary beggar objected to meat and wine and spices.

"Just listen to this glutton Zarathustra!" he said jokingly. "Is that why people go into caves and high mountains, to prepare such meals?

Now indeed I understand what he once taught us: 'Praised be a small poverty!' And why he wants to get rid of beggars."

"Cheer up," answered Zarathustra, "as I am cheered. Stick to your custom, you excellent man, crunch your grains, drink your water, praise your cuisine – if only it makes you cheerful!

I am a law only for my own, I am no law for everyone. But whoever belongs to me must be of strong bones, also light of foot –

– must be eager for wars and festivals, no gloomy Gus, no dreamy Joe, just as ready for what is hardest as for his festival, healthy and hale.

What's best belongs to mine and to me; if one doesn't give it to us, then we take it – the best food, the clearest sky, the strongest thoughts, the most beautiful women!" –

Thus spoke Zarathustra; but the king on the right retorted: "That's odd! Did anyone ever hear such clever things from the mouth of a wise man?

And truly, the oddest thing about a wise man is when, on top of everything else, he is also clever and not an ass."

Thus spoke the king on the right and he was amazed; but the ass responded to his remarks malevolently with "hee-yaw." And this was the beginning of that long meal which is called "the last supper" in the history books. During the same, however, nothing was discussed but *the higher man*.

On the Higher Man

1

When I came to mankind for the first time, I committed the hermit's folly, the great folly: I situated myself in the market place.

And when I spoke to all, I spoke to none. But by evening my companions were tightrope walkers, and corpses, and I myself almost a corpse.

But with the new morning a new truth came to me; then I learned to say: "What do the market place and the rabble and the rabble noise and long rabble ears matter to me!"

You higher men, learn this from me: in the market place no one believes in higher men. And if you want to speak there, well then! But the rabble blinks "we are all equal.

You higher men" – thus blinks the rabble – "there are no higher men, we are all equal, human is human, before God – we are all equal!"

Before God! – Now, however, this God has died. But we do not want to be equal before the rabble. You higher men, go away from the market place!

2

Before God! – But now this god has died! You higher men, this god was your greatest danger.

It is only now, since he lies in his grave, that you are resurrected. Only now the great noon comes, only now the higher man becomes – ruler![3]

Have you understood these words, oh my brothers? You are frightened; do your hearts become dizzy? Does the abyss yawn before you here? Does the hell hound yelp before you here?

Well then! Well now! You higher men! Only now is the mountain in labor with humanity's future. God died: now *we* want – the overman to live.

3

Those who care most today ask: "How are human beings to be preserved?" But Zarathustra is the only one and the first one to ask: "How shall human being be *overcome?*"

---

[3] Neither "lord" nor "master" fits here for *Herr*, "ruler." See "On the Three Evils" where Nietzsche defends *Herrschsucht*, "lust to rule," a noun based on *herrschen*, "to rule," which in turn is based on *Herr*, ruler. Nietzsche's motif for TSZ Part IV is "who shall be ruler of the earth." The earth can neither be "lorded" nor "mastered," but according to Nietzsche, it shall be ruled.

The overman is in my heart, *that* is my first and my only concern – and *not* human beings; not the neighbor, not the poorest, not the most suffering, not the best –

Oh my brothers, what I am able to love in human beings is that they are a going over and a going under. And in you, too, there is much that makes me love and hope.

That you despise, you higher men, that makes me hope. For the great despisers are the great reverers.

That you have despaired, there is much to revere in that. For you did not learn how to surrender, you did not learn petty prudence.

For today the little people have become ruler: they all preach surrender and resignation and prudence and industry and consideration and the long etcetera of little virtues.

What is effeminate, what comes from the servant's ilk and especially the rabble mishmash: *that* now wants to become ruler of all human destiny – oh nausea! Nausea! Nausea!

That asks and asks and does not tire: "How do human beings preserve themselves best, longest, most pleasantly?" With that – they are the rulers of today.

Overcome these rulers of today for me, oh my brothers – these little people: *they* are the overman's greatest danger!

Overcome for me, you higher men, the little virtues, the little prudence, the sand-grain sized considerations, the detritus of swarming ants, the pitiful contentedness, the "happiness of the greatest number"!

And despair rather than surrender. And truly, I love you for not knowing how to live today, you higher men! For thus *you* live – best!

4

Do you have courage, oh my brothers? Are you brave of heart? *Not* courage before witnesses, but the courage of hermits and eagles, which not even a god looks at anymore.

Cold souls, mules, the blind, the drunk – these I do not call brave of heart. Whoever has heart knows fear, but *conquers fear*; sees the abyss, but with *pride*.

Whoever sees the abyss, but with eagle's eyes, whoever *grasps* the abyss with eagle's talons: he has courage. –

5

"Human beings are evil" – thus spoke all the wisest to comfort me. Oh, if only it were still true today! Because evil is a human being's best power.

"Mankind must become better and more evil" – thus *I* teach. What is most evil is necessary for the overman's best.

It may have been good for that preacher of the little people that he suffered and labored under the sins of mankind. But I enjoy the greatest sin as my greatest *comfort*. –

But such things are not said for long ears. Every word does not belong in every snout. These are fine and faraway things: sheeps' hooves should not reach for them!

6

You higher men, do you think I am here to make good what you made bad?

Or that I have come henceforth to bed you suffering ones more comfortably? Or to show new, easier paths to those of you who are unsteady, lost, and have climbed astray?

No! No! Three times no! Ever more, ever better of your kind shall perish – for you shall have it ever worse and ever harder. Only thus –

– only thus do human beings grow into *that* height, where lightning strikes and breaks them: high enough for lightning!

My mind and my longing are trained on the few, the long, the distant: what do I care about your many little brief miseries?

You do not suffer enough in my opinion! For you suffer from yourselves, you haven't yet suffered *from human beings*. And you would be lying if you said otherwise! All of you do not suffer from what *I* suffered. –

7

It is not enough for me that lightning no longer causes damage. I do not want to divert it: it shall learn to work – for *me*.

My wisdom has gathered itself for a long time like a cloud, it becomes stiller and darker. Thus does every wisdom that shall *one day* give birth to lightning.

To these people of today I do not want to be *light*, nor be called light. *Them* – I want to blind: lightning of my wisdom – put out their eyes!

8

Will nothing beyond your capacity: there is a wicked falseness among those who will beyond their capacity.

Especially when they will great things! For they arouse mistrust against great things, these fine counterfeiters and actors –

– until at last they are false before themselves, cross-eyed, white-washed worm food, cloaked by strong words, by showy virtues, by gleaming false works.

Be very careful there, you higher men! For I regard nothing more precious and rare today than honesty.

Is this today not of the rabble? But rabble does not know what is great, what is small, what is straight and honest: it is innocently crooked, it always lies.

9

Have a good mistrust today, you higher men, you brave-hearted, you open-hearted ones! And keep your grounds secret! For this today is of the rabble.

What the rabble once learned to believe without grounds, how could anyone overthrow that with grounds?

In the market place one convinces with gestures. But grounds make the rabble mistrustful.

And if ever truth was victorious there, then ask yourselves with good mistrust: "Which strong error fought for it?"

And beware also of the scholars! They hate you, because they are sterile! They have cold, dried up eyes; before them every bird lies plucked.

Such types boast that they do not lie: but powerlessness to lie is by no means love for the truth. Beware!

Freedom from fever is by no means knowledge! I do not believe spirits that have cooled down. Whoever cannot lie does not know what truth is.

10

If you want to climb high and beyond, then use your own legs! Do not let yourselves be *carried* up, do not seat yourselves on strangers' backs and heads!

But you mount your horse? You ride swiftly up to your goal? Well then, my friend! But your lame foot is also mounted on your horse!

When you've reached your goal, when you leap from your horse, precisely at your *height*, you higher man – you will stumble!

11

You creators, you higher men! One is pregnant only with one's own child.

Do not let yourselves be misled and spoon-fed! Who after all is *your* neighbor? And even if you act "for your neighbor" – still you don't create for him!

Unlearn this "for," you creators; your virtue itself wants that you do nothing "for" and "in order" and "because." You should plug your ears against these false little words.

"For your neighbor" is the virtue of only small people; there they say "birds of a feather" and "one hand washes the other" – they have neither the right nor the strength to *your* self-interest.

In your self-interest, you creators, are the precaution and providence of the pregnant! What no one yet has laid eyes on, the fruit: your whole love shelters and spares and nourishes it.

Where your whole love is, with your children, there too your whole virtue is! Your work, your will is *your* "neighbor" – do not let yourself be spoon-fed any false values!

12

You creators, you higher men! Whoever must give birth is sick; but whoever has given birth, is unclean.

Ask women: one does not give birth because it is enjoyable. Pain makes hens and poets cackle.

You creators, in you there is much that is unclean. That's because you had to be mothers.

A new child – oh how much new filth also came into the world! Step aside! And whoever has given birth should wash his soul clean!

13

Do not be virtuous beyond your strengths! And will nothing of yourselves that is contrary to probability!

Walk in the footsteps where your fathers' virtue walked before! How could you climb high if your fathers' will did not climb with you?

But whoever would be a firstling should see to it that he does not also become a lastling! And where the vices of your fathers are, there you should not pretend to be saints!

If your fathers took to women and strong wine and boar swine, what would be the use of demanding chastity of yourself?

It would be a folly! To me it truly seems like much if such a man belonged to one or two or three women.

And if he founded monasteries and wrote above the door: "This way to sainthood" – I would still say: What for! It's a new folly!

He founded himself a guardhouse and safeguard: good for him! But I don't believe in it.

Whatever one brings into solitude grows in it, even the inner beast. On this score, solitude is ill-advised for many.

Was there ever anything filthier on earth than saints of the wilderness? *Around them* not only hell broke loose – but pigs too.

14

Timid, ashamed, awkward, like a tiger whose leap has failed; thus, you higher men, I often saw you slinking aside. A *throw* failed you.

But what does it matter, you dice throwers! You did not learn to gamble and banter as one should gamble and banter! Are we not always sitting at a great bantering and gaming table?

And when something great failed you, are you yourselves therefore – failures? And if you yourselves failed, did humanity therefore fail? But if humanity failed: well then, well now!

15

The higher its kind, the more seldom a thing succeeds. You higher men here, haven't all of you – failed?

Be of good cheer, what does it matter! How much is still possible! Learn to laugh at yourselves as one must laugh!

And no wonder that you failed and half succeeded, you half-broken ones! Does humanity's *future* not push and shove within you?

What is most distant, deepest, highest to the stars in humanity, its prodigious power: does all that not foam against each other in your pot?

No wonder many a pot breaks! Learn to laugh at yourselves as one must laugh! You higher men, oh how much is still possible!

And truly, how much has succeeded already! How rich is this earth in small, good, perfect things, in things that turned out well!

Place small, good, perfect things around you, you higher men! Their golden ripeness heals the heart. Perfection teaches us to hope.

16

What was the greatest sin here on earth until now? Was it not the words of him who spoke: "Woe to you who laugh now!"

Did he himself find no reasons to laugh on earth? Then he searched badly. Even a child finds reasons here.

He – did not love enough; or else he would have loved us too, we who laugh! But he hated and heckled us, howling and gnashing of teeth he heralded for us.

Must one curse right away where one does not love? That – seems to me in bad taste. But that is how he acted, this unconditional one. He came from the rabble.

And he himself just did not love enough; or else he would have been less angry that people did not love him. All great love does not *want* love – it wants more.

Get out of the way of all such unconditional ones! That is a poor sick kind, a rabble kind; they look harshly at this life, they have the evil eye for this earth.

Get out of the way of all such unconditional ones! They have heavy feet and sultry hearts – they do not know how to dance. How could the earth be light to them?

17

Crookedly all good things approach their goal. Like cats they arch their backs, they purr inwardly with their impending happiness – all good things laugh.

A person's stride betrays whether one is striding on *his* course: just look at me walk! But whoever approaches his goal dances.

And truly, I have not become a statue, I do not yet stand there stiff, stunned, stony, a column; I love swift running.

And even though there are bogs and thick depressions on earth, whoever has light feet runs over and past the mud and dances as if on clean-swept ice.

Lift up your hearts, my brothers, high! higher! And don't forget your legs either! Lift up your legs as well, you good dancers, and better still: stand on your heads too!

18

This crown of the laughing one, this rose-wreath crown – I myself put on this crown, I myself pronounced my laughter holy. I found no other strong enough for it today.

Zarathustra the dancer, Zarathustra the light one who waves with his wings, the flightworthy, waving to all birds, worthy and ready, a blissful lightweight –

Zarathustra the soothsayer, Zarathustra the soothlaugher, not impatient, not unconditional, someone who loves capers and escapades; I myself put on this crown!

19

Lift up your hearts, my brothers, high! higher! And don't forget your legs either! Lift up your legs as well, you good dancers, and better still: stand on your heads too!

Even in happiness there are heavy creatures, there are born ponderipedes. Quaintly they struggle, like an elephant struggling to stand on its head.

But it is better to be foolish with happiness than foolish with unhappiness, better to dance ponderously than to walk lamely. So learn this wisdom from me: even the worst thing has two good reverse sides –

– even the worst thing has good legs for dancing: so learn from me, you higher men, to stand yourselves on your right legs!

So unlearn moping and all rabble sadness! Oh how sad even today's rabble clowns seem to me! But this today is of the rabble.

20

Make like the wind when he plunges from his mountain caves: he wants to dance to his own pipe, the seas tremble and skip under his footsteps.

Praised be this good unruly spirit who gives wings to asses and milks the lionesses, who comes upon all that is today and all rabble like a storm wind –

– who is hostile to thistle-heads and hair-splitters and all wilted leaves and weeds: praised be this good, free storm spirit, who dances on bogs and depressions as upon meadows!

Who hates the rabble's mindless swindlers and all botched gloomy brood: praised be this spirit of all free spirits, the laughing storm who blows dust into the eyes of all fusspots and pus-pots!

You higher men, your worst part is that all of you have not learned to dance as one must dance – dance over and past yourselves! What does it matter that you didn't turn out well?

How much is still possible! So *learn* to laugh over and past yourselves! Lift up your hearts, you good dancers, high! higher! And don't forget good laughter either!

This crown of the laughing one, this rose-wreath crown: to you, my brothers, I throw this crown! I pronounced laughter holy; you higher men, *learn* – to laugh!

The Song of Melancholy

As Zarathustra made these speeches he stood close to the entrance of his cave; with the last words, however, he slipped away from his guests and fled for a short while into the open.

"Oh clean fragrance around me," he cried out, "oh blissful stillness around me! But where are my animals? Come here, come here my eagle and my snake!

Tell me, my animals: these higher men all together – do they perhaps not *smell* good? Oh clean fragrances around me! Only now do I know and feel how I love you, my animals."

– And Zarathustra spoke again. "I love you, my animals!" But the eagle and snake pressed up against him as he spoke these words, and they looked up at him. In such a manner the three of them together sniffled and sipped the good air. For the air here outside was better than among the higher men.

2

But scarcely had Zarathustra left his cave when the old magician stood up, looked around cunningly and said: "He's gone out!

And already, you higher men – if I may tickle you with this complimentary and flattering name, even as he did – already my wicked deceiving and magic spirit befalls me, my melancholy devil,

– who is an adversary of Zarathustra from the ground up: forgive him! Now he *wants* to conjure before you, right now is *his* hour; I wrestle in vain with this evil spirit.

All of you, whatever honors you may give yourselves with words, whether you call yourselves 'the free spirits' or 'the truthful' or 'penitents of the spirit' or 'the unbound' or 'the great longing ones' –

– all of you who suffer from *the great nausea* like me, for whom the old God died and no new god is lying yet in cradles and crib clothes – all of you are favored by my evil spirit and magic devil.

I know you, you higher men, I know him – I also know this monster whom I love against my will, this Zarathustra: he himself often seems to me like a beautiful mask of a saint,

– like a new wondrous masquerade in which my evil spirit, the melancholy devil, enjoys himself – I love Zarathustra, so it often seems to me, for the sake of my evil spirit. –

But already *he* befalls me and forces me, this spirit of melancholy, this evening twilight devil; and truly, you higher men, he is fond –

– just open your eyes! – he is fond of coming *naked*, whether male or female I do not yet know; but he is coming, he is forcing me, oh no! Open your senses!

The day is winding down, to all things evening now is coming, even to the best things; listen now and see, you higher men, what kind of devil, whether man or woman, this spirit of evening melancholy is!"

Thus spoke the old magician, glanced around cunningly and then reached for his harp.

3

When the air grows dim,[4]
When already the dew's consolation
Wells down to earth,
Invisible, and unheard –
For delicate shoes wears
The dewy consoler, like all who mildly console –
Do you recall then, do you recall, hot heart,
How once you thirsted,
For tears from the sky and dribbles of dew,
Parched and weary, thirsted
While on yellow grass paths
Malicious evening sun glances
Ran through black trees around you,
Blinding sun-ember glances, delighting in your pain?

"The wooer of *truth*? You?" – thus they mocked –
"No! Mere fool!
A beast, a cunning, preying, creeping beast
That must lie,
That must knowingly, willingly lie:
Lusting for prey,
Camouflaged,
A mask to itself,
Prey to itself –
That – the wooer of truth?
No! Mere fool! Mere poet!

---

[4] "Bei abgehellter Luft" means literally when the air has cleared or brightened. Nietzsche is borrowing the exact phrase used by the German poet Paul Fleming (1609–1640) in his sonnet "Auf Mons. Jakob Schevens seinen Geburtstag" (*Gedichte von Paul Fleming*, ed. Julius Tittmann (Leipzig: F. A. Brockhaus, 1870), p. 235). Grimms' *Deutsches Wörterbuch*, the authoritative dictionary of the German language, quotes both Fleming and Nietzsche for *abhellen*. However, in this context Nietzsche appears to use the verb *abhellen* to mean "dimming" or "darkening."

Merely speaking colorfully,
From fools' masks shouting colorfully,
Climbing around on lying word bridges,
On colorful rainbows,
Between false skies
And false earths,
Roaming around, hovering around –
Mere fool! *Mere* poet!

That – the wooer of truth?
Not still, stiff, smooth, cold,
Turned to statue,
To a pillar of God,
Not erected before temples,
A god's gatekeeper:
No! Hostile to such statues of truth,
More at home in any wilderness than before temples,
Full of feline mischief,
Leaping through every window
Swish! into every chance,
Sniffing toward every jungle,
Greedily, longingly sniffing,
So that in jungles
Among dappled beasts of prey
You could run, sinfully healthy and colorful and beautiful,
With lusty lips,
Blissfully mocking, blissfully hellish, blissfully bloodthirsty,
Run preying, creeping, lying –

Or, like the eagle that long,
Long gazes fixedly into abysses,
Into *its own* abysses –
Oh how they wind downward here,
Down low, down into,
Into ever deeper depths! –
Then,
Suddenly, straight and tight,
You spring to flight,
Pounce on lambs,
Steeply down, ravenously,
Lusting for lambs,
Wroth to all lamb souls,

Grimly wroth to everything that looks
Sheepish, lamb-eyed, curly wooled,
Gray, with lamb and sheep benevolence!

Thus
eagle-like, panther-like
Are the poet's longings,
Are *your* longings beneath a thousand masks,
You fool! You poet!

You who viewed mankind
As god and sheep – :
Tearing to pieces the god in mankind,
Like the sheep in mankind,
And *laughing* while tearing –

That, that is your bliss!
A panther's and eagle's bliss!
A poet's and fool's bliss!" –

When the air grows dim,
When already the moon's sickle
Creeps along green, between
Purple reds, and jealously:
– hostile to day,
With every step secretly
Scything away at rosy hammocks
Until they sink,
Sink down into night, sink down, pale –

Thus I myself once sank
From my own truth-madness,
From my longings of the day,
Weary of the day, sick from light,
– sank downward, eveningward, shadowward:
By one truth
Burned and thirsty:
– do you still recall, do you recall, hot heart,
How you thirsted then? –
To be banned
From *all* truth,
Mere fool!
Mere poet!

On Science

Thus sang the magician; and all who were together went unwittingly, like birds, into the net of his cunning and melancholy rapture. Only the conscientious of spirit was not captured; he snatched the harp away from the magician and cried: "Air! Let in the good air! Let Zarathustra in! You make this cave sultry and poisonous, you wicked old magician!

You seduce us, you faker, you fine one, to unknown desires and wildernesses. And watch out when such as you start making speeches and fuss about *truth*!

Woe to all free spirits who are not on their guard for *such* magicians! Their freedom is done for: you teach and tempt us back into prisons –

– you old melancholy devil, out of your lament rings a bird call; you resemble those who secretly incite sexual desires with their praise of chastity!"

Thus spoke the conscientious one; but the old magician looked around, enjoyed his triumph, and for its sake swallowed the annoyance that the conscientious one caused him. "Be quiet!" he said with a modest voice. "Good songs want to reverberate well; one should remain silent for a long time after good songs.

That is what all these do, the higher men. But you perhaps have understood little of my song? In you there is little of a magic spirit."

"You praise me," retorted the conscientious one. "In so far as you distinguish me from yourself, well good! But you others, what do I see here? You're all still sitting there with lusting eyes –

You free souls, where is your freedom now? Almost, it seems to me, you resemble those who have long watched wicked, dancing naked girls: your very souls are dancing!

In you, you higher men, there must be more of that which the magician calls his evil magic and deceiving spirit – we must surely be very different.

And truly, we spoke and thought enough together, before Zarathustra came home to his cave, to let me know that we *are* different.

We are *seeking* something different up here too, you and I. I for one am seeking *more security*, that is why I came to Zarathustra. For he is still the most solid tower and will –

– today, when everything is wobbling, when the whole earth is quaking. But you, when I look at the eyes that you make, it almost seems to me you are seeking *more insecurity*,

245

– more thrills, more danger, more earthquakes. What you are fond of, I almost suppose, but forgive my posing, you higher men –

– what you are fond of is the worst, most dangerous life, the one that frightens *me* the most; the life of wild animals, woods, caves, steep mountains and labyrinthine gorges.

And not the leaders *away* from danger do you like best, but instead those who lead you astray from all paths, the seducers. But, if such fondness is *real* in you, then it seems to me *impossible* nonetheless.

Fear, after all – that is a human being's original and basic feeling; from fear everything can be explained, original sin and original virtue. From fear *my* virtue also grew, it is called: science.

For the fear of wild animals – it was bred longest in human beings, including the animal that he conceals within himself and fears – Zarathustra calls it 'the inner beast.'

Such a long old fear, refined at last, made spiritual, intellectual – today, it seems to me, it is called: *science*." –

Thus spoke the conscientious one; but Zarathustra, who had just returned to his cave and heard and guessed the last speech, tossed a hand full of roses to the conscientious one and laughed at his "truths." "What!" he cried. "What did I hear just now? Truly, it seems to me, you are a fool or I myself am one; and your 'truth' I stand wham-bam on its head.

Fear you see – is our exception. But courage and adventure and pleasure in uncertainty, in what is undared – *courage* seems to me humanity's whole prehistory.

He envied and robbed the wildest, most courageous animals of all their virtues: only thus did he become – human.

This courage, refined at last, made spiritual, intellectual, this human courage with eagle's wings and snake's cleverness: *it*, it seems to me, today is called – "

"*Zarathustra!*" cried everyone sitting together, as if with one mouth, and they raised a great laughter then, and it rose from them like a heavy cloud. Even the magician laughed and said cleverly: "Well then, he's gone, my evil spirit!

And did I myself not warn you about him when I said that he was a deceiver and a cheat- and deceit spirit?

Especially, you see, when he shows himself naked. But what can *I* do about his tricks! Did *I* create him and the world?

Well then! Let's be good again and be cheerful! And even though Zarathustra looks angry – just look at him, he grudges me –

– before night comes he will learn again to love and laud me, he cannot live long without committing such follies.

He – loves his enemies: this art he understands best of all whom I have seen. But he takes revenge for it – on his friends!"

Thus spoke the old magician, and the higher men applauded him, such that Zarathustra went around and shook the hands of his friends with malice and love – like someone who has to make up for something and apologize to everyone. But when in doing so he reached the door of his cave, then once again he had a craving for the good air outside and for his animals – and he wanted to slip out.

Among Daughters of the Desert

1

"Do not go away!" said the wanderer who called himself the shadow of Zarathustra. "Stay with us, or else our old dull depression could befall us again.

Already that old magician has regaled us with his worst, and just look, the good pious pope there has tears in his eyes and once again he's completely shipped out on the sea of melancholy.

These kings may well put on a good face before us; of all of us today *they* learned that best after all! But if they did not have witnesses, I bet that the evil game would begin again with them too –

– the evil game of drifting clouds, of damp melancholy, of veiled skies, of stolen suns, of howling autumn winds,

– the evil game of our howling and crying in distress; stay with us, oh Zarathustra! Here there is much hidden misery that wants to speak, much evening, much cloud, much musty air!

You nourished us with strong, manly fare and strong sayings: do not permit the wimpy womanish spirits to befall us again for dessert!

You alone make the air around you strong and clear! Have I ever on earth found such good air as here with you in your cave?

Many lands indeed have I seen, my nose learned to test and assess many kinds of air; but in your cave my nostrils taste their greatest treat!

Unless – unless – oh forgive an old memory! Forgive me an old dessert song that I once composed among daughters of the desert –

– for among them there was likewise good, bright, oriental air; there I was furthest from cloudy, damp, melancholy old Europe!

Back then I loved such Oriental girls and a different blue sky, over which no clouds and no thoughts hang.

You wouldn't believe how decently they sat there when they weren't dancing; deep, but without thoughts, like little secrets, like beribboned riddles, like dessert nuts –

colorful and foreign to be sure! but without clouds; riddles that can be guessed: as a favor to such girls I then thought up a dessert psalm."

Thus spoke the wanderer and shadow; and before anyone answered him, he had already grasped the old magician's harp, crossed his legs and looked around dignified and wisely; but with his nostrils he slowly and questioningly inhaled the air like someone in new lands who savors the new, strange air. Then he began to sing with a kind of roaring voice.

2

The desert grows: woe to him who harbors deserts!

       – Ha! Solemn!
       Indeed solemn!
       A worthy beginning!
       African solemn!
       Worthy of a lion,
       Or of a moral howling monkey –
       – but nothing for you,
       My most lovely lady friends,
       At whose feet I,
       For the first time,
       A European among palm trees,
       Am permitted to sit. Selah.

       Wonderful truly!
       Here I sit now,
       Near the desert and already
       So distant again from the desert,
       Even in this nothingness ravaged:

Namely swallowed
By this smallest oasis –
– it just now yawned wide open
Its lovely mouth.
The most fragrant of all little mouths:
Then I fell in,
Down, down through – among you,
My most lovely lady friends! Selah.

Hail, hail to that whale
If he thus let his guest
Be comfortable! – you understand
My learned allusion?
Hail to his belly
If it was thus
Such a lovely oasis belly,
Like this one: which I doubt, however,
– that's why I come from Europe,
Which is more doubt ridden than all
Elderly married women.
May God improve it!
Amen!

Here I sit now,
In this smallest oasis,
Like a date,
Brown, sweetened through, oozing gold, lusting
For a rounded maiden's mouth,
But even more for maidenly
Ice-cold snowy-white incisor
Front teeth: for these, after all,
Languish the hearts of all hot dates. Selah.

To the aforementioned southerly fruits
Similar, all too similar
I lie here, little
Winged bugs
Dancing and playing around me,
Likewise even smaller
More foolish malicious
Wishes and fantasies –
Besieged by you,

You silent, you foreboding
She-cats,
Dudu and Suleika,
– *besphinxed*, to stuff much feeling
Into a single word:
(Forgive me God
This sin of language!)
– I sit here, sniffing the best air,
Paradise air truly,
Bright light air, streaked with gold,
Air as good as ever
Fell down from the moon –
Whether by chance,
Or did it happen from mischief,
As the ancient poets tell?
I the doubter, however,
Doubt it; that's why I come
From Europe,
Which is more doubt ridden than all
Elderly married women.
May God improve it!
Amen!

Drinking this most beautiful air,
With nostrils swollen like cups,
Without future, without memories,
Thus I sit here, my
Most lovely lady friends,
And watch the palm tree
As she, like a dancer,
Sways and dips and swivels her hips,
– one does it too if one watches too long!
Like a dancer who, it seems to me,
Already too long, dangerously long
Always, always stood on one foot only?
– which is why she forgot, it seems to me,
The other leg?
In vain, at least
I looked for the missing
Twin jewel
– namely the other leg –

In the holy proximity
Of her most lovely, most delicate
Little fan and flutter and flitter tinsel skirt.
Indeed, my beautiful lady friends, if you would
Believe me entirely:
She's lost it!
It's gone!
Forever gone!
The other leg!
Oh what a shame about this other lovely leg!
Where – might it while and grieve forlorn?
The lonely leg?
In fear perhaps of a
Grim golden blond-locked
Lion monster? Or perhaps even
Gnawed off, nibbled away –
Miserable, oh no! oh no! Nibbled away. Selah.

Oh do not weep,
Soft hearts!
Do not weep, you
Date hearts! Milk bosoms!
You licorice-heart
Little pouches!
Weep no more,
Pale Dudu!
Be a man, Suleika! Courage! Courage!
– Or is perhaps
Something fortifying, heart-fortifying
Called for here?
An anointed saying?
A solemn exhortation? –

Ha! Up now, dignity!
Blow, blow again,
Bellows of virtue!
Ha!
Roar once more,
Roar morally!
As a moral lion
Before daughters of the desert, roar!
– For the howling of virtue,

My most lovely lady friends,
Is more than all
European fervor, European voraciousness!
And here I stand already,
As a European,
I cannot do otherwise, God help me!
Amen!

The desert grows: woe to him who harbors deserts!

The Awakening

I

After the song of the wanderer and shadow all at once the cave became full of noise and laughter; and because the assembled guests all spoke at the same time, and even the ass no longer kept quiet amidst such encouragement, Zarathustra was overcome by a slight aversion and a bit of scorn for his visitors, even though he was glad for their cheerfulness. This, it seemed to him, was a sign of their convalescence. And so he slipped out into the open and spoke to his animals.

"Where is their distress now?" he said, and already he himself was relieved of his minor annoyance. "In my company, it seems to me, they have unlearned their crying in distress!

– Though unfortunately, not their crying." And Zarathustra covered his ears, for just then the hee-yaw of the ass blended oddly with the noisy jubilation of these higher men.

"They're having fun," he began again, "and who knows? Perhaps at the expense of their host; and if they learned to laugh from me, then still it is not *my* laughing that they learned.

But what does it matter? They're old people; they convalesce in their way, they laugh in their way: my ears have endured worse already without becoming testy.

This day is a triumph; he is already retreating, he's fleeing, *the spirit of gravity*, my old arch-enemy! How well this day wants to end, which began so badly and so hard!

And it *wants* to end. Already evening is coming; over the sea he rides, this good rider! How he sways, the blissful, homecoming one, in his purple saddle!

The sky looks on clearly, the world lies deep; oh all you strange people who came to me, it's worth it indeed to live with me!"

Thus spoke Zarathustra. And again the cries and laughter of the higher men came from the cave, so he began again.

"They are biting, my bait is working, their enemy is retreating from them too, the spirit of gravity. Already they're learning to laugh at themselves: do I hear correctly?

My manly fare is working, my vim and vigor sayings; and truly, I did not nourish them with gassy vegetables! But with warrior fare, with conqueror fare – I awakened new desires in them.

New hopes live in their arms and legs, their hearts expand. They are finding new words, soon their spirit will breathe mischief.

Such fare may not be for children, to be sure, nor for longing little women, old and young; their entrails are persuaded differently, their physician and teacher I am not.

Nausea retreats from these higher men – well then! That is my victory. In my kingdom they're becoming secure, all their stupid shame runs away, they're pouring themselves out.

They're pouring out their hearts, good hours are returning to them, they celebrate and ruminate – they're becoming *grateful*.

That I take as the best sign; they're becoming grateful. It won't be long now and they will invent festivals and erect monuments to their old joys.[5]

They are *convalescing*!" Thus spoke Zarathustra gaily to his heart and he gazed outward; but his animals pressed up against him and honored his happiness and his silence.

2

Suddenly, however, Zarathustra's ears were startled; for the cave which up till now had been full of noise and laughter became deathly still all at once – but his nose sensed an aromatic smoke and incense, as of burning pine cones.

"What is happening? What are they doing?" he asked himself and crept closer to the entrance, in order to watch his guests surreptitiously. But, wonder of wonders! What did he have to behold with his own eyes?

---

[5] "[S]ie denken sich Feste aus und stellen Denksteine ihren alten Freuden auf." Kaufmann misread *Freuden* (joys) as *Freunden* (friends).

"They've all gone *pious* again, they're *praying*, they're mad!" – he said and he was amazed beyond measure. And, in truth, all these higher men, the two kings, the retired pope, the wicked magician, the voluntary beggar, the wanderer and his shadow, the old soothsayer, the conscientious of spirit and the ugliest human being – they all kneeled there like children and devout little old women, and they worshiped the ass. And just then the ugliest human being began to gurgle and snort as though something unspeakable wanted to get out of him; but when he actually put it into words, behold, it was a pious, remarkable litany praising the worshiped and censed ass. This litany, however, sounded thus:

Amen! And praise and honor and wisdom and thanks and glory and strength be to our god, from everlasting to everlasting!
– But to this the ass brayed Hee-yaw.
He carries our burden, he adopted the form of a servant, he is patient from the heart and never says No; and whoever loves his god, chastises him.
– But to this the ass brayed Hee-yaw.
He does not speak, unless it be to say Yaw to the world that he created; thus he praises his world. It is his slyness that does not speak; this way he is rarely found to be wrong.
– But to this the ass brayed Hee-yaw.
Homely he walks through the world. Gray is the body color in which he cloaks his virtue. If he has spirit, then he conceals it; but everyone believes in his long ears.
– But to this the ass brayed Hee-yaw.
What hidden wisdom is it, that he has long ears and always says Yaw and never No! Has he not created the world in his image, namely as stupid as possible?
– But to this the ass brayed Hee-yaw.
You walk ways that are straight and crooked; it matters little to you what seems straight or crooked to us human beings. Your kingdom is beyond good and evil. It is your innocence not to know what innocence is.
– But to this the ass brayed Hee-yaw.
See now, how you push no one away, not the beggars, not the kings. The little children you let come to you, and when the mean boys bait you, then you simplemindedly say Hee-yaw.
– But to this the ass brayed Hee-yaw.

You love she-asses and fresh figs, you are no picky eater. A thistle tickles your heart if you happen to be hungry. Therein lies the wisdom of a god.

– But to this the ass brayed Hee-yaw.

The Ass Festival

1

At this point in the litany, however, Zarathustra could no longer control himself, cried Hee-yaw himself even louder than the ass, and leaped into the midst of his guests, who had gone mad. "But what are you doing, you mortal children?" he cried, as he pulled the praying men off the floor and to their feet. "Watch out that someone other than Zarathustra should see you:

Anyone would conclude that with your new faith you were the most vicious blasphemers or the most foolish of all old little women!

And you yourself, you old pope, how can you reconcile for yourself that you worship this ass here as God?" –

"Oh Zarathustra," responded the pope, "forgive me, but in matters of God I am more enlightened even than you. And that's how it should be.

Better to worship God in this form, than in no form at all! Think about this dictum, my exalted friend; you will quickly realize that there is wisdom in such a dictum.

He who said 'God is a spirit' – he took the biggest step and leap ever on earth toward disbelief: such words are not easy to rectify on earth!

My old heart leaps and skips at the fact that there is still something to worship on earth. Forgive, oh Zarathustra, an old pious pope's heart! –"

– "And you," said Zarathustra to the wanderer and shadow, "you call and consider yourself a free spirit? And yet here you perform such idolatry and popery?

Your performance here is more wicked indeed than it is with your wicked brown girls, you wicked new believer!"

"Wicked enough," answered the wanderer and shadow, "you're right; but what can I do about it? The old God lives again, oh Zarathustra, say what you will.

The ugliest human being is to blame for everything; he has awakened him again. And when he says that he once killed him: *death* is always a mere prejudice among gods."

– "And you," said Zarathustra, "you wicked old magician, what have you done! Who in these liberated times is supposed to believe in you anymore, if *you* believe in such asinine divinities?

What you did was a stupidity; how could you, you clever one, commit such a stupidity!"

"Oh Zarathustra," replied the clever magician, "you're right, it was a stupidity – and it's been hard enough for me."

– "And you most of all," said Zarathustra to the conscientious of spirit, "lean your head on your hand and consider! Doesn't anything here go against your conscience? Isn't your spirit too clean for this praying and the steam of these Holy Joes?"

"There is something about it," answered the conscientious one, leaning his head on his hand, "there is something about this spectacle that actually does my spirit good.

Maybe because I am not allowed to believe in God; but it is certain that God in this form seems most believable to me.

God should be eternal, according to the witnessing of the most pious; whoever has that much time, takes his time. As slowly and as stupidly as possible: *that way* such a one can indeed go very far.

And whoever has too much spirit, he may well become a fool even for stupidity and folly. Think about your own case, oh Zarathustra!

You yourself – indeed! Even you could well become an ass from superabundance and wisdom.

Does a perfectly wise man not like to walk on crooked paths? Appearances would indicate this, oh Zarathustra – *your* appearance!"

– "And finally you yourself," said Zarathustra and he turned toward the ugliest human being, who still lay on the floor, reaching up with his arm to the ass (for he was giving it wine to drink). "Speak, you unspeakable one: what have you done here!

You seem transformed to me, your eyes glow, the cloak of the sublime lies about your ugliness: *What* have you done?

Is what they say true after all, that you awakened him again? And why? Were there not good grounds for killing and getting rid of him?

You yourself seem awakened to me; what have you done? Why did *you* revert? Why did *you* convert? Speak, you unspeakable one!"

"Oh Zarathustra," replied the ugliest human being, "you are a rogue!

Whether *he* still lives or lives again or is thoroughly dead – which of us two knows that best? I ask you.

But I know one thing – it was from you yourself that I once learned, oh Zarathustra: whoever wants to kill most thoroughly, *laughs*.

'One kills not by wrath, but by laughter' – thus you once spoke. Oh Zarathustra, you hidden one, you annihilator without wrath, you dangerous saint – you are a rogue!"

2

But then it happened that Zarathustra, astounded by the sheer number of such roguish answers, bounded back to the door of his cave and, facing all of his guests, cried out with a strong voice:

"Oh you foolish rascals, the lot of you, you jesters! Why do you dissemble and disguise yourselves before me?

How the hearts of each of you squirmed with glee and malice that at last you had become as little children again, namely pious –

– that at last you did again as children do, namely prayed, folded your hands and said 'dear God!'

But now leave me *this* nursery, my own cave, where today all manner of childishness is at home. Cool your hot children's mischief and your heart's noise out here!

To be sure, unless you become as little children, you shall not enter *that* kingdom of heaven. (And Zarathustra gestured upward with his hands.)

But we don't want to enter the kingdom of heaven at all: we have become men – *and so we want the kingdom of the earth*."

3

And once again Zarathustra began to speak. "Oh my new friends," he said – "you strange, you higher men, how well I like you now –

– since you've become gay again! All of you have truly blossomed; it seems to me that flowers such as you require *new festivals*,

– a small brave nonsense, some kind of divine worship and ass festival, some kind of old gay Zarathustra fool, a sweeping wind that blows your souls bright.

Do not forget this night and this ass festival, you higher men! *This* you invented in my cave, this I take as a good omen – such things are invented only by the convalescing!

And if you celebrate it again, this ass festival, do it for your own sake, do it also for my sake! And in remembrance of *me*!"

Thus spoke Zarathustra.

The Sleepwalker Song

1

Meanwhile, however, one after another had stepped outdoors into the open and into the cool, pensive night; but Zarathustra himself led the ugliest human being by the hand, to show him his night world and the big round moon and the silver waterfalls near his cave. There at last they all stood together, nothing but old people, but with comforted, brave hearts and inwardly amazed that they felt so good on earth; but the mystery of the night came closer and closer to their hearts. And Zarathustra thought again to himself: "Oh how well I like them now, these higher men!" – but he did not say it aloud, for he honored their happiness and their silence. –

But then something happened that was the most amazing thing of that amazing long day: the ugliest human being began once more and for the last time to gurgle and to snort, and when he had managed to put it in words, behold, a question leaped round and ready from his mouth, a good, deep, clear question, which moved the hearts of all who were listening to him.

"My friends, all of you," spoke the ugliest human being, "what do you think? For the sake of this day – *I* am satisfied for the first time that I have lived my entire life.

And it's still not enough for me to attest as much as I do. It's worth it to live on earth: one day, one festival with Zarathustra taught me to love the earth.

'Was *that* – life?' I want to say to death. 'Well then! One More Time!'

My friends, what do you think? Do you not want to say to death, as I do: Was *that* – life? For Zarathustra's sake, well then! One More Time!" –

Thus spoke the ugliest human being; but it was not long before midnight. And what do you think happened then? As soon as the higher men had heard his question, all at once they became aware of their transformation and convalescence, and of who gave it to them. Then they rushed toward Zarathustra, thanking, honoring, caressing him, kissing his hands, each in his own manner; such that some laughed, some wept. But the old soothsayer danced with joy; and even if, as some chroniclers opine, he was full of sweet wine at the time, then he was certainly even more full of sweet life and he had renounced all weariness. There are even some who say that the ass also danced then; not for nothing, after all, had the ugliest human being earlier given it wine to drink. Now this may have happened thus or otherwise, and if in truth on that evening the ass did not dance, then clearly even greater and rarer wonders took place there, than the dancing of an ass would have been. In sum, as Zarathustra's saying goes: "What does it matter!"

2

But as this went on with the ugliest human being, Zarathustra stood there like a drunken man; his tongue slurred, his feet faltered. And who could even guess what thoughts were speeding then through Zarathustra's soul? Visibly, however, his spirit receded and flew ahead and was in remote distances and at the same time "upon a high ridge," as it is written, "between two seas,

– between the past and the future, wandering as a heavy cloud." Gradually, however, as the higher men held him in their arms, he came to himself a bit and used his hands to fend away the throng of the revering and the worrying; yet he did not speak. All at once though he quickly turned his head, because he seemed to hear something: then he put his finger to his lips and said: "*Come!*"

And immediately it became still and mysterious all around; but from the depths the sound of a bell rose slowly. Zarathustra listened for it, as did the higher men; then he put his finger to his lips once more and said again: "*Come! Come! It's going on midnight!*" – And his voice had changed. But still he did not stir from his place; then it grew even more still and mysterious, and everything listened, even the ass, and Zarathustra's animals of honor, the eagle and the snake, and also the cave of Zarathustra and the big cool moon and the very night. But Zarathustra put his hand to his lips for the third time and said:

"*Come! Come! Come! Let us walk now! It is the hour: let us walk now into the night!*"

3

You higher men, it's going on midnight; I want to whisper something in your ears, like that old bell whispers it into my ear –

– as secretly, as terribly, as cordially as that midnight bell, which has experienced more than any human, says it to me:

– which long ago tallied the heartbeat beatings of your fathers – oh! oh! how it sighs! How it laughs in dream delight, the old, the deep deep midnight!

Still! Still! Then things are heard that by day may not be said; but now, in the cool air, where the noise of your hearts has fled –

– now it speaks, now it listens, now it creeps into nocturnal, over-awake souls – oh! oh! how it sighs! How it laughs in dream delight!

– don't you hear, how it secretly, terribly, cordially speaks to *you*, the old, the deep deep midnight?

Oh mankind, pray!

4

Woe to me! Where has time gone? Did I not sink into deep wells? The world sleeps –

Alas! Alas! The dog howls, the moon shines. I would sooner die, die, than tell you what my midnight heart is thinking right now.

Now I've died already. It's gone. Spider, why do you spin around me? Do you want blood? Oh! Oh! The dew falls, the hour comes –

– the hour when I shiver and freeze, which asks and asks and asks: "who has enough heart for it?

– who shall be the ruler of the earth? Who wants to say: *thus* you shall flow, you great and little streams!"

– the hour approaches: oh mankind, you higher men, pray! This speech is for fine ears, for your ears – *what does deep midnight have to say?*

5

It carries me away, my soul dances. Day's work! Day's work! Who shall be ruler of the earth?

The moon is cool, the wind is silent. Alas! Alas! Have you flown high enough? You dance: but a leg is not a wing.

You good dancers, now all joy is gone, wine became resin, every cup became brittle, the graves stammer.

You did not fly high enough; now the graves stammer: "Redeem the dead! Why is it night for so long? Does the moon not make us drunk?"

You higher men, redeem the graves, awaken the corpses! Oh, why does the worm still bore? It approaches, the hour approaches –

– the bell growls, the heart still rattles, the wood worm still bores, the heart worm. Alas! Alas! *The world is deep!*

6

Sweet lyre! Sweet lyre! I love your tone, your drunken, sunken croaking tone! – From how long ago, from how far away your tone comes to me, from afar, from ponds of love!

You old bell, you sweet lyre! Every pain tore into your heart, father pain, fathers' pain, forefathers' pain, your speech grew ripe –

– ripe like golden autumns and afternoons, like my hermit's heart – now you speak: the world itself became ripe, the grape turns brown,

– now it wants to die, die of happiness. You higher men, do you not smell it? A fragrance wells up mysteriously,

– a fragrance and aroma of eternity, a rosy blissful, brown golden wine aroma of ancient happiness,

– of drunken, midnight, dying happiness, which sings: the world is deep *and deeper than the grasp of day!*

7

Let me be! Let me be! I am too pure for you. Do not touch me! Did my world not just become perfect?

My skin is too pure for your hands. Let me be, you stupid, clumsy, stifling day! Is midnight not brighter?

The purest shall be rulers of the earth, the least known, strongest, the midnight-souled, who are brighter and deeper than any day.

Oh day, you grope for me? You fumble for my happiness? I seem rich to you, lonely, buried treasure, a chamber of gold?

Oh world, you want *me*? Am I worldly to you? Am I spiritual to you? Am I godlike to you? But day and world, you are too crude –

– have smarter hands, reach for deeper happiness, for deeper unhappiness, reach for some kind of god – do not reach for me:

– my unhappiness, my happiness is deep, you strange day, but still I am no god, no god's hell: *deep is its pain.*

8

God's pain is deeper, you strange world! Reach for god's pain, not for me! What am I? A drunken sweet lyre –

a midnight lyre, a bell-toad that no one understands, but that *must* speak, before the deaf, you higher men! For you do not understand me!

Gone! Gone! Oh youth! Oh noon! Oh afternoon! Now evening's come and night and midnight – the dog howls, the wind:

– is the wind not a dog? It whimpers, it yelps, it howls. Alas! Oh how midnight sighs, how it laughs, how it rattles and wheezes!

How she speaks soberly just now, this drunken poetess! Perhaps she overdrank her drunkenness? She became over-awake? She ruminates?

– she ruminates her pain, in dream, the old deep midnight, and even more her joy. Because joy, even if pain is deep: *Joy is deeper still than misery.*

9

You grapevine! Why do you praise me! I cut you! I am cruel, you bleed – what does your praise want of my drunken cruelty?

"What became perfect, everything ripe – wants to die!" so you speak. Blessed, blessed be the vintner's knife! But everything unripe wants to live, alas!

Pain says: "Refrain! Away, you pain!" But everything that suffers wants to live, to become ripe and joyful and longing,

– longing for what is farther, higher, brighter. "I want heirs," thus speaks all that suffers, "I want children, I do not want *myself*" –

But joy does not want heirs, not children – joy wants itself, wants eternity, wants recurrence, wants everything eternally the same.

Pain says: "Break, bleed, heart! Walk, legs! Wings, fly! Up! Upward! Pain!" Well then, well now, old heart! *Pain says: "Refrain!"*

10

You higher men, what do you think? Am I a soothsayer? A dreamer? A drunk? A dream interpreter? A midnight bell?

A drop of dew? A haze and fragrance of eternity? Do you not hear it? Do you not smell it? Just now my world became perfect, midnight is also noon –

Pain is also a joy, a curse is also a blessing, night is also a sun – go away or else you will learn: a wise man is also a fool.

Have you ever said Yes to one joy? Oh my friends, then you also said Yes to *all* pain. All things are enchained, entwined, enamored –

– if you ever wanted one time two times, if you ever said "I like you, happiness! Whoosh! Moment!" then you wanted *everything* back!

– Everything anew, everything eternal, everything enchained, entwined, enamored, oh thus you *loved* the world –

– you eternal ones, love it eternally and for all time; and say to pain also: refrain, but come back! *For all joy wants – eternity!*

11

All joy want the eternity of all things, wants honey, wants resin, wants drunken midnight, wants graves, wants tomb-tears' solace, wants gilded sunset –

– *what* does joy not want? It is thirstier, heartier, hungrier, more terrible, more mysterious than all pain, it wants *itself*, it bites into *itself*, the ring's will wrestles in it –

– it wants love, it wants hate, it is super-rich, bestows, throws away, begs for someone to take it, thanks the taker, it would like to be hated –

– so rich is its joy that it thirsts for pain, for hell, for hate, for disgrace, for the cripple, for *world* – this world, oh you know it well!

You higher men, it longs for you, does joy, the unruly, blissful one – for your pain, you failures! All eternal joy longs for failures.

For all joy wants itself, and therefore it wants all misery too! Oh happiness, oh pain! Oh break, my heart! You higher men, learn this, joy wants eternity,

– Joy wants the eternity of *all* things, *wants deep, wants deep eternity!*

12

Have you now learned my song? Have you guessed what it means? Well then! Well now! You higher men, then sing me my new roundelay!

Sing me this song yourselves now, whose name is "One More Time," whose meaning is "in all eternity!" – sing, you higher men, Zarathustra's roundelay!

> Oh mankind, pray!
> What does deep midnight have to say?
> "From sleep, from sleep –
> From deepest dream I made my way: –
> The world is deep,
> And deeper than the grasp of day.
> Deep is its pain –,
> Joy – deeper still than misery:
> Pain says: Refrain!
> Yet all joy wants eternity –
> – Wants deep, wants deep eternity."

The Sign

But in the morning after this night Zarathustra sprang from his sleeping place, girded his loins and came out from his cave, glowing and strong, like a morning sun that emerges from dark mountains.

"You great star," he said, as he had said before, "what would all your happiness be if you did not have *those* for whom you shine?

And if they stayed in their rooms while you are already awake and come and bestow and distribute – how would your proud shame be angered!

Well then! They're sleeping still, these higher men, while *I* am awake: *they* are not my proper companions! Not for them do I wait here in my mountains.

I want to go to my work, to my day; but they do not understand what the signs of my morning are, my step – is not a wake up call for them.

They are sleeping still in my cave, their dream still ruminates on my midnights. The ear that hearkens for *me* – the *heeding* ear is still lacking in their limbs."

– Thus Zarathustra spoke to his heart as the sun was rising; then he glanced questioning into the heights, for he heard above him the sharp call of his eagle. "Well then!" he shouted upward, "thus it pleases and suits me. My animals are awake, because I am awake.

My eagle is awake and like me he honors the sun. With eagle's talons he grasps for the new light. You are my proper animals; I love you.

But I still lack the proper human beings!" –

Thus spoke Zarathustra; but then it happened that he suddenly heard himself swarmed and fluttered around as if by countless birds – but the whirring of so many wings and the thronging around his head was so great that he had to close his eyes. And truly, like a cloud it descended upon him, like a cloud of arrows pouring down upon a new enemy. But see, here it was a cloud of love, and it poured over a new friend.

"What is happening to me?" thought Zarathustra in his astonished heart, and he sat down slowly on the big stone that lay near the exit of his cave. But as he reached with his hands around and above and below himself, warding off the affectionate birds, something even more extraordinary happened to him: he reached unwittingly into a thick, warm tangle of hair, and at the same time a roar sounded before him – a soft, long lion's roar.

"*The sign is coming*" said Zarathustra and his heart transformed. And in truth, as it grew brighter around him, there at his feet lay a yellow, powerful beast, and it pressed its head against his knee and did not want to leave him out of love, acting like a dog that finds its old master again. And the doves with their love were no less eager than the lion; and each time when a dove flitted over the nose of the lion, the lion shook its head and was amazed and laughed.

To all of this Zarathustra had only one thing to say: "*My children are near, my children*" – then he became completely mute. But his heart was freed, and from his eyes tears dropped down and fell onto his hands. And he heeded nothing more and sat there, unmoving and not even warding off the animals. Then the doves flew back and forth and lighted on his shoulders and caressed his white hair and did not tire of tenderness and jubilation. But the strong lion kept licking the tears that fell onto Zarathustra's hands, roaring and growling bashfully. Thus acted these animals. –

All this lasted a long time, or a short time: for, properly speaking, there is *no* time on earth for such things –. Meanwhile, however, the higher men in Zarathustra's cave had awakened and were forming a procession, in order to approach Zarathustra and offer their morning greeting. For they had discovered, when they awakened, that he was no longer among them. But as they reached the door of the cave, and the noise of their footsteps preceded them, the lion started violently, turned suddenly away from Zarathustra and leaped, roaring wildly, toward the cave; and the higher men, when they heard it roaring, all cried out as if with one voice, and fled back and disappeared in a flash.

Zarathustra himself, however, dazed and disoriented, rose from his seat, looked around, stood there astonished, questioned his heart, reflected, and was alone. "What did I hear?" he said at last, slowly, "what just happened to me?"

And right away he remembered, and he grasped in a single glance all that had transpired between yesterday and today. "Here is the stone," he said, stroking his beard, "*that's* what I sat on yesterday morning; and here's where the soothsayer approached me, and here's where I first heard the cry that I heard just now, the great cry of distress.

Oh you higher men, it was *your* distress that this old soothsayer foretold yesterday morning –

– to your distress he wanted to seduce and tempt me. Oh Zarathustra, he said to me, I come to seduce you to your last sin.

"To my last sin?" cried Zarathustra, and laughed scornfully at his own words. "*What* has been left me now as my last sin?"

– And once more Zarathustra became immersed in himself and sat down again on the great stone, and he reflected. Suddenly he jumped to his feet –

"*Pity! Pity for the higher men*!" he cried, and his face transformed to bronze. "Well then! *That* – has its time!

My suffering and my pity – what do they matter! Do I strive for *happiness*? I strive for my *work*!

Well then! The lion came, my children are near, Zarathustra became ripe, my hour came –

This is *my* morning, *my* day is beginning: *up now, up, you great noon!*" –

Thus spoke Zarathustra and he left his cave, glowing and strong, like a morning sun that emerges from dark mountains.

***

The end of *Thus Spoke Zarathustra*

Index

CAMBRIDGE TEXTS IN THE HISTORY OF PHILOSOPHY

Titles published in the series thus far

Aquinas *Disputed Questions on the Virtues* (edited by E. M. Atkins and Thomas Williams)
Aquinas *Summa Theologiae, Questions on God* (edited by Brian Davies and Brian Leftow)
Aristotle *Nicomachean Ethics* (edited by Roger Crisp)
Arnauld and Nicole *Logic or the Art of Thinking* (edited by Jill Vance Buroker)
Augustine *On the Trinity* (edited by Gareth Matthews)
Bacon *The New Organon* (edited by Lisa Jardine and Michael Silverthorne)
Boyle *A Free Enquiry into the Vulgarly Received Notion of Nature* (edited by Edward B. Davis and Michael Hunter)
Bruno *Cause, Principle and Unity* and *Essays on Magic* (edited by Richard Blackwell and Robert de Lucca with an introduction by Alfonso Ingegno)
Cavendish *Observations upon Experimental Philosophy* (edited by Eileen O'Neill)
Cicero *On Moral Ends* (edited by Julia Annas, translated by Raphael Woolf)
Clarke *A Demonstration of the Being and Attributes of God and Other Writings* (edited by Ezio Vailati)
Classic and Romantic German Aesthetics (edited by J. M. Bernstein)
Condillac *Essay on the Origin of Human Knowledge* (edited by Hans Aarsleff)
Conway *The Principles of the Most Ancient and Modern Philosophy* (edited by Allison P. Coudert and Taylor Corse)
Cudworth A *Treatise Concerning Eternal and Immutable Morality* with *A Treatise of Freewill* (edited by Sarah Hutton)
Descartes *Meditations on First Philosophy,* with selections from the *Objections and Replies* (edited by John Cottingham)
Descartes *The World and Other Writings* (edited by Stephen Gaukroger)
Fichte *Foundations of Natural Right* (edited by Frederick Neuhouser, translated by Michael Baur)
Fichte *The System of Ethics* (edited by Daniel Breazeale and Günter Zöller)
Herder *Philosophical Writings* (edited by Michael Forster)
Hobbes and Bramhall on Liberty and Necessity (edited by Vere Chappell)
Humboldt *On Language* (edited by Michael Losonsky, translated by Peter Heath)
Kant *Critique of Practical Reason* (edited by Mary Gregor with an introduction by Andrews Reath)
Kant *Groundwork of the Metaphysics of Morals* (edited by Mary Gregor with an introduction by Christine M. Korsgaard)
Kant *Metaphysical Foundations of Natural Science* (edited by Michael Friedman)
Kant *The Metaphysics of Morals* (edited by Mary Gregor with an introduction by Roger Sullivan)
Kant *Prolegomena to any Future Metaphysics* (edited by Gary Hatfield)
Kant *Religion within the Boundaries of Mere Reason and Other Writings* (edited by Allen Wood and George di Giovanni with an introduction by Robert Merrihew Adams)
Kierkegaard *Fear and Trembling* (edited by C. Stephen Evans and Sylvia Walsh)

La Mettrie *Machine Man and Other Writings* (edited by Ann Thomson)

Leibniz *New Essays on Human Understanding* (edited by Peter Remnant and Jonathan Bennett)

Lessing *Philosophical and Theological Writings* (edited by H. B. Nisbet)

Malebranche *Dialogues on Metaphysics and on Religion* (edited by Nicholas Jolley and David Scott)

Malebranche *The Search after Truth* (edited by Thomas M. Lennon and Paul J. Olscamp)

Medieval Islamic Philosophical Writings (edited by Muhammad Ali Khalidi)

Melanchthon *Orations on Philosophy and Education* (edited by Sachiko Kusukawa, translated by Christine Salazar)

Mendelssohn *Philosophical Writings* (edited by Daniel O. Dahlstrom)

Newton *Philosophical Writings* (edited by Andrew Janiak)

Nietzsche *The Antichrist, Ecce Homo, Twilight of the Idols and Other Writings* (edited by Aaron Ridley and Judith Norman)

Nietzsche *Beyond Good and Evil* (edited by Rolf-Peter Horstmann and Judith Norman)

Nietzsche *The Birth of Tragedy and Other Writings* (edited by Raymond Geuss and Ronald Speirs)

Nietzsche *Daybreak* (edited by Maudemarie Clark and Brian Leiter, translated by R. J. Hollingdale)

Nietzsche *The Gay Science* (edited by Bernard Williams, translated by Josefine Nauckhoff)

Nietzsche *Human, All Too Human* (translated by R. J. Hollingdale with an introduction by Richard Schacht)

Nietzsche *Thus Spoke Zarathustra* (edited by Adrian Del Caro and Robert B. Pippin)

Nietzsche *Untimely Meditations* (edited by Daniel Breazeale, translated by R. J. Hollingdale)

Nietzsche *Writings from the Late Notebooks* (edited by Rüdiger Bittner, translated by Kate Sturge)

Novalis *Fichte Studies* (edited by Jane Kneller)

Reinhold *Letters on the Kantian Philosophy* (edited by Karl Ameriks, translated by James Hebbeler)

Schleiermacher *Hermeneutics and Criticism* (edited by Andrew Bowie)

Schleiermacher *Lectures on Philosophical Ethics* (edited by Robert Louden, translated by Louise Adey Huish)

Schleiermacher *On Religion: Speeches to its Cultured Despisers* (edited by Richard Crouter)

Schopenhauer *Prize Essay on the Freedom of the Will* (edited by Günter Zöller)

Sextus Empiricus *Against the Logicians* (edited by Richard Bett)

Sextus Empiricus *Outlines of Scepticism* (edited by Julia Annas and Jonathan Barnes)

Shaftesbury, *Characteristics of Men, Manners, Opinions, Times* (edited by Lawrence Klein)

Adam Smith, *The Theory of Moral Sentiments* (edited by Knud Haakonssen)

Voltaire *Treatise on Tolerance and Other Writings* (edited by Simon Harvey)